Critical Readings in
Bodybuilding

Routledge Research in Sport, Culture and Society

Critical Readings in Bodybuilding

Edited by
Adam Locks and
Niall Richardson

Routledge
Taylor & Francis Group

NEW YORK AND LONDON

First published 2012
by Routledge
711 Third Avenue, New York, NY 10017

Simultaneously published in the UK
by Routledge
2 Park Square, Milton Park, Abingdon, Oxon OX14 4RN

*Routledge is an imprint of the Taylor & Francis Group,
an informa business*

Library of Congress Cataloging-in-Publication Data
Critical readings in bodybuilding / edited by Adam Locks and
Niall Richardson.
    p. cm. — (Routledge research in sport, culture and society; 9)
Includes bibliographical references and index.
    1. Bodybuilding—Social aspects. 2. Human body—Social aspects.
I. Locks, Adam. II. Richardson, Niall.
GV546.5.C75 2011
796.41–dc22   2011001224

ISBN13: 978-0-415-87852-4 (hbk)
ISBN13: 978-0-203-80945-7 (ebk)

Typeset in Sabon
by Glyph International

Printed and bound in the United States of America on acid-free
paper by IBT Global

Contents

List of Illustrations

Figures

Tables

Acknowledgments

An earlier version of Chapter 3 was published as Monaghan, L.F. (2002) 'Vocabularies of Motive for Illicit Steroid Use among Bodybuilders', *Social Science & Medicine* 55: 695–708 (Elsevier).

Chapter 7: 'The Self Contained Body: the Heroic and Aesthetic/Erotic modes of representing the muscular body' is a slightly edited version of the chapter entitled 'The Self-Contained Body' in the work by Kenneth R. Dutton entitled *The Perfectible Body: The Western Ideal of Physical Development* (1995), published in the UK by Cassell, in the USA by Continuum and in Australia by Allen and Unwin.

Chapter 11 is an excerpt from 'Aphrodisia and Erotogenesis', in Joanna Frueh (2001) *Monster/Beauty: Building the Body of Love*. Copyright 2001 by the Regents of the University of California. Berkeley, Los Angeles, London: University of California Press: 59–88.

Figure 0.1 James Llewellin. Courtesy of Rebecca Andrews.

Introduction

Adam Locks

In recent years the body has become one of the most popular areas of study in the arts, humanities and social sciences. There are presently many undergraduate and postgraduate university modules in film, cultural studies, gender studies, visual culture, sociology, and sports science devoted to the study of the body in representation and cultural practice. As can only be expected, the activity of bodybuilding continues to be of interest to scholars of gender, media, film, cultural studies, and sociology. However, there is surprisingly little scholarship available on *contemporary* bodybuilding. For example, much of the existing cultural studies literature on bodybuilding addresses the performances of Arnold Schwarzenegger and the gender politics of the *Pumping Iron* documentaries and therefore addresses the practice of bodybuilding as it was in the 1970s. Yet as many of my students have remarked, Arnold's physique looks 'sylph like' in comparison to the bodies flexing on the current Mr. Olympia stage. Similarly, much of the existing writing on female bodybuilding simply praises the activity as feminist resistance: female bodybuilders are actively challenging traditional feminine iconography. Yet there is little attention paid to the eroticism of the built physique and the recently labeled form of sexual fetish known as 'muscle worship'. *Critical Readings in Bodybuilding* is intended, therefore, to be the first collection to address the contemporary practice of bodybuilding with specific attention to these issues, especially the way in which the activity has become increasingly more extreme and "freaky" and to consider much neglected debates of eroticism and sexuality related to the activity.

Second, the collection is intended to offer "critical" readings of the activity. Much of the writing on bodybuilding is often art historical, addressing the idea of the "perfectible" body as found in fine art and emulated by bodybuilders. This collection is not intended to provide a history of bodybuilding (although this introduction will offer a historical overview for the reader) but to critically investigate current debates in the contemporary activity. Similarly, there exist a number of ethnographic style studies in which the subcultural lifestyle politics of hardcore bodybuilders, including their nutritional and drug regimes, have been investigated. This collection will not attempt to replicate this work but instead focus on current critical debates related to the activity. One of the strengths of the collection is that it unites a broad range of methodologies with some of the contributors drawing upon qualitative research, quantitative research, textual analysis and some empirical work inspired by personal experience.

Therefore, the collection will be divided into two parts. The first part, 'Practices,' addresses a range of bodybuilding topics related to the cultural activity itself. This part differs from a lot of previous work on bodybuilding as its analysis will not simply be limited to a consideration of the finished "product" – that is, the physique. Other topics which will be addressed in this part include: bodybuilding as "immersive" practice; how 'figure' competitions have eclipsed 'female bodybuilding competitions'; shame and pride; the gender politics of the gym itself and a consideration of drug use including recent developments in steroids and growth hormones. The second part, 'Representations,' is devoted to an analysis of bodybuilding representations and, as such, is more textually driven. As the introduction to this part will explain, the ever-increasing availability of media imagery, especially the internet (sites such as YouTube.com), has increased the number of representations of competitive bodybuilding physiques. It is important to remember that many people may never have seen a competitive physique (certainly not a professional bodybuilder's physique) in real life and so for many fans of the activity these bodies exist only in the hyperreal sense of media representation. Chapters in this part will therefore address such topics as the erotics of female muscle and 'muscle-worship'; competitive bodybuilders represented as "freaks"; and a discussion of the bodybuilding physique as avant-garde representation.

All the contributors to this collection are active researchers in the debates of bodybuilding. Many are widely published in this area and some contributors (Anne Bolin, Kenneth Dutton, Joanna Frueh, Leslie Heywood and Lee Monaghan) are authors of highly respected books and articles on bodybuilding. They have all agreed to contribute to this collection as they feel there is a need to address recent developments and, in some cases, revise or reconsider their original positions on this topic. Given that there have been so many developments in the activity of bodybuilding, we believe that a new collection, addressing contemporary representations and practices, is a necessary addition to the existing literature.

WHAT IS BODYBUILDING?

One of a number of "most muscular" poses, the crab brings everything to the surface, making the crabber look like a human anatomy chart. I'd start with a deep breath, then, bending forward at the waist, fiercely thrust my arms before me like a crab's pincers and watch. The inevitable result was veins shooting like lightning across the skin of my chest and shoulders, muscle fibers dancing just beneath my skin, my whole body shuddering. Bodybuilders call this veiny look "vascularity", and it is prized as proof that a bodybuilder can be huge without being fat.

(Sam Fussell 1991: 65)

To a casual observer, male and female bodybuilding might seem simple enough: the attempt through training, nutrition, and self-discipline to attain the heavily muscled body which the bodybuilder considers "ideal" or "perfect"; professionally this body is then exhibited in competition to be appreciated for itself, much as a spectator (or owner) might cherish the form of a thoroughbred horse, or the line of a classic car. However, as Sam Fussell's description reveals, this would be too static a perception: building up the body is about attaining the dynamic moment of "vascularity," itself the product of many months and many stages of training and nutrition. Therefore, to appreciate bodybuilding properly (most especially in the professional realm) first requires a recognition that it is concerned with both practice and a product. Through its practices of training and dieting, bodybuilding for men and women involves the labor-intensive process of attaining the imagined "perfect" muscular body, but the product, in effect the climax of a fundamentally aesthetic moment, is extremely fleeting. In fact, it can only be given lasting substance in the photographic image, which is why the visuality of the body and its representation in photographs of bodybuilders and magazines devoted to such have been essential to the subculture of bodybuilding, right from its very beginnings. However, as Fussell's valuation of this crucial moment reveals – in being 'huge without being fat' – there is an additional dimension to these endeavors, since the sought-after ideal body also involves the pursuit of a dynamic target. In bodybuilding more than anything else size matters, and so any perfection which is attained in the moment of the pose must be seen as doubly fleeting. This is because the history of bodybuilding has been one of continual increase – in the size, weight, muscle mass and body measurements which constitute the dynamic aesthetics of the ideal bodybuilder's physique.

In this introductory part I want to provide a brief history of bodybuilding for men and women, and explain how for the male, there was a movement from a bodybuilding aesthetic based upon an imagined classical archetype to a far more excessive representation. Although bodybuilding remains rooted in the classical style, the far larger and defined bodies represented in bodybuilding magazines, gyms and on the stage during competition have begun to overwhelm classical codes that, historically, have operated as an aesthetic blueprint. Irrespective of classical lineage, bodybuilding is based upon the increasingly fragmented body with over-developed body parts often celebrated and displayed over the whole. This fragmentation of the body is what I term "Post Classic."

ORIGINS OF BODYBUILDING

Without doubt, the most important factor in the emergence of body-building was the popularity in late nineteenth-century America of the coiner of the term, Eugene Sandow. Sandow developed an act based on displays of strength and muscular poses and he met with some success on the stage in Europe, but it was through an American that Sandow found fame and fortune. In 1887 while in search of a new act for his father's Trocadero Theatre in Chicago, the American promoter Florenz Ziegfeld went to a performance of the musical *Adonis* in London and saw Sandow posing on the stage in between acts, gaining applause and admiration from both men and women in the audience (Dutton 1995: 121). Ziegfeld was struck by the potential for exhibition in the United States and he went on to establish Sandow as one of the most well-known bodies in the world. Ziegfeld invested $5,000 to put Sandow on a tour of American and European theatres; he was a sensation and his popularity was such that the tour netted $30,000 in six weeks, with Sandow eventually receiving $1,500 a week (Webster 1982: 33). Sandow signed a four-year contract with Ziegfeld and spent the few years constantly touring America and England.

While Sandow occasionally took part in typically vaudevillian displays – notably his "fight" with a lion in 1894 (Chapman 1994: 88) – his real importance lies not in being a weightlifter, but more significantly as some-one whose physique was viewed as an object of interest in its own right. Emmanuel Cooper comments: 'Sandow was not described as a strong man but as "the world's most perfect man", someone who could lift weights and demonstrate strength, but who was also aesthetically pleas-ing' (1990: 92). This distinction – between the celebration of strength demonstrated by an activity such as weightlifting and the appreciation of its results in a body built by such an activity – would become crucial to bodybuilding's definition of itself. Success brought forth a plethora of magazines, books, and fitness products from Sandow (and a slew of imita-tors), all aiming to make the practice of physical culture, its subject, the body, and its object, images of the body, into marketable commodities.

To accentuate his body, Sandow did not wear the usual leopard skins and white tights, but brief shorts or even just a faux fig leaf while on stage (Budd 1997: 42). If near naked display was central to Sandow's popularity, so were the photographs that recorded his muscular poses off stage. In 1899 the French writer and traveler Paul Bourget commented on how during a visit to a group of American millionaires in Newport,

Rhode Island, he was astonished to find that most of the various houses he visited had photographs of the semi-nude Sandow prominently on display (Chapman 1997: 4). Photography allowed the dissemination and sale of Sandow's body outside the theatre, and it has been the primary medium for displaying bodybuilding ever since. This extended the very practices of popular consumption, which William Ewing suggests had invented the sports star in the mid-1860s when photography had become less expensive and its products more widespread (1996: 168). By the 1880s, particular interest was already being shown in photographs of male and female athletic bodies shown by *cartes de visite*, cabinet cards, and cigarette cards (ibid.: 168). Given the long exposure times and primitive flash devices of early photography, it was impossible to capture anyone in any bodily pose except by requiring them to sit or stand still for at least several seconds. Working within such static impositions, the poses adopted by Sandow (and soon his many imitators) included elements drawn from classical statuary which provided a set of recogniz-able codes for the representation of muscularity that remain highly influential for bodybuilding even today.

It's probably fair to say that bodybuilding would likely never have achieved the success it did if it had not been for photography – a body-builder might hold a pose for a few seconds, but the photograph held the pose forever. Thus to understand the aesthetic of bodybuilding it is necessary to examine not just the live body in the event, but the body as represented in the photographic image (see Part 2 'Representations,' this volume). Furthermore, it is important to consider what both the actual bodies and the images of bodies reveal in terms of the inscription of the effort in the gym which has made the body what it is. Popular photog-raphy at the turn of the century had already given significant attention to the body, most especially in regard to the female nude. Pornographic images became available almost from the first advent of the photography – the earliest dates from 1855 (Koetzle 1994: 47). However, more aesthetic images of naked or semi-naked women at this time often used classical settings and props to legitimize their subject matter. Nevertheless, as Isabel Tang observes, unlike painting where the artist's model was often idealized, photography showed *real* women, resulting in a body seen with all its imperfections. She writes:

> The problem with photography was that it was too candid; it showed too much. And a surfeit of the real made it impossible to sustain the ideal. Instead of the painter's ability to idealize the human form, in a photograph the blemishes and the imperfections of the actual woman were on full view. Instead of alabaster skins, there were blemished ones; instead of idealized limbs, they were awkward, foreshortened ones . . . This was the shock of the real.
>
> (1999: 105, 107)

But if the female form often seemed let down by photography, it proved an ideal medium for displaying images of the muscularity which bodybuilders devoted such efforts to making real. Cooper comments that: 'The camera was perfect for documenting the success and development of the individual bodybuilder' and that 'the photographic process could flatter particular muscle development and show body proportions at their best by the use of angled lighting and so on' – particularly true of black and white photography (1990: 92). However, photographs also validated bodybuilding because as a medium they were considered to show the "real." Alan Thomas writes: 'An awareness of the remarkable fullness of the power born into his [Victorian] hands is plainly evident in the exclamations of delight with which the early photographer noted in his diary his ability to record with the camera every line and crack of the brickwork of his neighbour's chimney' (1978: 11). Due to this realism, photographers of the body had to use ways to prove the "artistic" veracity of photographs. Photographs of the body used props and heroic poses based on Western high art to suggest that photography was a continuation of painting and sculpture. Unlike the tradition of Western art where the artist idealized the body via brushwork (or carving), the bodybuilders created an aesthetic ideal in the flesh; hence the precise suitability of the photographic medium in recording this realization. Once again, Sandow was the primary originator of the photographic pose as a means of displaying developed muscles. In a fashion akin to the female nude, he was often photographed copying a variety of classical Greek statuary in poses. Such photographs of Sandow and his contemporaries thus provided a set of recognizable codes for the representation of muscularity that would become highly influential for bodybuilding, particularly within an American context.

AMERICAN MUSCLE

An American named Bernarr Macfadden had been strongly influenced by Sandow's bodybuilding contest and it inspired him to organize the first American bodybuilding competition in 1903. In an advertisement for the event, Macfadden wrote: 'In nearly every country in these great United States there is held an annual fair in which prizes are offered for the best specimens of the various domestic animals – horses, cows and pigs. But never on a single occasion has a prize been offered for the best specimen of man or woman' (Adams 2009: 50). As Kenneth Dutton notes:

> Macfadden, never a man to let pass an opportunity for self-promotion, was not long in organising a series of similar contests in America. Hiring Madison Square Gardens as the venue, he offered a

prize of $1,000 (an immense sum at the time) for the winner of his title as the 'Most Perfectly Developed Man in America'. The victor was a physical education graduate of Harvard University, Albert Treloar (1873–1960), a former assistant to Sandow, who was to capitalise on this newly-won title by the publication of *Trelaor's Science of Muscular Development* (1904) and a series of theatrical bookings under the name, 'Albert, the Perfect Man'. In 1906, he became Director of Physical Education at the Los Angeles Athletic Club; it was from this location that he was to introduce the practice of bodybuilding to Southern California, where it was later to establish its unofficial world headquarters.

(1995: 128)

(The contest would later produce the most famous advocator for building up the body: Charles Atlas.) It was shortly after the 1903 competition that Sandow first coined the term "bodybuilding" in a book of the same name. Sandow refers to bodybuilding as part of Physical Culture commenting: 'Physical Culture means all-round development whereby the organisms of the body, are brought into a thoroughly healthy condition, so enabling one to realise to the full what real health is' (1904: 2). In Sandow's description, bodybuilding is concerned with health and, as a result of this, an improved appearance. (This link to bodybuilding and health is still important in contemporary culture as Bailey and Gillett analyze, Chapter 4, this volume.) But bodybuilding was also about displaying the body as an object for contemplation and enjoyment (in either the competition or photograph); and most importantly for Sandow (and later Macfadden), it was a lucrative marketing concept. Sandow and Macfadden epitomized the fitness entrepreneur, but it would be in the mid-1940s that the dominant cultural narratives of bodybuilding would shift almost exclusively to America, and to West Coast America at that.

Why did the possession of a muscular body appeal so much to twentieth-century America? (See Heywood, Chapter 6, this volume, for further consideration of these debates.) To understand this it is instructive to briefly examine the history of the Italian immigrant Angelo Siciliano, who would popularize the image of the bodybuilder while simultaneously, locating such a figure firmly within American popular culture. Born in 1893, Siciliano came to prominence in 1921 when he won "The World's Most Beautiful Man" contest organized and sponsored by Macfadden. Siciliano had changed his name shortly before he won Macfadden's first contest. While walking on the beach, a friend commented that Siciliano resembled a statue of Atlas which was placed on top of a local hotel. He liked the name, which symbolized strength and power; it also had the advantage of sounding American as with his other adopted name of Charles.[1] In 1928 Atlas met Charles Roman, a New York University Business School graduate, and together they decided to exploit Atlas' popularity as bodybuilder and strongman. They devised an advertisement cartoon strip entitled 'The Insult That Made a Man out of "Mac"' (based on a personal incident experienced by Atlas when he was 16 years old) depicting a skinny boy named Mac having sand kicked in his face on the beach by a brawny male. This humiliation leads the young man to take up the course of exercises promoted by Charles Atlas which result in him gaining a muscular body, a battered and shamed "bully," and the adoration of his girlfriend and others watching on the beach. (For more in-depth examination of how bodybuilding relates to dynamics of shame and pride, see Sparkes et al., Chapter 5, this volume.)

Atlas' greatest achievement was turning the image of the bodybuilder into a populist representation more associated with America than ancient Greece. The predominance of Atlas' image in the advertising pages of comic books shifted associations of the muscular body from the high art of classical statuary to the low art of popular culture. It is striking that in the comic books, the bodies of superhero characters such as Superman (emerging in 1934) and Batman (materializing in 1939) took on the same physical characteristics of heavily muscled arms, chests and thighs that Atlas was often advertising on the facing page. Other characteristics reveal this Americanization. Early bodybuilders such as Sandow had covered their bodies in chalk to pale the skin in emulation of Greek statuary. However, in America pale was replaced by the "healthy" tan, and chalk was replaced by sunbathing. The mahogany tan of Charles Atlas pointed less to ancient Greece and classicism than to the Californian beaches which were to become the home of bodybuilding in the 1940s. Atlas' body most of all demonstrated that bodybuilding was starting to depart significantly from the classical ideals of Apollonian perfection which Sandow had sought to copy (even if Atlas' adverts suggest otherwise in their reference to Greek bodily ideals).

BOB HOFFMANN AND THE WEIDER BROTHERS

Although Sandow should be regarded as an inaugural figure in bodybuilding, he was nevertheless still seen by many as a strongman, albeit one with a remarkable physique. This is not surprising: from its beginnings, bodybuilding was an activity with a fundamental relationship to strength-based routines of exercise and the display of muscle would remain secondary to displays of strength until 1946 and the emergence of a dedicated bodybuilding association – the International Federation of Bodybuilders (IFBB). The IFBB emerged from the revival in the 1930s of physique magazines in America and Europe. However, the magazines rarely existed in themselves – they were usually closely linked to the promoters of bodybuilding products and organizers of small-scale competitions. The first such entrepreneur was the American Bob Hoffmann, owner of the profitable and well-known York Barbell Company, who in 1932 began publication of the photo magazine *Strength and Health*.

In 1946 came the formation of an alternative professional association, the IFBB by two Canadian brothers, Joe and Ben Weider, publishers of the magazines *Your Physique* (starting in 1940) and *Muscle Power* (beginning in 1945). The relationship between Hoffman and the Weiders was never cordial as Joe Weider explains in his autobiography:

> I'd rather keep Hoffman out of my story because I don't like conflict and badmouthing people. But this would be like David not mentioning Goliath, or like leaving the Nazis out of a history of World War II. If he could have, Hoffman would have squashed me like a bug when I started to get successful and threaten his position. For years and years he did everything in his power to smear my name and tear down my reputation and discredit all that Ben and I did for the sake of bodybuilding. Hoffman was an egomaniac, a faker, a hypocrite – this is not to mention an anti-Semite, anti-Black, anti-foreigner bigot.
>
> (Weider et al. 2006: 38–39)

Both organizations and their promoters relied heavily on recruiting star bodybuilders to their stable to market their publications, the products on sale within, and most of all the identity for bodybuilding which their associations stood for. Hoffmann, operating through the Amateur Athletic Union (AAU) and thus with connections to established sports organizations, used his magazines to focus more directly on practices such as weightlifting. The Weider magazines in contrast were the first to devote their entire content to its result – the body built by bodybuilding. Likewise as promoters, the Weiders wanted bodybuilding contests to be the main event without the incorporation of weightlifting displays. This distinction was a crucial recognition that the muscular body was an object that could be admired – and judged – in its own right. As such, the muscular body originated by Sandow was reified by rules, regulations, competition practices and regularized training regimes. Both the AAU and IFBB provided competitions with regulations and classifications, but with the IFBB becoming the dominant awarding body from the 1950s.

The Weiders have retained significant political and economic control over bodybuilding to a degree which cannot compare with other professional athletic activities, although in 2003 there was the acquisition of the IFBB by the publishing company America Media, Inc. (AMI) – and then the death of Ben Weider in 2008. The IFBB still remains the controlling influence and it regulates all the major bodybuilding competitions in America including: IronMan Pro Invitational, The Arnold Classic, Night of Champions, Masters Olympia, Mr. Olympia, and the Grand Prix contests (the latter held in numerous European countries including England). As a result of the competing promotional activities of the AAU and IFBB, bodybuilding became much more visible in America from the late 1940s onwards.[2]

THE AMERICAN CLASSIC AESTHETIC

Through the late 1930s and 1940s a stretch of beach in Santa Monica – "Muscle Beach" – became one of the defining locations for American bodybuilding. Beginning in 1934, an enclosure on the beachfront became a space for exercise and posing in front of the public by bodybuilders – John Grimek in the 1940s, Steve Reeves in the 1950s, and Larry Scott in the mid-1960s. Muscle Beach was transplanted a few miles down the coast to a better site at Venice Beach in 1959. In the 1970s, Arnold Schwarzenegger and other popular bodybuilders such as Dave Draper, Franco Columbo, Ken Waller, and Frank Zane were, as one observer from the period remarks, regularly to be seen at Venice in the 'open-air Muscle Beach weight-lifting pen' (Ray 1997: 133). From Venice emerged not only muscle beach, but also numerous bodybuilding contests and a number of gymnasiums – the most successful and popular (amongst hardcore bodybuilders) being Gold's Gym opened by Joe Gold in 1965. Soon to become known as the Mecca of Bodybuilding, Gold's Gym gained further iconic status when the bodybuilding documentary *Pumping Iron* was filmed there to record Arnold Schwarzenegger's training for the 1975 Mr. Olympia contest.

The most significant bodybuilder to emerge in the new Californian climate was Steve Reeves. Born in Montana in 1925, Reeves had only a comparatively short bodybuilding career. Working in the IFBB, Reeves became the first bodybuilder to be famed entirely for his body without recourse to any strength-based routines. Richard Dyer writing about bodybuilding of the 1950s notes that a muscular body was a sign of a wealthy body and such a look became strongly associated with America, the nation of conspicuous consumption (1997: 155). The greater size of American bodybuilders more generally was partly due to a greater abundance of foods available in America, unlike Europe where many countries after the Second World War were affected by food shortages and rationing. American bodybuilders who visited England in the late 1940s to compete quickly found themselves losing weight because of food rationing. Dyer thus writes that Reeves' popularity was predominantly due to this 'Americanness' (ibid.: 174). Nevertheless, it is striking that compared with the other bodybuilders of the day such as Reg Park and

Clancy Ross, Reeves' body was of small stature. It was because of the superior muscular definition of his body that he won titles; in effect he won on his aesthetic appeal alone. Of course compared with a non-bodybuilder, Reeves was still exceptionally well built, but his reluctance to add mass to his frame did make his career in competitive bodybuilding fluctuate between success and failure, and he lost in the finals of competitions such as the 1948 Mr. Universe and the 1949 Mr. USA (Webster 1982: 91).

Therefore, compared with Park, Ross and other professional bodybuilders of the time, and alongside maverick figures such as Charles Atlas, Reeves' physique was much more in keeping with the earlier ideals of classical beauty venerated in Greek statuary and emulated by Eugene Sandow. Reeves is still used as a point of reference for the Apollonian ideal in contemporary bodybuilding magazines. His broad shoulders, muscular and defined body, and small waist revealed that 1950s American bodybuilding had produced a more symmetrical, V-tapered (i.e. wide shoulders and narrow waist), and aesthetically shaped body than Europe, and Reeves was continuously praised in bodybuilding magazines. He remains seen as typifying the classically developed body that, like the ancient Greeks, placed emphasis on proportion, shape and symmetry rather than size. As such Reeves was the epitome of, what I term, the "American Classic" aesthetic.

However, in the early 1960s professional bodybuilding underwent two significant changes which, in other ways, make Reeves seem obsolete. First, bodybuilders started to appear much more defined because of the introduction of diuretics that rid the body of excess water fluid, revealing far greater levels of muscularity and definition. Second, if one looks at bodybuilding magazines from this era, the physiques on display quite abruptly changed, with an even greater impetus on mass than had been seen before. Larry Scott, winner of the first two Mr. Olympia contests in New York in 1965 and 1966 typified the direction which bodybuilding was going with his enormous upper arm development, earning him the nickname 'Master of Biceps' (Grannis 1998: 117). Other much larger bodybuilders began to appear, including Dave Draper, Boyer Coe, Sergio Oliva, Harold Poole, Wilf Sylvester, Serge Nubret, Rick Wayne, Chris Dickerson, Al Beckles, and Arnold Schwarzenegger. The reason for this change was partly due to more effective exercise and better diet, but significantly to the emergence of anabolic steroids, a factor that irreparably cut off the sport from its classical roots and would function as the primary armature of a new American Classicism which made Reeves only a nostalgic ideal. The American physician Dr John Ziegler is principally accountable for steroids being introduced into bodybuilding during the 1950s.

During the 1950s, athletes from the Eastern bloc became notorious for their alleged use of drugs to enhance their performance. In collaboration with Swiss pharmaceutical manufacturer CIBA, in 1958 Ziegler produced an oral steroid called Dianabol (nicknamed "D-Bol"), which was made widely available to American weightlifters (Woodland 1980: 54). Les Woodland reports:

> The results were impressive at first, but Ziegler was reportedly horrified to discover changes to more than the weights lifted. Among the effects he noted were the shrinking of the testes. The trouble was that the lifters, delighted at the result of Ziegler's experiments, had abandoned all caution and started swallowing the drugs like peppermints. Their enthusiasm ran unbridled and Ziegler withdrew hurriedly.
>
> (1980: 54)

Ellis Cashmore defines steroids as 'a compound considered to be responsible for the particular synthesis that causes the construction of muscle mass' (1990: 146). As he continues: 'The idea behind using an anabolic steroid is to mirror the chemical action of the male hormone testosterone in the body and facilitate muscle growth' (ibid.: 146). Yet the side effects of testicular atrophy first noticed by Ziegler were due to the drugs anabolic properties which are impossible to completely stop. The anabolic effects of steroids – getting bigger, stronger and changing shape – have been compared to forcing the body to go through puberty again (Thorne and Embleton 1997: 551).

By 1969, *Track and Field News* would observe that steroids had become the 'breakfast of champions', a phrase which then gained ironic popularity in American gyms during the 1980s. For the journalist Ron Harris, the very size of American bodybuilders since the late 1960s has 'flaunted their criminal activity through their very physiques' (1995: 7). For bodybuilding, the 1960s has sometimes been called the "Dianabol decade" but in fact while bodybuilders took a wide selection of steroids, it was usually in much lower dosages than later generations would use. The dosage, like the bodies themselves, has dramatically increased over the years. In 1977 Schwarzenegger admitted some use of steroids: 'I will not speak for my colleagues but I will write about my experience with tissue-building drugs. Yes, I have used them, but no, they didn't make me what I am. Anabolic steroids were helpful to me in maintaining muscle size while on a strict diet in preparation for a contest.'[3] By the mid-1970s the muscular bodies on show at competition level on stage and in magazines were getting significantly larger than before due to bodybuilders taking a cocktail of steroids with a variety of other drugs, a method otherwise known as "stacking" (Zulak 1999: 99). Stacking refers to making extra muscle gains through mixing oral and injectable steroids with other drugs (such as insulin and growth hormones). According to steroid "experts" such as John Romano, this alone has been the foundation of success for many professional bodybuilders in competition since the end of that decade (1996: 136). (For an analysis of the use of steroids in contemporary bodybuilding culture, see Monaghan, Chapter 3, this volume.)

Yet despite the rise in drug-taking in the sport, bodybuilding gained a new respectability in the 1970s with the emergence of the fitter body as general ideal for men and women alike and the parallel rise of Arnold Schwarzenegger, the first superstar bodybuilder. Looking back, many bodybuilding commentators seem to see the era as the Golden Age of bodybuilding. However, this attitude is not fulfilled by a reading of George Butler and Charles Gaines' 1974 book *Pumping Iron* (followed in 1975 by a documentary of the same name.). In their introduction, Butler and Gaines remark that while researching the book, they had 'felt at times like 19th Century explorers . . . because we found bodybuilding to be as primeval and unmapped as parts of Labrador' (1991: n. pag.). Remarkably *Pumping Iron* was the first book length attempt to report on and analyze American bodybuilding, even though the practice had emerged almost 80 years before. In their text, Butler and Gaines' would compare bodybuilding to 'dwarf-tossing and midget-wrestling,' a connection which not only signifies a relationship to the freak show, but also, by using such an outlandish example, to the ludicrous, the kitsch, and the marginal. (See Richardson, Chapter 9, this volume, for a consideration of how bodybuilding maintains this "freak show" status.)

However, the mid- to late 1970s saw the arrival of a time in which fitness was more generally gaining a cultural currency and in which bodybuilding came to be seen as a more mainstream pursuit. This metamorphosis in the 1970s and 1980s was dramatic and the American fitness industry today has a massive turnover. Recognizing this shift, in 1980 Joe Weider cannily changed the title of his leading magazine from *Muscle Builder* to *Muscle and Fitness*.

ARNOLD SCHWARZENEGGER AND THE POST CLASSIC AESTHETIC

Schwarzenegger was born in Thal, Austria in 1947 and his first physical contest was aged 16 years old as a weightlifter in a beer hall in Graz near Thal (McGough 1997: 48). He continued to compete successfully in powerlifting events between 1966 and 1968, even though by then he had decided to commit himself to bodybuilding (Dobbins 1997a: 96–97). In 1966, aged 19 years old, Schwarzenegger traveled to England to compete in the top amateur class European bodybuilding contest, the NABBA Amateur Mr. Universe (Roark 1999: 134). He lost to Ivan Dunbar, but Schwarzenegger returned to win the contest the following year, and then moved into the professional division where he won three consecutive

Mr. Universe titles – the youngest winner of the title. One week after winning the 1967 NABBA Mr. Universe, Joe Weider, interested in the Austrian's European success, flew him to compete in the 1968 IFBB Mr. Universe contest in Miami (Schwarzenegger 1993: 47). By all accounts to Schwarzenegger's apparent surprise, he lost to a bodybuilder named Frank Zane who, at 190 lbs, was 45 lbs lighter than his rival (McGough 1997: 52). This defeat would prove a crucial experience not just for Schwarzenegger but also for the future development of the sport. As Joe Weider recalls: 'Arnold was huge . . . He had some definition, but not a lot. Europeans at that time concentrated almost totally on size and mass, so Arnold was surprised when he was beaten by Frank Zane, who was so much smaller but in terrific shape' (Dobbins 1997b: 63). Eventually Schwarzenegger's body would triumph by combining European size with American vascularity, and in doing so would revolutionize professional bodybuilding.

In the opinion of most bodybuilding commentators, Schwarzenegger is still considered the most important bodybuilder in history (and further emphasized when a meeting was immediately arranged between American Media, Inc. and Schwarzenegger to utilize his image and expertise as 'an anchoring force' for the seven fitness and bodybuilding publications which the company had recently purchased) (Leamer 2005: 277). No doubt some of this comes from his success beyond bodybuilding: following his retirement from competition in 1975, Schwarzenegger appeared in a succession of Hollywood films that were hugely important in imbuing an excessive muscularity with the hyper-visibility that presented the bodybuilder as a figure of staggering power. But if Schwarzenegger's bodybuilding career led him (like many predecessors) towards Hollywood and wider popularity from non-bodybuilders, within the field he was one of a number of men whose physical development would send bodybuilding on a different and more exclusive trajectory from the 1980s onwards.

I am not suggesting that the top professional bodybuilders intentionally pushed the sport to the extremes of today; indeed, many of the champions of the 1960s and 1970s (including Schwarzenegger) have shown distaste for the current appearance of professional bodybuilders. But, the example Schwarzenegger set to other bodybuilders was clear and to win a professional bodybuilding contest a competitor must invariably improve on what has come before. The history of the sport reveals that since the 1940s, the bodies on display (and those judging them) have equated progress with an increase in size or vascularity. Schwarzenegger was the first bodybuilder to place stress on achieving not just much greater muscle proportions and bulk, but also significantly higher levels of muscular delineation and definition (or vascularity). Thus he succeeded by combining what had previously been separate elements – a bodybuilder was either big and not too defined, or was well defined but not very big. Possessing mass with vascularity made Schwarzenegger so unbeatable that he finally decided to retire after his 1975 Mr. Olympia victory against Lou Ferrigno (later to play the *Incredible Hulk* on television). Schwarzenegger was the largest body-builder competing throughout his career weighing at his peak 250 lbs. At the time Schwarzenegger was clearly perceived by many as "freakish," yet he was one of the last winners of the Mr. Olympia contest who could be likened to Greek art by mainstream commentators. Like Sandow before him, he was declared 'the world's most perfectly developed man' and invited to pose at the Whitney Museum of American Art in New York for a series of lectures on Greek statuary during 1976 (Roark 1997: 80, 82). This would be an unimaginable tribute for the professional bodybuilders of today. The post-Schwarzenegger bodybuilder is only residually associated with the aesthetics of Greece, and only a little more with that of the classic bodybuilders of the 1940s and 1950s.

Therefore, it is ironic that the very person who helped provide body-building with its greatest publicity since the turn of the last century, should be significantly responsible for encouraging the aesthetic by which professional bodybuilding has become severed from much of its classical lineage, and thereby promoting a look that would ostracize it again from the mainstream which it (and Schwarzenegger) had just found entry into. Equally, it is important to realize that once Schwarzenegger embarked on a film career after retiring from competi-tion, his muscular body became, to some degree, normalized by its very popularity in the space of the cinema. As such, the hyper-mesomorphic aesthetic Schwarzenegger represented appeared to have lost its subcul-tural status, providing another spur for professional bodybuilding to move beyond even Schwarzenegger's physical accomplishments. This is why I suggest that Schwarzenegger is both the apex and the nadir of American bodybuilding and the American Classic body. Thus, while working out did became a much more common pastime for those not normally partaking of weight training, the bodybuilding subculture has – inevitably perhaps – become more extremist. In a guest editorial in *Musclemag* in 1995, bodybuilding writer Ed Fortney asked: 'Is body-building really growing as a sport? Well, that depends on what type of bodybuilding. If you're talking about weight training, bodyshaping and definition training, then the answer is yes. Hardcore bodybuilding, on the other hand, is slowly crawling its way back into a dark and mysteri-ous place' (1995: 7).

The contemporary bodybuilding aesthetic – which I term Post-Classic – focuses on the body as an incongruent set of muscles, a fragmentary physique which is now so defined that during various poses, the muscle fibers are clearly visible beneath the skin. With their broad shoulders and narrow hips and enormous muscles of the torso (chest and back), together with bodies so defined that substructures of muscles reveal

further substructures, these bodies exemplify the most desired hypertrophic look of the contemporary bodybuilder: a "shredded mass."
What is most remarkable about this is the extent to which it has taken
bodybuilding away from the popularity and even respectability which it
seemed to have gained by the early 1980s, one which had led to the
muscular mainstream evident in Hollywood cinema, toys, advertising,
and the like. While the classical body signifies order, proportion and
symmetry, so the new hypermorphic body of Post-Classicism signifies
excess, disproportion, and exaggeration. While today's professional
bodybuilder retains some of the aesthetic traits of American Classicism
(e.g. broad shoulders and defined abdominals), because of an ever-
increasing quest for size and vascularity, other traits have become visible.
By classical definitions, many professional bodybuilders today possess
extremely massive and disproportionate physiques. Thus the image of
the male professional bodybuilder has become, to use a phrase from the
film critic Jack Hunter's history of human oddities, a 'freak of conformity' which I use as another component of Post-Classicism (1995: 100).
Hunter suggested that the freak of conformity is marked out by figures
such as Schwarzenegger (as the hyper-mesomorph) and the super-model
(anorexic chic). Writing in 1995, for Hunter, such figures heralded a
period where the traditional 'freak of deformity' has been superseded by
the 'freak of conformity' in an age where the search for perfection has
become gradually more excessive (ibid.: 100). For this reason many
outside professional bodybuilding who are not used to seeing such
bodies (particularly during periods of competition) view professional
bodybuilders as taking ideals of bodily perfection to such an extreme
that these very attributes begin to invert themselves. The mesomorphic
body shape which became so prized in the visual discourse has become
a "freakish" image of shock value.

FEMALE BODYBUILDING

Women's bodybuilding emerged in the late 1970s (see Bunsell and
Shilling, Chapter 2, and also Chare, Chapter 10, this volume, for developments since in relation to gym culture and in relation to female muscle
worship). Despite it being deemed inappropriate, throughout the late
1980s and 1990s size and ultra definition became the chosen standard of
the female competitors entering competitions (see Bolin, Chapter 1, this
volume). Bodybuilders such as Debbi Muggli, Laura Creavalle, Denise
Rutkowski, Sandy Riddel, and Kim Chizevsky displayed massively thick
muscles, large striated thighs, "razor cut" definition, pronounced
V-tapers and tiny waists with detailed midsections. Since 2000 – and as
clear backlash against women such as former Ms. Olympia Kim
Chizevsky – the main female bodybuilding contests held by the IFBB,

in addition to other bodybuilding organizations, have firmly insisted that women must be less muscular and shredded to encourage a more feminine element back into the sport. Due to the smaller physique being rewarded by the judges, competitors from the past returned who had been out-sized and muscled by their rivals. The first was Juliette Bergmann who won the 2001 Ms. Olympia; the second, was the surprise return of Lenda Murray – previously too small to continue to win – and able to regain her Ms. Olympia "crown" in 2002.

Somewhat ironically, the current female bodybuilder perhaps better represents the American Classic ideal than the men. This was an observation first stated for the 1997 Ms. Olympia when it was commented:

> There were lat spreads, delts, legs, traps and arms the like of which I would have given my right arm to own as a young man. Yes, as a young man, because if you take away the breast and add a little extra here and there, today's top women have the most classic male physiques a man could ever ask for. I hope not to offend any woman bodybuilder by stating such views. Indeed, I don't think I will . . . Women's bodybuilding has reached such a high masculine standard that they have now cornered the market on classical male physiques.
> (Fitness 1998: 54)

With the reduction in mass and extreme definition, these comments seem more apt for the female bodybuilder since 2000. There are also similar developments taking place with the representation of the female fitness and figure competitors. For example, several bodybuilding journalists have noted how the physiques of female fitness competitors (during competition) have gradually become increasingly similar to those of female bodybuilders. Bill Dobbins, for instance, writes how 'it is ironic that over the past several years fitness competitors have got more and more muscular, looking like bodybuilders from a decade earlier, but when you see their pictures in the magazines little of this is evident.'[4] Johnny Fitness also comments that though it is generally well known that the difference between female bodybuilders and fitness competitors has reduced since the mid-1990s, it is the extent of the increasing muscularity of the latter which is less recognized (2001: 9). Part of this reason is due, as Fitness observes, to the reduction in size and condition of female bodybuilders because of changes to the rules by the IFBB (ibid.: 9). Concurrently when in competition, female competitors are shown increasingly muscular and "cut" with highly defined bodies that, as Fitness observes, has removed the previously marked physical difference between 'the most muscular fitness girls from the least muscular women bodybuilders' (ibid.: 9).

The current paradox is that female bodybuilding and fitness (and now figure) contestants seem to be nearer in representation to the American

Classic ideal than the male bodybuilder. Fundamentally these women adhere to the classical mesomorphic shape with wide shoulders, thin waist, a V-taper, muscular thighs, and overall muscular balance, muscle separation, and proportion. On the contrary, male bodybuilding continues to be dominated by larger, ever more disproportionate, and exceptionally ripped and shredded bodies. The 2010 Mr. Olympia – Jay Cutler – possesses a physique that renders the triumphant body of Arnold Schwarzenegger a historical curiosity. The changing aesthetic in men's bodybuilding serves to shed light not only on the entrenchment of male chauvinism in bodybuilding, but also on a competitive idiom that begs questions about the status of an aesthetic that amalgamates with "freakery."

Notes

1 Information taken from the documentary *Charles Atlas: Modern Day Hercules* (2003), Biography Channel (Sky, UK).
2 I should stress that for reasons of economy, I have not mentioned Peary Rader. Rader started one of the most successful and influential American bodybuilding magazines, *Iron Man* (1938–), and it helped shape bodybuilding subculture in a variety of ways.
3 Quote taken from http://www.bodyfatguide.com/ArnoldSteroidConfession. html (last accessed 22 October 2007).
4 See Dobbins' discussion at http://www.billdobbins.com/PUBLIC/pages/ coolfree/mso_canc.html (last accessed 10 August 2010).

Part 1

Practices

Figure I.1 Noel Gordon. Courtesy of Rebecca Andrews.

Introduction to Part 1
What is the "Practice" of Bodybuilding?

Niall Richardson

When I teach classes on the "body," I always try to emphasize to my students that we are all body-builders. In other words, we all "build" the body on a daily basis. For example, we decide how we make-up our skin and we tan it, paint it or even modify its appearance with cosmetic procedures; we decide whether to shave or wax the hair on our bodies; we style and/or color the hair on our heads; we ornament the body with jewelry or piercings; we choose clothes which re-shape the body's silhouette, and nearly all of us, at some time or other, are involved in a process of dietary manipulation and exercise in order to lose fat and tone/shape the voluntary muscles of the body. In contemporary culture the "body" is now viewed as a project, rather than an essential or fixed attribute, and all of us, to some degree or other, are involved in the practice of body-building in that we are shaping or styling the tissues of our body.

However, bodybuilding is usually read as an area of body-modification in which a person engages in a regime of resistant weight-training exercises, and follows a very specific diet, in order to build and shape the voluntary muscles of the body. Of course, many people engage in a process of diet and resistance weight training for purposes other than that of bodybuilding. Dancers and athletes, for example, will all "work out" in order to support or enhance their performance on the stage or the track. Yet the difference is that although other athletes and sports people may employ bodybuilding practices, they do so in order to supplement or enhance the performance in their specific sport. Bodybuilding, by contrast, holds the sculpted physique *as* the final product of the activity rather than the additional gains in strength or endurance which the activity may promote. While other activities may require a highly muscular physique in order to enhance performance; in bodybuilding the development of the muscular physique *is* the final goal.

For this reason, much academic writing to date has focused on one possible final product of bodybuilding: the competition level physique. Understandably, critics and writers have been intrigued by the semiotics of the competition-level physique, especially how it challenges or conforms to traditional gender iconography. While male bodybuilding has often been viewed as the assertion of hegemonic masculinity (Bridges 2009; Gillett and White 1992; Wiegers 1998), female bodybuilding has been regarded as feminist resistance and critics have considered how/if it challenges traditional feminine iconography (see Brook 2001; Coles 1999; Grogan et al. 2004; Guthrie and Castelnuovo 1992; Ian 2001; Schulze 1990; St. Martin and Gavey 1996). Other critics have been interested in the debates about gendered spectatorship and gazing which are implicit in the dynamics of bodybuilding competitions/representations (Brady 2001; Chare 2008; Holmlund 1989; Patton 1994; Richardson 2008; Simpson 1994) while some have attempted to "queer" the body-building physique (Richardson 2004; Shippert 2007). Most importantly, it is often assumed that bodybuilding simply *is* the competition-ready physique.

Arguably, there are a few problems with this assertion. For example, underpinning much of the writing which focuses simply on the "competition" physique is an assumption that the bodybuilder will look like this all year long. As any of us who have been competitive bodybuilders ourselves will know, this is not the case. First, these bodies are the product of an intense period of dieting and dehydration and if the bodybuilder attempted to maintain this "condition" for a prolonged period, s/he would create considerable health problems. Second, this physique is very much the product of "staging" techniques – especially tanning/make-up and stage lighting. Much of bodybuilding is about "illusion" – the appearance of dense slabs of muscle flexing beneath paper-thin skin. In day-to-day activities, however, many bodybuilders, dressed as they do in "baggies" (loose bodybuilding clothes which cover their pumped-up muscles) will have a very different appearance and, if anything, merely appear bulky (see Locks 2003 and Chapter 8 this volume).

Therefore, this part is an attempt to broaden much of the existing writing on bodybuilding by widening the focus so that the only consideration is *not* simply the politics of the stage-ready, oiled and flexing physique. Indeed, most of the bodybuilding work takes place in the gym, these modern-day torture chambers where bodybuilders push themselves to the absolute limit every day of their lives. As Bunsell and Shilling in Chapter 2 of this collection asks, what are the politics of the gym in relation to training regimes and how does the gender of the bodybuilder inflect this space? Similarly, how do bodybuilding regimes map onto health and fitness ideologies and the self-identifications which body-builders make in this respect (Bailey and Gillett, Chapter 4)? What about the other factors which deserve consideration in the forging of a bodybuilding physique, such as the personal emotions (shame/pride) experienced by the athlete (Sparkes et al., Chapter 5) and his/her "possible" use of pharmaceutical, performance-enhancing drugs (Monaghan, Chapter 3)? Of course, there are many people who train regularly in the gym but never intend to step onto a competition stage in their life. How do these people identify? Can bodybuilding be deemed an identity if its participants never move into the competition stage (Heywood, Chapter 6)? All these questions are at the forefront of the following chapters.

One aspect which we hope will distinguish this book from previous collections is that this part will maintain a focus upon bodybuilding life outside of the competition stage. Although some contributors are considering the dynamics of competition level bodybuilding (Bolin, Chapter 1), the focus of many of the chapters will be on bodybuilding identifications and gym culture. One of the most interesting aspects of gym culture is that although many people are actively engaged in bodybuilding (i.e. following an ascetic diet and a program of resistance weight training in order to build and shape the voluntary muscles of the body), they tend to avoid identifying as bodybuilders. Most people prefer to say that they 'go to the gym' or 'work out' or 'weight train' rather than claim the identity of being a bodybuilder. There are a number of probable reasons as to why this is the case. First, as I have already pointed out, the idea of bodybuilding as something linked to the competition stage is ingrained in much contemporary culture. Can someone identify as a bodybuilder if he/she has never stepped onto the competition stage? One possible comparison could be with someone identifying as a 'writer' when he/she has never had anything published. Related to this is the area which the second part of the book will address in more detail: the idea of bodybuilding *as* representation. If the image of the competition-ready bodybuilder is canonized as *the* look of bodybuilding, then most people would acknowledge that their off-season physique does not match up to the recognized norm and so feel a sense of embarrassment in failing to compare. Obviously it is rather humiliating to identify as a bodybuilder and receive a puzzled stare from someone who then says, 'Oh really? I hadn't noticed.'

Second, bodybuilding has always been a "suspect" activity. For men, it is dogged by the stigma of homoeroticism (see Richardson, Chapter 9 this volume), while for women it is gender transgression and, given that gender is the scaffold for heterosexuality, then female bodybuilding is also dismissed as sexually "deviant." What problems do female bodybuilders encounter, not only in the competition circuit, but also in the gym itself? Likewise, *can* a male bodybuilder identify beyond the two stereotypes of either metropolitan gay "gym-bunnies" or narcissistic, vacuous "muscle-hedz?" Related to the last stereotype is, of course, the stigma of illicit steroid use. Most towns or cities will have one "hardcore" bodybuilding gym which is synonymous with steroid use. Parents may well quiver with fear that their teenage son might be enticed into such a gym which is "filled with steroids." In other words, there has always been something rather "deviant" about bodybuilding. Many times I have had middle-class acquaintances frown with disgust when they learn that I engage in the activity of bodybuilding. Surely this is not a suitable pastime for a university academic? In this respect there may be a problem for many people in finding a space (often a literal gym space) in which they *can* identify.

Related to this has been the challenge posed by the rise of "middle-class" health clubs in Anglo-American culture from the 1980s onwards (see Heywood, Chapter 6, this volume). Far from promoting the practice of bodybuilding, these venues often operate as a defining other against the bodybuilder who is usually not welcome in such establishments. When I asked a local "health club" why they did not have heavier dumb-bells, the manager informed me that they did not want to encourage bodybuilders around the place. This was a "nice" establishment. In this respect, despite the legacy of Arnold Schwarzenegger as Governor of California, and the mainstreaming of the bodybuilder physique in 1980s Hollywood, the practice of bodybuilding still remains a subcultural activity in which it is difficult to find space for identification. The following contributions hope to address some of the difficulties surrounding the practice of bodybuilding and its enthusiasts.

Anne Bolin is a name familiar to many of us – whether scholars of bodybuilding or competitors on the US competition circuit. Bolin starts this part with her consideration of female bodybuilding competitions and how "fitness" competitions have eclipsed female bodybuilding comps. In 'Buff Bodies and the Beast: Emphasized Femininity, Labor and Power Relations among Fitness, Figure and Women Bodybuilding Competitors,' Bolin considers how inauguration of the sport of women's bodybuilding in 1975 gave women the chance to push the perimeters on femininity with their unruly bodies; challenging the hegemonic gender order. Indeed, much of the writing on female bodybuilding viewed it simply as feminist resistance to traditional feminine iconography and it was often the case that female bodybuilding was a key topic on Women's Studies or Gender Studies academic programs. Bolin, however, suggests that by the new millennium, a bodily backlash in feminine ideals of beauty had begun to perforate this trend of transgressive embodiment and this is registered in the relative eclipsing of women's bodybuilding through the increasing popularity of fitness contests and the recent intro-duction of figure competitions. Bolin's chapter provides a very important cultural history of female bodybuilding and focuses on four watersheds in women's bodybuilding.

While Bolin's chapter focuses on the evolution of the female body-building competition circuit, Tanya Bunsell and Chris Shilling's chapter considers how female bodybuilders identify within the gym. In 'Outside and Inside the Gym: Exploring the Identity of the Female Bodybuilder,' Bunsell and Shilling explore how female bodybuilders seek to develop and maintain a viable sense of self despite being stigmatized for non-conformity to traditional gender iconography. Bunsell and Shilling consider the workout; a ritualized activity-space which allows the female bodybuilder to be distanced from the gendered demands of public life. Bunsell and Shilling argue that this activity is central to the identity-affirming activities female body builders engage in. Drawing on Victor Turner's (1992) analysis of liminality, Bunsell and Shilling argue that while the workout is key to the creation and sustenance of female body builders' identities, providing a form of physical capital within this milieu and a relative autonomy from wider interactional norms, the experiences associated with, and the social consequences of, this activity remain culturally ambivalent. Immersion in the rituals and routines of weightlifting provide female body builders with what Turner (1992) describes as a temporary, 'liminoid' escape from daily life, but they offer no permanent solution to the "deviant" role these women are often seen to occupy in society.

From the politics of the competition circuit and the space of gym floor, Lee F. Monaghan broadens the debates by considering the open secret of *much* of the world of bodybuilding: steroid use. In 'Accounting for Illicit Steroid Use: Bodybuilders' Justifications,' Monaghan considers that although the illicit use of anabolic-androgenic steroids, for purposes of performance and physique enhancement, is widely deemed unnecessary, wrong and dangerous, many bodybuilders do make use of these drugs. Indeed, there seems to be a tension within contemporary culture in that there exists, simultaneously, both a romanticization and demonization of steroids. For example, someone might describe a state-of-the-art computer as being 'on steroids' – suggesting that the computer was exceptionally effective/impressive. By contrast, nobody would ever say 'that's a computer on MDMA.' In other words, there is a romantic investment in the "power" of steroids but yet their use is culturally vilified. Monaghan explores bodybuilders' vocabularies of motive for illicit steroid use and how their accounts justified, rather than excused, steroid use. Monaghan finds that supporting the fundamental tenets of their drug subculture, and as part of the underlying negotiation of potentially deviant identities, bodybuilders espoused three main justifications for illicit steroid use: self-fulfillment accounts, condemnation of condemners, and a denial of injury. Here steroid use was rationalized as a legitimate means to an end, people who passed negative judgments were criticized and it was claimed steroid use does not (seriously) harm health or threaten society more generally.

Brian Bailey and James Gillett offer the other side of the bodybuilding coin and, from a discussion of "roids" and the idea of bodybuilding as "harmful" to either the self or society, their chapter considers the idea of bodybuilding as something practised for health. In 'Bodybuilding and Health Work: A Life Course Perspective,' Bailey and Gillett point out that the body image portrayed as ideal in bodybuilding magazines is often closely associated with notions of health. Bailey and Gillett's chapter explores the health dimensions of bodybuilding for men who are at different stages of their life course. Their research builds upon existing social scientific research that has examined the meaning of bodybuilding practices for men who work out regularly but do not compete professionally. In this literature, questions have been posed about the health benefits and risks of the sport for participants. Bailey and Gillett's chapter sheds light on this issue by exploring the meaning of health for men who engage in bodybuilding practices. While bodybuilding is usually recognized as being appearance driven, Bailey and Gillett point out that the ideal of an aesthetic body was understood among younger men as achieving a healthy body. Indeed, for older men, aesthetics was secondary to the development of a functional body which was understood as key to preventing health problems.

From considerations of "roids," supplements, and the relation bodybuilding holds to perceived notions of health, Andrew Sparkes, Joanne Batey and Gareth Owen's chapter discusses the *emotional* investment in the activity of bodybuilding. Most bodybuilders would assert that bodybuilding is not simply an activity which somebody "does" in the gym for a few nights in the week, but is a lifestyle which performatively shapes identification. Sparkes, Batey and Owen's chapter addresses a timely topic in cultural studies: the cultural politics of emotions. In 'The Shame–Pride–Shame of the Muscled Self in Bodybuilding: A Life History Study', Sparkes, Batey and Owen draw on the life history of an elite, black, male bodybuilder in order to explore the association of pride and shame in the construction of this man's bodybuilder identity. A cycle of shame–pride–shame is identified which begins in childhood from the shaming experiences of being small, black and "Other" in an overwhelmingly hostile environment. These experiences of shame motivate the beginning of the bodybuilding project to create a stronger "protected" self-identity and, as the proud muscled body emerges, bodybuilding becomes increasingly linked to self-esteem and shame avoidance. When the successful muscled body is interrupted by a fateful moment that prematurely ends his bodybuilding career, pride turns again to shame as the body is once more experienced as unsuccessful, small, black – the shameful "Other." Considering the influences of racism and social class, the chapter concludes by offering a bio-psychosocial process model to illustrate the competitive dynamic of shame–pride–shame in the "looking-glass self" of this bodybuilder's life history.

Leslie Heywood is certainly a name which requires no introduction for scholars of bodybuilding, having contributed extensively to the existing debates about female bodybuilding and its relationship to feminism and femininity. Here Heywood revisits many of her original arguments and offers some self critique. In 'Building Otherwise: Bodybuilding as Immersive Practice,' Heywood addresses the very issue which this introduction has tried to flag up: if competitive bodybuilding is situated at the top of the gym pyramid, how do non-competitive bodybuilders identify other than through the derogatory label of "gym rat"? Heywood points out that bodybuilding as an activity practiced for health of body and mind has remained relatively unexplored – in fact, without drugs and competitions, "lifting weights" is the operational term rather than "bodybuilding." Heywood wants to move away from the usual explorations of bodybuilding as a form of plastic art (see Locks, Chapter 8, this collection) or else the critique of weightlifting/bodyshaping as a form of self-improvement and begin to formulate a crucial doubleness that shapes the athletic experience in the gym. Rather than occupying a wholly co-opted space or an entirely transformative space, the non-competitive athlete oscillates between transcendence and immanence, tech time and biological time. A sense of immanence, a reconnection to biological time as experienced through physical activity, has been termed by sociologist Nigel Thrift as an 'immersive practice.' Arguably, the immersive is the alternative to the competitive model of sport and its relentless focus on the bottom line of winning. If one shifts the lens away from a bottom-line focus on competition and the zero-sum game of winning, a different experiential model based around the idea of immersive practices begins to emerge within sporting practices that reconnects us with biological time (this is why "being in the zone" is also experienced as being "out of time") and sheds some light on why the "gym rat" makes the gym his or her home away from home.

All of the contributions evidence the love/hate relationship which I myself have always held with bodybuilding. Indeed, many of the contributors are bodybuilders (either competitive level, ex-competitive level or engaged in the 'immersive practice') and continue to be inspired and horrified by bodybuilding culture. Yet whether we are still bewitched by the euphoria of the workout and its beloved "pump," mesmerized by the condition of the bodies on the competition stage, or awed by the activity's whirlpool of emotions, we will always be *intrigued* by bodybuilding. As something which can be *both* normative and transgressive, dissident and contained, ugly and beautiful, bodybuilding will remain one of the most troubling and fascinating practices of contemporary Western culture.

1 Buff Bodies and the Beast

Emphasized Femininity, Labor, and Power Relations among Fitness, Figure, and Women Bodybuilding Competitors 1985–2010

Anne Bolin

INTRODUCTION: THE ATHLETIC AESTHETIC

The women's movement of the 1960s, conjoined with Title IX and the subsequent fitness revolution, gave impetuous to alternative ideals of feminine beauty whose scope has widened to include an athletic aesthetic of toned and taut muscle. The athletic aesthetic was reproduced in diverse popular discourses such as fashion magazines, which described the 1970s somatic ideal of women as the "Action Beauty," and in the inauguration of the sport of women's bodybuilding. Women bodybuilders pushed the perimeters on femininity even further. Their bodies argued that muscles are not the exclusive domain of men. These athletic contours were culturally unruly and contained elements of subversion that challenged the patriarchal hegemony of the Western bio-reductivist gender order.

Research suggests that by the new millennium an embodied backlash in ideals of feminine beauty had occurred (Faludi 1991; Bolin 1998). The body backlash, initiated in the early 1990s and gaining momentum in the new millennium, has undermined these earlier transgressive trends representing women's corporeal power. I argue here that the bodybuilding stage registers an ongoing enfleshed debate through three women's physique sports: bodybuilding, fitness, and figure competitions. In contrast to women's bodybuilding, the fitness and figure competitors somatic contours are much more culturally compliant than those of women bodybuilders. This buttresses a paradigm of what Connell (1987) terms 'emphasized femininity', an accommodation to hegemonic masculinity that yields to the interests and desires of men, and dominates the industrial nexus of femininity/beauty/ heterosexuality. In this regard, Dworkin and Wachs (2009: 32–33) contend that those women positioned to fit the ideal of emphasized femininity are "privileged" even if paradoxically "disempowered" by patriarchal objectification.

METHODS

Reflexive participant observation in the sporting culture of bodybuilding informs the media and textual analysis undergirding this research. My ethnographic research spans 22 years, where I have shared my posing oil and mirrors with fitness competitors since 1994 and figure competitors since 2002. It includes immersion in the locker-room society of "hard core" gyms in several areas of the United States, participation as a training partner, judging and expediting bodybuilding competitions, choreographing routines, helping competitors with posing, and many community ritual events involving food. I have also competed in bodybuilding shows since 1988 on a regular basis (approximately every two years) in a variety of organizations including the National Physique Committee at the local, state, and regional levels (qualifying for national level competition) and in natural organizations (drug tested) including the Natural Physique Association in which I am currently a professional.

Archival and media information comes from a variety of resources. The most important data come from the major organization dominating the sport of bodybuilding, fitness and figure. The brainchild of the Weider brothers, the International Federation of Bodybuilding and Fitness controls amateur level bodybuilding and the physique sports of fitness, figure, and bikini, and organizes over 2,500 national, regional, and global competitions. Under its umbrella are 182 national/international affiliates including regional and continental federations (IFBB Executive Committee 2009–10). The US affiliate, The National Physique Committee (NPC), transmits IFBB rules and regulations and USA rules, updates, and changes through its official website, the state websites, magazines, and related bodybuilding websites (NPC News On-Line). Letters to athletes from the NPC president, Jim Manion, also announce changes. As a competitive amateur bodybuilder and member of the NPC for more than 20 years, I am fortunate in receiving these letters over the years facilitating my documentation of the nuances and changes occurring in the history of the physique competitions for women. The NPC official website only maintains an approximately two year history of changes in rules and regulations.

At the professional level, the IFBB is constituted by the IFBB Professional League (IFBB Professional League). The rules and regulations relevant to this research include *IFBB Rules Men and Women Bodybuilding, Men Classic Bodybuilding, Women Fitness, Men Fitness, Women Body Fitness* 2009, IFBB Professional League Rules 2009, IFBB Professional League News that features advisories and rules changes. These advisories are intermixed and interspersed with diverse other information and must be mined.

Rules continue to be adjusted to promote the sport/industry and to facilitate events management. It is through the NPC and IFBB at the amateur local, regional, national, and international levels that the aesthetics for the women's physique sports are created, transmitted, and carried forth into the pro level. The pro rules themselves do not articulate these standards. The September 27, 2007 Minutes of the IFBB Pro League Committee meeting are illustrative. Betty Pariso, a pro woman bodybuilder proposed '. . . that the "desired look" for female bodybuilding be formalized in writing as part of the IFBB Pro Rules.' An explanatory note stated: '*After some discussion, the committee held the majority opinion that the judges were already shaping the look for female bodybuilding with the winners they choose and therefore, there was no need for additional criteria other than what is currently expressed in the Pro Rules.*'

BACKLASH: THE FASHION INDUSTRY AND MEDIA

Consider the timing. Professional women's bodybuilding in the Ms. Olympia, the zenith of women's bodybuilding titles, took a turn for mass after 1992 just as the athletic aesthetic in wider discourses such as fashion began to wane after fluorescence in the 1980s. My research has situated 1992–1994 as landmark years for the decline of the athletic aesthetic and the reintroduction of a more conventional corporeality for women emphasizing slenderness in the fashion media. This embodiment that combines slim contours and "significant" breasts has gained momentum and continues to dominate the first decade of the new millennium as a "hegemonic" form of femininity in diverse discourses and rhetorics of beauty. The "Stepford" wives are in vogue as seen in fashion magazines. Content analysis of fashion discourses offers several lines of evidence. In 1992, Lenda Murray pumped up for her 1992 third win as Ms. Olympia. The swimwear maker, Cole, suggested a less subversive way to pump up with an inflatable bikini top that created instant cleavage. In the words of Cole 'pump it a little to turn heads. Pump it a lot of cause frenzy' ("New Inflatable Bikini Will Pump!-You Up" 1992). By 1994, '[t]he message at the haute couture collections in Paris was clear: It's time to get back into shape. And supermodels did just that as designers from Karl Lagerfeld to Michel Klein laced, zipped and squeezed them into curvy corsets . . . Whether women will want to squeeze back into this constricting silhouette doesn't matter. "You can't wear these clothes without a corset,"' explained Lagerfeld in an article in *Vogue* (*Vogue* 1994: 244). In April 1994 Sara Lee released the Wonderbra super uplift brassier and Sacks 5th Avenue sold 489 on the first day and apparel buyers could not keep up with the demand. The fashion director for Donna Karan remarked that 'Womanliness is back with a vengeance. What's selling? Products to maximize breasts – and minimize everything else' (Kanner 1994: 197).

These trends are also illustrated in the embodiments of two iconic supermodels: Cindy Crawford and Kate Moss. In interviews, Crawford has on numerous occasions maintained that she transgressed the ideal of the thin model by offering a heavier and bigger model of womanhood – an athletic and healthy look that became known as the 'athletic aesthetic' (Bolin 1998: 202–203). This more robust physique ideal was seriously challenged in 1992–1993 when Kate Moss heralded in the ethereal waif look. The Periodical Abstract index of popular magazines offers evidence of this change in bodily ideals. The number of times over a ten-year period Cindy Crawford's and Kate Moss's names appeared in articles was assessed as a measure of embodied popularity. Crawford dominated from 1986 to 1992 with 35 references to Moss's one. By 1993, Moss began to appear more frequently and jumped to 17 from December 1992 to December 1994, compared to Crawford's, nine. Further support was provided by a spokesperson for a major New York modeling agency who in an interview with the author regarding somatic trends stated: 'The fuller models went out of style in 1992 and 1993, which is when the waif look came into style. The thinner models are more in demand now.'[1]

This trend for slenderness has continued into the new millennium in the pages of fashion magazines. While mention is made on counter discourses on curvaceousness and "booty" (see Arnaut 2009: 168–171); the covers of magazines such as *Vogue* continue to display slender women as ideals of beauty. Despite *Vogue*'s practice of expanding the covers to feature popular culture women celebrities in addition to models, svelte and slim women continue to dominate the covers (e.g. Blake Lively (February 2009); Sarah Jessica Parker (July 2008); Keira Knightley (September 2008); Gwyneth Paltrow (May 2008)). In December 2008, *Vogue International* featured Kate Moss, the iconic waif on its cover. This is symbolic testimonial to the continued deification of slenderness since the mid-1990s into the first decade of the millennium.[2]

BODYBUILDING HISTORY

At the historical moment of this embodiment backlash, women bodybuilders contested this return to the tyranny of slenderness. In contrast to men's bodybuilding that may largely but not invariably reproduce and amplify Eurocentric bio-reductivist beliefs essentializing gender difference, women's bodybuilding represents a different cultural agenda. The female bodybuilders' somatic contours are transgressive and disruptive to the gender order wherein muscularity embodies power and privilege as the natural purview of men and hence masculinity (cf Richardson (2004) on queer muscles).[3] Women bodybuilders challenge the industrialized view of women as the weaker sex; instead, they live and embody a femininity that includes strength and power. They are indeed "testy" bodies.

Since its inception in the 1975, the sport of women's bodybuilding has been transformed from one in which the competitors wore high heels and rarely performed the muscular poses such as the iconic front double biceps with closed fists, which was discouraged as too masculine. These early bodybuilding contests were more akin to beauty pageants than the subversive displays of strength and muscularity that they have become today, in spite of efforts by the bodybuilding industry to curtail these trends. It was not until the 1980s that women's bodybuilding contests were legitimized as competitions in their own right, not just as auxiliaries for male competitions. The first Miss (now Ms.) Olympia was held in 1980 and set the standard for women's international and professional titles that continues today.

Over time, the women competitors have achieved degrees of muscularity, symmetry, and definition once believed impossible for women. Since its beginnings, women bodybuilders have been involved in a debate over the issue of muscularity and femininity that has reached elevations of a "moral panic" at various times in the sporting industry of bodybuilding (cf. Herdt 2009). The debate over masculinity and femininity has plagued the sport of women's bodybuilding from its inception. The basic question is: how muscular can a woman be and not forfeit her femininity? The response of women bodybuilders has been to redefine notions of femininity to include strength and muscularity. In 1979, after winning the first major women's bodybuilding competition, Lisa Lyon stated, 'Women can be strong, muscular and at the same time feminine.' Women bodybuilders continue to echo this concern. This sentiment continues to be voiced today by women bodybuilders and their allies that contend that muscularity and femininity not only can co-exist, but that they are also changing wider cultural contours of femininity. Such a strategy may indeed be a form "physical feminism," in which the physicality that lies beneath bodybuilding in the hard-core gym is expressed in the desire and pleasure of strength and power (McCaughey 1997). However, as representation, such an approach is easily subverted into "glamour jock" and a hegemonic mandate for "emphasized femininity" that equates the "doing of gender" with the "doing beauty and sexiness" and also supports the bi-polar gender order. Although the debate over femininity and muscularity has been inflamed by anabolic steroid use among women competitors, this debate was well underway prior to the reported use of steroids among women competitors during the latter part of the 1980s. Time has shown that virtually any activity that threatens the hegemonic gender order will call into question the gender authenticity of its participants. This debate surfaced in the infancy of women's bodybuilding when Gloria Miller Fudge took off her high heels. It arose again when Cammie Lusko (1980 Miss Olympia) presented a "hardcore muscular routine" using poses associated with men's bodybuilding and displaying her muscularity; she drove the audience wild, but did not even place in the competition.

Between 1980 and 1989, the sport of bodybuilding as epitomized in the Ms. Olympia contest deferred to conventional notions of femininity. The judges selected athletic, slim, and graceful women reflected in the physiques of Rachel McLish and Cory Everson, in contrast to the more muscular physiques of competitors such as Bev Francis. This embodiment reproduced without challenging the borders of the "fashion" of the athletic aesthetic popular in the 1980s. The debate over the direction the sport would take was resolved with the retirement of Cory Everson in 1989. Cory Everson, six-time Ms. Olympia champion, was not known for having a great deal of muscle mass but was said to embody the perfect combination of symmetry, muscularity, and femininity.

FOUR WATERSHEDS IN THE HISTORY OF WOMEN'S BODYBUILDING

Four critical watersheds resonate in the sport of women's bodybuilding, dramatizing "events," positions (cf. Salzman 1999), and relations in strategic defiance and compliance to emphatic femininity. Following Hochschild (1994: 4, quoted in Messner 2004) and Messner (2004: 88), these watersheds may be regarded as 'magnified moments . . . episodes of heightened importance, either epiphanies, moments of . . . unusual insight, or moments in which things go intensely but meaningfully wrong. In either case, the moment stands out; it is metaphorically rich, usually elaborate and often echoes [later]' (Hochschild 1994, in Messner 2004: 88). As magnified moments, these four watersheds foreground women's bodybuilding as a stage for symbolic debate over the borders of corporeal femininity. As such, the magnified moments registered theoretical issues of personal agency and structural containment as women bodybuilders performed gender and did indeed influence judging standards in bodybuilding. Yet, paradoxically, their transgressive bodies were simultaneously constrained by masculine systems of power and labor including the hegemony of bodybuilding sporting organizations, specifically the International Federation of Bodybuilders and National Physique Committee that establishes judging standards and protocols, and access to industry sponsorships, endorsements, appearances media coverage, and other industry careers (cf. Messner 2004; Connell 1987). These, as Lafferty and McKay (2004) argue regarding women boxers, are the 'formidable structures of patriarchy' that are very difficult but not impossible to resist.

These four watersheds in women's bodybuilding are:

1   The 1992 International Federation of Bodybuilding Ms. Olympia Contest (IFBB) (the zenith of professional women's bodybuilding titles).

2 The adoption of new guidelines for judging women's bodybuilding by the International Federation of Bodybuilders and its amateur arm in the United States, the National Physique Committee (NPC), the largest and arguably premier bodybuilding organization in the world.

3 The introduction of NPC fitness competitions (originally pageants) in 1992 and the inauguration of the Fitness Olympia in 1995 as the premier fitness title.

4 The 2001 introduction of figure competitions by the NPC and the inauguration of the Figure Olympia in 2003 as the apex of figure titles.[4]

By 2000, the backstage of a bodybuilding contest was getting crowded. It could include women bodybuilders, fitness competitors, and figure competitors (and more recently in 2009 bikini competitors, see note 2). As magnified moments, these watersheds foreground women's bodybuilding as a stage for anatomical debates over the borders of corporeal femininity. Theoretical issues of personal agency and structural containment are indexed somatically as women bodybuilders incongruously performed gender conformity yet subverted judging standards. Their progressively transgressive bodies are simultaneously contained by masculine systems of power (implicit and explicit modes of social control) and labor (stratification of paid and unpaid work) including the hegemony of bodybuilding's sporting organization specifically the International Federation of bodybuilders and the National Physique Committee that establishes judging standards and protocols, and also facilitates access to industry sponsorships, endorsements, appearances, media coverage, and other industry related careers. These watersheds represent somatic debates and a politics of gendered corporeality as women bodybuilders encounter masculine hegemony in the industry and compete for media attention and resources with fitness competitors and more recently figure competitors.

A rough chronology of events follows, arguing that bodybuilding as sport is a paradoxical gender regime (after Connell 2000, 2002) that incorporates disruption and reproduction at the symbolic, representational, and structural level of embodiment and agency, and cooptation simultaneously at the micro and macro level as per Lafferty and McKay's (2004) analysis of women boxers in the context of labor, power, and representation.

1 Watershed: The 1992 International Federation of Bodybuilding Ms. Olympia Contest – The Turn to Mass

Between 1980 and 1989, the sport of bodybuilding as epitomized in the Ms. Olympia contest deferred to more orthodox notions of femininity. The judges selected athletic, slim, and graceful women (Rachel McLish and Cory Everson) as opposed to the more muscular physiques of competitors such as Bev Francis (Bolin 1992, 1998, 2003). With Cory Everson's retirement in 1989 after six straight wins as Ms. Olympia, it was an open question as to what direction the question of muscularity would take in women's bodybuilding. Would the judges reward another whose physique was very much like Everson, or would a more muscular ideal reign? The period of 1990 to 1992 may be interpreted as a period of uncertainty in which the debate over the direction of the sport was embedded in diverse discourses such as gym talk, media rhetoric, and interpretations of the physiques of competitors and their placing in contests. Various groups had vested interests in the direction women's bodybuilding would take, from the sports organizations (especially the IFBB/NPC that was eclipsing all other bodybuilding organizations by the 1990s) and their promoters, the producers of services and products, the industry sponsors, the media, the judges, the competitors and audiences from the health and fitness consumers to the hard-core gym culture bodybuilding audience. Each of these sectors had different concerns and avenues in which to influence the somatic debate.

In 1990, Lenda Murray won the Ms. Olympia over Bev Francis, a woman whose hyper-built muscle was ahead of its time as demonstrated in her role in the bodybuilding cult movie *Pumping Iron II: the Women* (Butler and Gaines 1985.) Bev Francis, who had the year before trimmed her physique down to be competitive with Cory Everson, lost to the heavily muscled Lenda Murray because she was ironically not muscular enough. For the 1991 Olympia, Francis read the bodytalk as a welcome change toward more muscularity. Again she lost to Murray, coming in a close second. With Lenda Murray and Bev Francis as first and second place Ms. Olympians respectively, their physiques offered a somatic text of muscle mass unparalleled by Everson at her most muscular. Francis subsequently retired and the 1992 Olympia became the stage on which the debate was resolved in favor of muscularity (although not without some embodied skirmishes, see Bolin (1992, 1998). Lenda Murray won yet again and remained undefeated until Kim Chizevsky claimed the title in 1996 with a more muscular but also ultra-ripped (lean) and hard physique. The symmetry, shape, size, and rock-hard separation of Chizevsky dominated the Olympia stage through 1999 when Chizevsky retired from bodybuilding to go into fitness competitions.[5]

During Chizevsky's reign (1996–1999) professional women bodybuilders showed they were willing to take their physiques up a notch, getting even bigger and harder in the course of three years of Ms. Olympia contests. As Bill Dobbins, advocate of women's bodybuilding and social critic states: 'Lenda Murray . . . surpassed all other women competitors with her display of muscularity, shape and symmetry. Then Kim Chizevsky entered the picture . . . and proved to be bigger and harder than anyone else, looking as somebody said recently [as] "carved out of ice," and everyone has been chasing this new standard since' (Dobbins, n.d.d). Despite concern by the industry gatekeepers, the women bodybuilders resisted admonitions regarding their extreme muscularity, offering the judges the choice of large and extra large; providing impetus to the small-scale muscle rebellion taking place within bodybuilding that had been on a roll since 1992. Their bodies dared the judges and assaulted wider North American notions of traditional slender embodiments of women that had gained ascendancy since 1992 with Kate Moss's "waif look" that continues to dominate feminine body ideals in the fashion industry. The escalation of muscle mass can be read in the bodyweights of the professional competitors. For example, at the 1997 Ms. Olympia, Kim Chizevsky weighed in at 165 lbs, Lenda Murray at 160 lbs, Laura Creavalle at 145 lbs, and Vicki Gates at 150 lbs. The average bodyweight of the Ms. Olympia top six in 1997 was 155 lbs, while in 1983, it was 121 pounds (McGough 1998: 116–117). The baseline criteria for qualifying for the Ms. Olympia became large and full muscles, with hardness, leanness, vascularity, and symmetry. This was the very same criteria used in judging the men, but with a subtext.

In addition to women bodybuilders' agency in influencing the judging standards, the bodybuilding sub-cultural fans also influenced the trend for the increasing muscularity of the women despite the efforts of the IFBB/NPC at the end of 1992 for a more widely appealing and commercial model of buff femininity. As one of my collaborators states: 'the bodybuilding audience wants to see "freaks" – women or men. You don't go to go-cart races when you can see the Indianapolis 500.' The bodybuilding industry, including organizations, promoters, sponsors and media, has had to contend with ways to make this enhanced muscularity more marketable to the broader health and fitness consumer that represented a huge market share – how to do that? Several avenues suggest themselves as will be discussed.

Glamour Jock: Issues Underlying Women's Bodybuilding

It is not argued here that women's bodybuilding is an entirely resistant or transgressive gender regime but rather that it is a paradoxical one in which resistance is countered by systems that promote conformity to the "doing of beauty" as a core feature of heterosexual femininity. Elsewhere I have presented this impetus as one of "beauty and the beast" (Bolin 2004). Bodybuilding is a paradoxical gender regime whose corporeal nexus contains both resistance and cooperation (Lafferty and McKay 2004; Connell 1987). Despite trends for enhanced muscularity, women bodybuilders must default to embodying some elements of traditional feminine iconography that are never clearly articulated but which underpins access to financial rewards and survival as a professional through the bodybuilding media, sponsors, vendors, and promoters. Despite their agency in developing phenomenal muscularity, women bodybuilders feel the tug from this cultural mandate for an emphasized femininity.

From its inception, and throughout its history, women bodybuilders have been plagued by demands to be feminine and to do beauty in order to succeed in the body marketplace. They do this by neutralizing their muscles with superficial insignias of femininity and heterosexual beauty for their public and media personas with breast implants and adornments. Women competitors are self-aware manipulators of their embodied presentations and they know that "femininity" lies beyond muscle (Bolin 1997: 189). Competitors will deliberately offset hypertrophied muscles with attributes associated with conventional femininity and beauty: pink posing suits, highlighting and dying their hair blond, long and fluffy hairstyles, long fingernails and other glamour jock insignias (Bolin 1992, 1998). However, a third-wave feminist stance does not regard these attributes of conventional femininity as neutralizing the power and strength of women bodybuilders. Their bodies are not insignias of a passive femininity by any means. This trend for glamour jock has been escalated from within the industry by the introduction of two new physique contests: fitness in 1995 and figure competitions in 2000 – an important nexus for women's bodybuilding.

2 Watershed: The Adoption of New Guidelines for Judging Women's Bodybuilding by the IFBB in 2000

On January 5, 2000, the NPC, in conjunction with the IFBB, offered new criteria for judging women that not only included attention to 'healthy appearance, the face, makeup, and skin tone' but emphasized 'symmetry, presentation, separations and muscularity but not to the extreme' (Manion 2000). In the IFBB Rules for Bodybuilding section 1.4, judges are reminded:

> First and foremost, the judge must bear in mind that this is a women's bodybuilding competition, and that the goal is to find an ideal female physique. Therefore, the most important aspect is shape – a muscular yet feminine shape. The other aspects are similar to those described for assessing the male physique, but muscular development must not be carried to such an excess that it resembles the massive muscularity of the male physique. Competitors shall also be assessed on whether or not they carry themselves in a graceful manner while walking to and from their position onstage.
>
> (IFBB Amateur Rules for Bodybuilding 2001)

In directives for Assessing the Female Physique (Appendix D): judges are cautioned that although "too big" is a term that applies only to whether or not a competitor has developed too much muscle mass for her skeletal structure and proportions '. . .women are encouraged to develop their physique to the limits of their individual potential, keeping in mind all of the aspects of the criteria to which they will be judged: size, symmetry, proportion and definition. They should not be too thick or bulky or depleted or emaciated. . .' (ibid.: 52).

Bill Dobbins (1999) has argued that women bodybuilders are victims of their own success. They are just too good at building muscle. The changes the IFBB enacted in 2000 must be considered in relation to the embodied trends from Ms. Olympia during the preceding four years. In 1996 Kim Chizevsky set what could be perceived by the IFBB as a dangerous precedent by achieving a size and hardness that had never been equaled on a bodybuilding stage. It was not long before the other professional women competitors followed suit. Chizevsky's new standard of muscularity and hardness prevailed until her retirement in 1999. I argue that it was Chizevsky and her colleagues' agency in pushing somatic boundaries that propelled the IFBB 2000 directive to rein the women in. In an article titled 'Kim Chizevsky: the Best Female Bodybuilder of All Time', Bill Dobbins (n.d.a) maintains that no other woman bodybuilder could match her in terms of her spectacular size, symmetry and sheer crispness of her definition. Unlike her Ms. Olympia predecessors (Rachel McLish, Cory Eversen, and Lenda Murray), Kim Chizevsky was not conventionally pretty and marketable in industry terms. During the off-season she bulked up to over 180 pounds, challenging emphasized femininity and a gender regime that conflates femininity, slenderness, and beauty.

In 2000, the IFBB reorganized the Ms. Olympia to include both a lightweight and a heavyweight title, followed in 2001 with an overall title that pitted the light- and heavyweight winners against one another. Although the impact of the new judging standards was touted in the IFBB/NPC media discourses, it was only briefly somaticized in the smaller and softer physiques of the women. Valentina Chepiga beat the more muscular Vickie Gates in the heavyweight class of the 2000 Ms. Olympia. In the 2001 Ms. Olympia, Juliette Bergmann, who last competed in 1989, won the overall title with an aesthetic and softer look than her competition. As a lightweight (under 135 lbs); her win over heavyweight Iris Kyle was testimony to the 2000 directive for muscular downsizing. Lenda Murray returned to the Ms. Olympia stage after a four-year hiatus to capture the 2002 crown and win her seventh Ms. Olympia against Juliette Bergmann, with a repeat performance in 2003. Murray is known for having the complete package of symmetry and proportion as well as the "cover girl" beauty that guarantees the endorsement success of women athletes in the contemporary world of commodification.

Certainly Murray was a bigger and "crisper" competitor than Juliette Bergman, although her physique was not up to the standard of muscularity and hardness established by Kim Chizevsky during her Ms. Olympia reign. Murray's physique is indeed far more extreme than the prevailing ideals of femininity writ large in the fashion magazines and other popular discourses; but it was an embodiment that inscribed the cultural and industry mandate for beauty. Murray was known in bodybuilding circles for her facial beauty as well as her proportions, conforming to the 2000 IFBB guidelines for judging women in terms of 'overall appearance, attention to face, makeup, skin and a healthy appearance' (Manion 2000).

On a cautionary note, women bodybuilders are agentic and proactive in increasing the level of muscularity, density, and definition offered on the competitive stage and in the gym backstage. Since the beginning of the sport, women's body weights have continued to escalate. This trend for increasing muscle mass is illustrated in the increasing body weights of the competitors; in 1983 the average weight of the Ms. Olympia contenders was 121 lbs while in 1997 it was 155 lbs. Kim Chizevsky competed at 165 lbs on a 5'7" frame. The NPC official weight categories for women have been climbing gradually over the years in response to the women's increasing muscularity. A comparison of the weight categories over time reveals this trend.

Between roughly 1985 (see note in Table 1.1) and 2004, the NPC offered three weight categories for women. At several different junctures, weight categories were modified to reflect the escalating muscle density of the women over time. By 1990, the women's weight classes had increased to the following: lightweights (less than 114½ pounds), middleweights (114½ to 125½) and heavyweights (over 125½ pounds). In 1994, the middleweight class expanded upward to 135 pounds causing the heavyweight to increase to 135 and over. In 1995, the weight categories were again adjusted so that the lightweight division was capped four pounds heavier than the year before with the middleweight concomitantly adjusted to reflect this change; although the upper end of middleweights and the lower end of the heavyweights was reduced by three pounds. Yet another historical moment occurred in 2004 (and currently stands in 2009): the light-heavyweight class was reintroduced resulting in the readjustment of all the weight categories (see Table 1.1). A comparison over time with the 1984 weight categories provides evidence of significant change in weights of the competitors over 20 years – lightweight and middle-weight categories increased by approximately nine pounds with an increase of eight pounds for the light-heavy and a 16 pound increase for the heavyweight category.[6]

Following Connell in her eloquent discussion of body-reflexivity (Connell 2002: 46–52), this history of weight divisions is presented as a dynamic cultural circuit of bodily practices in which the agency of women bodybuilders has been reproduced, ramified, and reconstituted in systemic/structural changes. It is contended that the NPC had

Table 1.1 Comparison of Women's Bodybuilding Weight Classes 1984–2009

Weight Category*	1984 Weight in Pounds	1990 Weight in Pounds	1994 Weight in Pounds	1995 Weight in Pounds	2004–2009 Weight in Pounds
Lightweight	Up to/including 105¾	Up to/including 114½	Up to/including 114	Up to/including 118	Up to/including 115
Middleweight	Over 105¾ to 116¾	Over 114½ to 125½	Over 114 to 135	Over 118 up to/ including 132	Over 115½ to 125
Light-heavyweight (1984–1987)**	Over 116¾ to 123¾	N/A	N/A	N/A	Over 125½ to 140
Heavyweight	Over 123¾	Over 125½	Over 135	Over 132	Over 140

* These weight classes vary depending on the number of divisions in a competition.
** The light-heavyweight class was incorporated as a NPC weight division in 2004. However, this class had an earlier incarnation; it was included in the NPC USA Bodybuilding Championships from 1984 to 1987 and at the NPC Nationals in 1984 and 1985 (Wennerstrom 2004: 219).

implemented these rule changes in responses to the increasing muscle mass and hence bodyweights of the women competitors. The addition of the light-heavyweight division offers the NPC promoters more flexibility to accommodate the distribution of competitors across weight classes and offers an additional class winner an opportunity to compete for the overall title and advance to the national level as well as pro level. This evidence supports general trends in women's sports that suggest enhanced longevity of sports and increases in resources and opportunities will result in women's enhanced sporting performances. In addition, it may also be viewed as an incentive to the flagging of women's bodybuilding discussed in watershed 3 and 4.

3   Watershed: The Introduction of NPC Fitness Competitions (Originally Pageants) in 1992 and the Inauguration of the Fitness Olympia in 1995 as the Premier Fitness Title

Fitness competitions have their origin in Wally Boyco's Fitness Pageants (of the early 1980s), Lou Zwick's Fitness America Pageants and the Ms. Galaxy (introduced in 1993). These contests combined elements of beauty pageants (evening gown and bathing suits) with aerobics competitions/fitness routines. Beginning in the early 1990s, the IFBB grew the sport of fitness from the amateur to the professional level, offering the first Ms. Olympia Fitness Competition (1995). It is asserted that the IFBB/NPC and the bodybuilding industry embraced fitness contests because the fitness corporeality is a much more docile and conventionally feminine one than that of women bodybuilders, offering a more naturalized, appealing and hence marketable somatic ideal.

At the amateur level, NPC fitness competitors are judged by three height classes: 5'2" and under, over 5'2" and up to and including 5'4½", and over 5'4½". At the pro level there are no height classes (NPC 2009a:140). Pro Fitness competitors were judged in four rounds until September 24, 2009: Rounds One and Two (Judging Rounds) and Rounds Three and Four (Finals) occurring at different time periods in the competition. They were judged on their appearance (physique rounds): in a two piece bikini (Round Two) and one piece swimsuit (Round Four) and in two performance routine rounds: (Round One) a 45-second fitness routine performed in a black full-length leotard with five prescribed mandatory moves (three strength and two flexibility moves) to one continuous piece of music and (Round 3) a 2-minute routine with costume that is choreographed with one or more music changes and includes '. . . elements of strength, flexibility, dance, gymnastics, aerobic movements and cardiovascular endurance' (IFBB Professional League 2009: 29). These four rounds were each worth 25 percent of the total score. However, more recently in Advisory Notice 101409, the IFBB Pro

League made significant changes for 2010. The changes do not reflect any modifications to aesthetics of judging. In fitness, the 45-second mandatory routine round and the one-piece swimsuit rounds were eliminated, leaving two rounds at 50 percent each. This will undoubtedly facilitate the production of pro and amateur bodybuilding shows whose numbers of competitors have burgeoned with the addition of figure and bikini competitions. Likewise, the NPC also introduced modifications in fitness designed to increase NPC revenues and participation. The phenomenal growth of figure competitions has resulted in events management/organizational issues in the production of bodybuilding shows. Changes in fitness and figure rules represent a response to these constraints at the national as well as professional levels. Fitness competitors are currently judged in two rounds at the amateur level; a 2-minute fitness routine and a two-piece physique round, keeping the NPC in line with changes made at the professional level (*Hard Body News* 2008).

In addition to the demonstration of strength, flexibility, dance, gymnastics, aerobics, and cardiovascular endurance in the routine rounds, fitness competitors are judged on their costumes including the fit and style of the one-piece (until its elimination in 2009), the two-piece suit and the costume worn during the fitness routine performance (Round Three) (IFBB Professional Rules 2003: 39). In contrast to the barefooted women bodybuilders, the women fitness competitors must wear high heels for the physique rounds.

As one IFBB official stated: 'the Fitness Olympia is about appearance, performance, and feminine grace. We don't want women thinking they have to build muscle to win this' (Clive 1997: 88–89). 'Judges will be looking for the best toned body (not the most muscular) . . . [for] total tone and shape,' while 'overt muscularity will be marked down' (Kindela 1996: 163). Fitness judge and former competitive bodybuilder Carla Dunlap-Kaan has maintained that the primary rational behind women's fitness competitions is to offer a venue for women with fitness modeling aspirations to display a marketable appearance emphasizing beauty (Weber 1992: 9).

IFBB judges 'are strongly reminded that they are judging a woman's FITNESS competition and not a woman's BODYBUILDING competition.' According to the IFBB Amateur Rules for Bodybuilding, Women's Fitness, Body Fitness, Men's Fitness, Code of Ethics, Directives, The Deviation Method, Judging Forms (2006: 31) 'the type of muscularity, vascularity, muscular definition, and leanness appropriate for a female bodybuilder will not be considered acceptable if displayed by a fitness competitor and will result in a reduced score. Competitors are assessed on their overall appearance from head to toe including skin, proportion, and degree of athleticism. . .' The degree of athleticism includes 'assessing the degree of firmness, symmetry, proportion and the overall physical appearance including complexion, poise and overall presentation.'

In scoring, the judges include face, makeup, skin tone and costume in the athletic routine. Again 'facial beauty is attended to and there should be smooth and tight skin without the presence of "cellulite"' (see IFBB 2010: 8; Amateur Rules for Women's Fitness 2001: Appendix 2).

According to IFBB/NPC guidelines, the physique should show a 'small degree of muscularity with separation, no visible striations, and again it is reiterated there should be no extreme muscularity. . . . Judges are reminded that this is not a bodybuilding contest. The competitors should show shape to the muscle but not the size, definition, and vascularity that is seen at a bodybuilding competition. Any competitors who exhibit these qualities shall be marked down' (IFBB Amateur Rules 2001; NPC 2009a: 140). The NPC reinforces these somatic parameters at the amateur level stating: 'The contestants should have shape to their muscles but not the size, definition or vascularity as in the bodybuilding physique. If these are present the contestant will be scored down' (NPC 2009a: 140). As in the IFBB and the IFBB Pro League, fitness, symmetry, proportion and overall physical appearance including complexion and poise are the essential criteria. These rules clearly establish the distinction in physiques between bodybuilders and fitness competitors. An emphatic femininity is at play here selecting for pretty, athletic but not too muscular women and this is clearly built into the judging criteria where facial beauty is articulated as part of the winning package.

The IFBB/NPC emphasize that one need not be a gymnast to compete in fitness. 'Routines may include aerobics, dance, gymnastics or other demonstrations of athletic talent and that judges will be looking for style, personality, athletic coordination, strength moves, endurance and overall performance' (Manion 2001: 2). In the years since fitness first appeared, the criteria have not remained static. Women fitness competitors have upped the ante on the routine, which initially was more akin to an aerobics routine. Fitness judges soon began to reward women with gymnastics ability. This unwritten criterion has come to dominate the judging and the wider discourses on fitness competitions within the media and magazines (e.g. *Joe Weider's Flex*) and in cyberspace. One *Flex* writer stated, regarding the 1999 Fitness Olympia: '[It] has become more gymnastically orientated as Monica Brant gets 4th place, [and] Kelly Ryan and Susie Curry tumble their way to victory with gymnastic routines. . .' (Rosenthal 2000: 238). Monica Brandt retired from fitness in 1999 stating 'The fact that I'm not a gymnast doesn't make things any easier for me to continue . . . It concerns me that gymnastics has become such a big part of the sport' (ibid.: 242). She switched to figure competitions in 2003. Susie Curry, known for her extreme gymnastic ability, won her first Fitness Olympia in 2000 and then continued to claim three more titles against her arch enemy, Kelly Ryan, known as "flyin' Ryan" for her acrobatic expertise. Subsequent winners continue to display astute aerial abilities. The bar on the Ms. Fitness Olympia has clearly been moved up in the direction of gymnastic ability from the first Ms. Fitness in 1995. Like Brandt, Susie Curry retired in 2004 from fitness and switched to the new figure competitions after her four straight wins of the Fitness Olympia.

By emphasizing acrobatic capability in the routine rounds, small and petite fitness athletes, just as Olympic gymnasts, have become smaller and lighter over time (Burstyn 1999: 158–159; Dobbins n.d.b). The height classes at the non-pro level substantiate this: 5'2" and under, 5'2" up to and including 5'4½", over 5'4½" tall. If there are only two categories then these are 5'3" and under, and over 5'3" (NPC 2009a: 140). In counteracting the infantilization that tiny and slender gymnastic bodies animate, fitness athletes, such as women bodybuilders and figure competitors, have become active consumers of breast implants. Physique athletes must keep a low body-fat level to be competitive, and consequently breast size is reduced. To create a more "feminine" appearance, breast augmentation has become normalized as part of the fitness, figure, and bodybuilding regimens. By 1994, this trend was readily visible on the stages of the incipient fitness shows, continuing a well-established body practice among bodybuilders and continues as a current trajectory in the more recent figure competitions (cf. Burstyn 1999: 155).

Although the fitness competitors and their somatic ideal is a more diminutive and obedient aesthetic in comparison to the rambunctious muscle of women bodybuilders, they too are dedicated athletes as their physiques and gymnastic routines demonstrate. Although commanding awe for their aerial expertise, the fitness competition is clearly framed as a feminine regime in terms of accenting dance, costumes, beauty, and grace. Fitness does not challenge or subvert the gender order as does women's bodybuilding. The conformity of fitness physiques with current somatic ideals of femininity and the attendant privileging of fitness competitors over bodybuilders in media and industry visibility, combined with the escalating muscular size of professional bodybuilders has taken its toll on the sport of professional women's bodybuilding. The 1999 Ms. Olympia was nearly canceled due to lack of sponsors and tickets sales and was only salvaged by the efforts of the IFBB. In addition to fitness competitions, women's bodybuilding must add figure competitors into the industry mix of power, labor, and capital. The 2010 pro venues substantiate this trend with six pro women's bodybuilding events in contrast to seven fitness pro contests and 16 figure pro contests (2009 IFBB 2010: 217–218). These dynamics are discussed in greater depth below.

4 Watershed: The Introduction of NPC Figure Competitions (2001) and the Inauguration of the Figure Olympia in 2003 as the Apex of Figure Titles

More recently a new form of physique competition has been added to the bodybuilding venue – figure competitions. Figure competitions or body fitness (IFBB) are in essence fitness competitions without the required routine. Introduced at the NPC amateur level in 2001 and IFBB professional level in 2003 with the inaugural Figure Olympia, figure is arguably the fastest growing sector of the three physique events with the most robust number of competitors. Like fitness, figure competitions attract women who want to succeed in an industry where beauty and an embodied athletic aesthetic provide career/economic opportunities such as modeling, promoting, endorsing, acting, and other activities related to selling fitness products (i.e. clothing, supplements, weight-loss programs, equipment, etc.). Because figure competition does not require the performance of an increasingly gymnastically oriented routine, it is far less physically demanding than fitness. It does not draw women with the muscular development of bodybuilders, although cross-over is permitted at the NPC amateur and pre-national level. Figure competitions are the legacy of fitness competitions, with the same judging criteria only without the routine (Lindsay 2009).

Figure competitors are judged in terms of an overall athletic appearance. The criteria at the amateur and the pro levels remain consistent. The judges are asked to:

1   . . . take into consideration the hair and facial beauty; the overall athletic development of the musculature, the presentation of a balanced, symmetrically developed physique, the condition of the skin and the skin tone; and the athletes ability to present herself with confidence, poise and grace . . .

2   . . . The muscles groups should have a round and firm appearance with a small amount of body fat. The physique should neither be excessively muscular nor excessively lean and should be free from deep muscle separation and/or striations. Physiques that are considered too muscular or too lean must be marked down. . . .

3   . . . The skin tone should be smooth and healthy in appearance and without cellulite. The face, hair and makeup should complement the 'Total Package' presented by the athlete . . .

4   Judges are reminded that this is not a bodybuilding contest. The competitors should have shape to their muscle but not the size, definition or vascularity that is seen at bodybuilding competitions. Any competitor who exhibits these features is to be marked down.

(IFBB Rules Men and Women Bodybuilding,
Men Classic Bodybuilding, Women Fitness,
Men Fitness, Women Body
Fitness 2009: 67–81)

Emphasized femininity penetrates the competition attire. For competitions, as stated earlier, the NPC eliminated the one-piece posing suit round for 2009. At the time of this research, the one-piece round continues at the IFBB professional level but may change in the future (IFBB 2009: 30). Suits may be solid or multi-colored with sequins, rhinestones, and other decorations and jewelry may be worn. Women display their physiques by walking to the center of the stage, doing individual turns followed by comparison judging typically in groups of five to seven (amateur level) and three to five (professional). Figure competitor are required to wear high heels during their posing rounds in the NPC and the IFBB Professional League (NPC Women's Figure Competition Guidelines n.d.; IFBB 2009: 31).

While the specific rules regarding shoe style vary among IFBB amateur organizations, clear heels have come to dominate the NPC competitions and the IFBB Professional League. The shoe parameters include a 0.75 to 1 inch platform and 5 inch clear heels (IFBB 2010: 4; Aliotti 2007; 'Choosing the Right Figure Shoes' n.d.). Although the pro competitors have no restrictions on shoe style, there is substantial discourse on the importance of attention to detail in selecting shoes (e.g. 'Choosing the Right Figure Shoes' n.d.). Brenda Kelly (pro-figure competitor) offered as evidence the case of Monica Brandt who nearly missed first place because her platform and heels were too high: '. . .the judges told her to lower her heel and platform height' (Kelly n.d.). One cannot overlook the resonance to Cinderella here, nor paradoxically should the expertise, balance, and practice required to walk gracefully in skyscraper heels be forgotten.

Amateur figure competitions in 2001 included three height classes. The response of women to the new figure competitions was phenomenal and soon the NPC and IFBB added additional opportunities to this new physique sport. Initially in the 2001 inaugural pro qualifying National Figure Championships, the top two in each of three height classes received pro cards. By 2002, more opportunities to turn pro were created so that at the second annual National Figure Championships, the top three in each of three height classes qualified to turn pro in anticipation of the first professional championships beginning in 2003 (this ruling was made retroactive to 2002 to allow even more women to compete as professionals). By 2003 the IFBB/NPC increased the number of height classes at the amateur level in pro qualifying events from the three established in 2001 to four height classes. By expanding the height categories this extended the number of possibilities to turn professional. In 2004 the IFBB added two more height classes for national level figure competitions for a total of six height classes: A, up to and including 5'2"; B, over 5'2" and up to and including 5'3"; C, over 5'3" and up to and including 5'4"; D, over 5'4" and up to and including 5'5"; E, over 5'5" and up to and including 5'6"; F, over 5'6" (NPC 2004: 'New NPC Rule Changes for 2004') resulting in even more opportunities to compete at the national and professional levels. The number of classes has remained to date. However, in 2008, the heights were modified to include: A, up to and including 5'1"; B, over 5'1½" and up to and including 5'2½"; C, over 5'2½" and up to and including 5'4"; D, over 5'4" and up to and including 5'5½"; E, over 5'5½" and up to and including 5'7"; and F, over 5'7" (NPC 2009a: 146).

In 2009, two additional NPC changes occurred reflecting the dramatic increase of figure competitors and their impact on the sport. Cross-overs between bodybuilding, fitness, figure, and the new bikini division were no longer allowed at national contests and the one-piece round was eliminated from the Fitness and Figure (NPC 2009c: 1). Both changes reflect the increasing difficulties of orchestrating a competition with large volumes of figure competitors added to the mix of bodybuilding and fitness. For example, at one 2006 bodybuilding show in which the author competed, the scheduling of the bodybuilding divisions had to be altered to allow the figure competitors to cross-over and change into bodybuilding posing suits causing confusion and an extended show length. This has consequences for the success of the shows, not only for the dehydrated and depleted bodybuilders, figure and fitness athletes but also for the audience. As one lifter remarked to me after a NPC state show that lasted close to six hours: 'Doc, I never thought I'd get tired of looking at beautiful women's buttocks, but I sure did with those figure gals.' These two rule changes may be regarded as a strategic step by the NPC in managing the expansion of figure in such a short period of time. The incremental increase of figure categories and prospects to turn professional facilitates the industry as well as serving the interests of the consumers who want to compete at the professional level. Because of the additional classes, figure competitors have far more possibilities to turn pro than fitness competitors with only three height classes and body-builders with four height classes. For example, by the end of 2005, the number of figure pro cards offered were 27. This compared to 18 pro cards given in a year to fitness competitors whose professional debut was in 1992 and to six pro cards offered to women bodybuilders whose pro competitions debuted in 1980 (Contest Activity Report 2005: 238, 240). By 2010, fitness competitors could earn ten pro cards and women's bodybuilding eight, in comparison to figure competition's 32 pro cards.

Figure competitions can draw on a much less specialized niche of expertise than either professional bodybuilding (requiring genetic poten-tial, extreme discipline, an extraordinary workout ethic, and a willing-ness to use illegal pharmaceuticals) or fitness (requiring beauty, an aesthetic physique and a gymnastics/dance background). This is not to suggest that figure competitors are not disciplined and dedicated, but they are not compelled to have the muscle and definition of a body-builder. The dieting is not as extreme and the training very different. In contrast, fitness competitions are also incredibly demanding and more mature bodies are prone to injury and possible accident from the fitness routine. Figure physique competitions have attracted former fitness competitors such as Monica Brant who found themselves unable to meet the accelerating standard for gymnastic skill dominating the routine rounds (Dobbins n.d.c: 3–4). Others such as Suzie Curry, four-time fitness Olympia Champion, switched to figure competitions to spare their bodies from injury (Schmaltz 2003: 50). The first year in which pro figure was offered (2003) Wayne DeMilia, IFBB vice-president of the Pro Division, noted that 'About 25–30 percent of last year's Fitness girls switched to Figure' (Wilkins n.d.: 2).

Ben Wider, deceased former president of the IFBB, regarded the addition of figure as 'yet another way to promote the sport of bodybuilding and fitness worldwide' (ibid.: 1–2). The success of the NPC in promoting the figure division at the amateur level paved the way for the establishment of the professional division under the IFBB by bringing in 'more competitors, sponsors, fans, and money into the sport' according to IFBB vice-president Wayne DeMilia (ibid.: 1–2). In addition, a prominent subtext is that figure may have been regarded as a means to attract a more mainstream audience to bodybuilding's more marginalized muscle cult.

Figure competitions have begun to eclipse both fitness and bodybuilding since its inception in 2001. In a report to *Southern Muscle* (2004: 50) regarding the 2004 Junior USA Contest, Peter Potter noted: '. . . the growing importance of the women's Figure athletes, they accounted for slightly over 62% of the entire contest entries.' To verify the claims by promoters and reporters of the increasing popularity of figure competitions, in its first three years I collected data using a convenience sample of 12 issues of *Southern Muscle Magazine* (June 2002–May 2004). I used *Southern Muscle* because this magazine lists the names of all the competitors for a competition whether they place or not, as opposed to other magazines such as *Joe Weider's Flex*, *NPC News* and NPC/IFBB internet sites that list only the winners, not the total number of competitors in a systematic manner. The number of women bodybuilders, fitness, and figure competitors from 59 shows was assessed. This data indicates the astounding popularity of figure competitors in contrast to the other women's physique sports of bodybuilding and fitness. The total numbers of competitors from June 2002 to May 2004 from 59 shows were as follows: women bodybuilders numbered 383, compared with 66 fitness competitors and 707 figure competitors (see Table 1.2).

Fitness and figure competitors are a far more compliant embodiment than the testy corporeality of women bodybuilders. And their more compliant physiques are taking their toll on women's bodybuilding in the competition for attention and resources of the industry, as well as on fitness. I will turn my lens to bodybuilding, fitness, and figure as somatic debates illuminated through these four magnified moments. My theoretical prism continues to incorporate a Connolesque approach that attends to the representational, the structural, and the cultural context of the gender order as well as to the opportunities for play and agency.

Table 1.2 Convenience Sample: Total Number of Competitors
June 2002–May 2004 in 59 Shows

Women Bodybuilders	383
Figure	707
Fitness Competitors	66

Source: Twelve issues of *Southern Muscle* 2002–2004.

BODYBUILDING, FITNESS AND FIGURE AS PUSHBACK AND DEBATE

We are in the midst of somatic history where muscle density is debated by athletic beauty contests and where glamour and sex emerge as the championship qualities. Women's bodybuilding is at the core of this debate as they paradoxically embody and defy these ideals. As an embodiment, bodybuilding has relations with and in some ways compels fitness and figure. The metaphor of a somatic "beauty or the beast" skirmish between fitness and bodybuilding emerged early in the history or fitness competitions. For example, fitness competitions began drawing into their ranks former bodybuilders such as Raye Hollitt who stated 'I . . . want to get smaller. I don't want to have such a hardcore image anymore. I want to be toned and fit, like Rachel and Cory. Big and bulky just doesn't get it anymore' (quoted in Dayton 1994: 73). In reflecting on fitness competitors, Melissa Coates gave voice to the continuing double bind of women's bodybuilding, all the more critical with the emergence of fitness contests stating:

> When I saw the type of girls who were winning at the Arnold Classic, I thought I would have to compromise myself and get bigger and thicker. That would make me less marketable for the magazines; you are damned if you do and damned if you don't . . . Sometimes people would come up to me and ask me if I was a fitness girl. I used to take it as an insult, but now I realize it's a compliment. The fitness girls get more work because they spend more time presenting themselves as a mainstream look. More people can identify with the fitness look.
>
> (in Gallagher 1997: 121)

In 1999 Kim Chizevsky retired from bodybuilding after four straight Ms. Olympia titles; wearing an unofficial crown as "the best woman bodybuilder of all time" in terms of muscular development, proportion, and definition, she turned to fitness competitions (Dobbins n.d.a: 1–2). According to interviews in *Flex*, several motives were suggested: she was ready for a change after ten years of bodybuilding, the prize money for the Ms. Olympia title had been reduced from $115,000 to $60,000 (1997) and to $50,000 (1998) to $25,000 (1999) with near cancelation in that year as well; and she was uncomfortable with how large she had to get in the off season in order to present a competitive look for the stage (over 180 lbs and some have hinted more). This switch allowed for lively magazine discourse (*Flex* 2000 and 2001) with before and after photos with an emphasis on her transformation from "the beast" to "the beauty" in which she dropped 30 lbs of muscle. One magazine story reports: '. . .a fan had gasped, "Is that Kim? That's not Kim. My god, it is Kim – she's beautiful."' When she was dominating bodybuilding, nobody ever called her beautiful. Awesome, freaky, massive – all accolades within the sport – but never beautiful' (McGough 2001: 88). This discourse reproduces a dominant metaphor of the physique competitions: fitness and figure are diminutive, complaint and contained while bodybuilding women are larger than life, visible and intimidating in their heroic and Amazon proportions (Thomas 1999: 88–99).

The metaphor of debate between bodybuilding and fitness has been articulated since fitness first shared the bodybuilding stage. Not only is the debate presented through the stories of individuals such as Kim Chizevsky who made the switch from the beast to the beauty, but also other forms and representations abound. For example, Australian *Ironman Magazine* asked: 'Who's Sexier: Women Bodybuilders or Fitness Women?' (Teper and Silverman 1996: 52–63). Bill Dobbins posited 'Muscle . . . or Fitness?' (1997: 158–161, 239) and a *Flex* 'Power and Sizzle' sponsored contest queried: 'Who is the sport's sexist fittest woman? Not only do you get to sort through the hottest array of shots we've ever published, but you can vote for the winner' (*Flex* 1998). By presenting a media discourse on bodybuilding and fitness as in mortal combat for "hotness," the sexualization of women physique competitors was elaborated at the expense of their athletic abilities. As an aside, historically fitness pageants subverted the athletic with the sexual. For example, the Taj Mahal Fitness pageant offering the first 1994 Ms. Exercise title to its winner included a bathing suit competition in thong bikini bottoms and high heels with several references to "sultry" bodies (Downs 1994: 52). The editors of popular bodybuilding magazines admit that sex sells magazines. The *Flex* 'Power and Sizzle' contest encouraged the women to display themselves provocatively and semi-nude. In contrast to the early days of women's bodybuilding, the NPC had rules prohibiting women bodybuilders from posing in the nude.

The privileged position of emphatic femininity as a romaticized gender discourse in the sporting industry is implicated in the pared down physiques of fitness pageant competitors and the landslide growth of figure competitions. It infiltrates judging and embodiment in fitness and figure competitions, saturates women's access to economic opportunities within the sporting industry, and sustains the "formidable structures of patriarchy." Even transgressive bodies are tamed by exposing their sexuality for the male gaze, commodified and objectified and this serves the interests of the industry in terms of women's access to labor and capital.

Fitness and more recently figure competitors have offered a renewed and emboldened somatic challenge to women bodybuilders. Will the fitness and figure physique overshadow that of the hypertrophied muscle of the competitive women bodybuilder? The fitness and subsequent figure soma as a pushback embodiment to women's bodybuilding is far less testy and more compliant with the wider asymmetric social hierarchy of the hegemonic gender order. Women bodybuilders' extreme muscularity and quest for largesse is subversive to the gender order of an emphatic femininity that includes the intersection slenderness, smallness, and conventional beauty (Bolin 1992, 1998, 2003, 2004).

In this regard, the industry media, specifically the major bodybuilding magazines, have been accused of reducing their coverage of women's bodybuilding at the expense of fitness and, more recently, figure competitors. Earlier, bodybuilder Kim Chizevsky argued that 'Fitness competitors have taken over the pages [of *Flex*] we used to fill. My main concern is that it seems to have been decided that the magazine can only promote one, not both streams of the female sport.' *Flex* magazine responded that 'magazines are in the business of selling magazines, and the change in emphasis – featuring fitness competitors in pictorials rather women bodybuilders – was made for that reason' (McGough 2000: 106–107).

Despite the agency of women bodybuilders in pushing the borders of femininity through this muscular massiveness, the patriarchal structures of the bodybuilding organizations and the health and fitness industry – a financially prolific array of interested parties – contain women bodybuilders in various ways. As discussed, one avenue is through judging standards and policy (cf Dobbins n.d.d). Although women bodybuilders have offered resistance to these measures by offering large and extra large embodiments, other efforts at subverting gender containment are not so easily overcome. For example, the industry media, specifically the NPC/IFBB controlled bodybuilding magazines, have reduced their coverage and inclusion of women bodybuilders. Women bodybuilders are seldom pictured in the "Around the NPC" the "tattler section" of the *NPC News,* a member's only publication. As an illustration, out of 82 photographs featuring women physique competitors in the January 2006 issue, only six of these photographs included women bodybuilders. In addition, guest posing and endorsements are currently dominated by figure and fitness professionals. The 2006 Pittsburgh Championships selected as guest poser Olympia Pro Fitness winner Adela Garcia, while the vendor booths included Olympic Figure Pro (2005) Davana Medina and Jenny Lynn. In contrast, bodybuilding Olympia winner Iris Kyle was relegated to a small, unsponsored booth where she sold her own sporting products.

Content analysis of 299 covers of *Flex* magazine from April 1985 through March 2010 comparing the number of images of women bodybuilders with the number of fitness/figure competitors also provides evidence of women bodybuilders increasing marginalization. Large cover photos as well as smaller photographic insets of various sizes were coded in the analysis (see Table 1.3).

The yearly data spanning March through April from these covers converged into four distinct historical phases representing: the Golden Age of Women's Bodybuilding (April 1985–March 1994); the Transitional Phase (April 1994–March 1998); the Decline of Women's Bodybuilding (April 1998–March 2004); and Erasure (April 2004–March 2010).

Table 1.3 Comparison: Women Bodybuilders, Fitness, Figure Competitors and Models

	Women Body-builders in Large Photographs, Cover	*Women Fitness/Figure Competitors and Models in Large Photographs, Cover*	*Women Bodybuilders in Small Photographs, Inset*	*Women Fitness/Figure Competitors and Models in Small Photographs, Inset*
Golden Age of Women's Bodybuilding (April 1985– March 1994)	27	1	0	0
Transitional Phase NPC and IFBB Introduce Fitness Olympia 1995 (April 1994– March 1998)	4	6	26	10
Decline of Women Bodybuilding NPC and IFBB Introduce Figure Olympia 2003 (April 1998– March 2004)	0	12	4	47
Erasure (April 2004– March 2010)	0	8*	0	36**

Covers of Joe Weider's *Flex* Magazine (1985–2010)

* Of these cover models, one is a World Wrestling Entertainment competitor and one an Ultimate Fighting champion.
** Of these inset photographs, three are World Wrestling Entertainment competitors and one is a bikini pro competitor.

April 1985 through March 1994 is the Golden Age of Women's Bodybuilding. During this period 27 women bodybuilders graced the covers of *Flex* with only one fitness/figure/model competitor shown. The period spanning April 1994 through March 1998 is categorized as the Transition Phase since it includes the introduction of fitness and a substantial increase of fitness images over the previous period. During this period, women bodybuilders' large cover photos are reduced from 27 to four and fitness large cover photographs eclipse bodybuilding for the first time with six covers. During this phase, *Flex* adopted a new photo strategy of including smaller photographic insets. These smaller insets illustrate the gradual introduction and media interest in women fitness and figure competitors. Bodybuilders maintain their dominance in small insets during the Transitional Phase with 26 bodybuilders compared to ten fitness/figure models in small inset photos. The period of April 1998 through March 2004 is regarded as the Decline of Women's Bodybuilding on *Flex*'s covers as the number of images indicates in both the large cover photographs and the smaller inserts. Women bodybuilders have disappeared completely from the large covers and have been replaced by 12 large photograph covers of fitness/figure competitors and models. In the small insets there are only four women bodybuilders in comparison to 47 fitness and figure competitors. In a related piece of evidence that also testifies to the disappearance of women's bodybuilders from bodybuilding magazines during this period, *Joe Weider's Flex* Magazine, which had been routinely running two distinct departments for the reigning Mr. and Ms. Olympia to offer training tips and advice, dropped the "Ask Ms. Olympia" in the February 2001 edition.

The period of Erasure occurs from April 2004 through March 2010. Women bodybuilders have disappeared completely not only in large covers but from the small photographic insets as well. Women Fitness/Figure Competitors are "cover girls" on eight covers and are included in 36 small insets. The numbers are compelling. The cover and insert images of women bodybuilders have been all but replaced by fitness/figure competitors. This has clear implications for the profession of women's bodybuilding as a viable occupation relating directly to issues of inequity in power and labor relations. Media coverage for competitors is an avenue to capital through endorsements, promotions, modeling and access to other career opportunities in the beauty-fitness arena of products and services. As previously mentioned, these trends are reproduced in the professional venue offerings such as in the 2010 schedule with six pro women's bodybuilding events in contrast to seven fitness pro contests and 16 figure pro contests (IFBB 2009: 217–218). The national level competitions suggest this as well. For example, GNC, the sponsors of a major professional bodybuilding competition known as the GNC Show of Strength, has decided to eliminate the women's bodybuilding component, claiming that ticket sales would not be high enough to justify including them in the program. In the words of IFBB Professional Lisa Bavington, they have 'add[ed] insult to injury' when the women's bodybuilding show was replaced with a figure competition, yet the fitness competition portion of the show was retained (2004: 1–3).

Women's bodybuilder physiques continue to be "problematized" in IFBB and NPC criteria, and they are subject to special admonitions in both organizations. The most recent IFBB rules for women's bodybuilding retains the wording from 2001 discussed earlier: '. . .the goal is to find an ideal female physique . . . a muscular yet feminine shape . . . muscular development must not be carried to such an excess that it resembles the massive muscularity of the male physique. . .' (IFBB 2010: 48). The NPC reiterates this concern with women bodybuilders' muscular propensities to challenge the somatic gender order with a section in *The National Physique Rules and Guidelines for Judging Competitions* entitled "Judges Message Concerning Female Bodybuilders." Judges are advised that women bodybuilders '. . .should have female looking muscles . . . When a judge looks at a female bodybuilder, she or he must have no doubt in their minds they are looking at a woman. . .' (NPC 2009d).

CONCLUSION

This analysis has focused on the physical self as it is culturally constituted in terms of metaphor and embedded in social structure. This combined data creates a grim picture for women bodybuilders in terms of their access to power, labor, and capital in an industry that sustains the dominant gender order that privileges and offers opportunities to those women whose embodiments animate and reproduce an emphatic femininity (despite its expanded borders of buff). No matter how much the grand bodies of women bodybuilders are adorned with insignias of femininity, their transgressive bodies are regarded as less marketable than the relatively docile and compliant embodiments of the fitness and figure physique competitors. I have discussed physique competitions and women's bodybuilding as a paradoxical body regime that transgresses yet indulges the gender order. I have also approached the subject relationally, arguing that embodiments of fitness and figure competitors represent somatic pushback to the testy and disobedient bodies of women bodybuilders and that women's bodybuilding is a corporeal nexus that responds and relates to historical processes in the sport and wider society. Amidst processes of commodification, power, and labor that sustain hegemonic masculinity and a collateral emphasized femininity lurks resistance and agency, embedded in specific moments in history and culture, and in the unruly and heroic bodies of women bodybuilders.

Notes

1 This line of evidence, along with some of the other historical evidence on bodybuilding prior to 1997, has been previously discussed in Bolin (1998: 187–212).

2 The purpose of my research is not to investigate *Vogue*, however, this information is offered as evidence of the continual emphasis on "thin" as an embodied ideal in the popular fashion media. For a more detailed discussion of cultural-historical trends in body ideals for women that spans a wider range of time beginning with the eighteenth century in the United States, refer to Bolin (1998).

3 There is a cogent argument to be made that male bodybuilding is not the essentializing masculinity it superficially appears to be but is more akin to the somatic ambiguity and subversiveness of women's bodybuilding. In this regard Niall Richardson (2004) has convincingly contended that male bodybuilding is simultaneously queer (non-normative), suggesting 'incoherencies between sex, gender and sexuality' (ibid.: 50), and gender orthodox through conterminously and paradoxically affirming masculinity and femininity in terms of sporting practice and embodiment. Extending Richardson's work, Schippert subsequently (2007) also applied the queer lens for understanding male and female built bodies, gendered normativities, and sexualities as these intersect in complicated and shifting milieus. For example, Schippert notes that '...the equation of muscles with male makes the realm of men's muscularity significantly vaster and more elastic than women's' (2007: 162). Time and length constraints prevent a thorough review of muscles as queer, although this stance is not antithetical to my inquiry. I have noted earlier that 'The bodybuilders' somatic standard transgresses cultural images of males and females alike by creating an ideal that represents both and neither of them' (Bolin 1997: 189). My research argues that women's bodybuilding is a paradoxical regime that must be understood not only in historical context but also in relation to fitness and figure embodiments (and more recently bikini competitors, although I did not address the latter specifically). I offer my research as contributing to Schippert's (2007) interests in the "how" of subversion and conformity in women's bodybuilding by attention to relations between fitness (also Bolin 1998) and figure as they are configured in terms of power and labor. Finally, for further complication of the bipolar gender paradigm and the transgressive potential of embodiment, see Bolin's (1994: 478–482) discussion of the impact of women's bodybuilding and the "athletic aesthetic" on the transgender community.

4 In 2009, the National Physique Committee sanctioned a new division for the amateur and professional level: the Bikini Division to be held in conjunction with other NPC divisions, that is, bodybuilding, fitness or figure. The Bikini Division follows the same height class regulations of fitness and figure competitions. Judging is based on 'balance and shape; and overall physical appearance including complexion, skin tone, poise and overall presentation' (NPC Bikini Division 2009b). Mike Davis, co-promoter of the Arnold Amateur competition, remarked that Bikini competitors are '... athletes who train to achieve a sleek yet less athletic physique. Their body fat tends to be a bit higher ... There are many athletes who wish to compete on stage without the intense training required for Figure and Fitness competitions' (NPC Amateur Bikini Division Competition at the 2009 Arnold Sports Festival). The introduction of Bikini Division has all the earmarks of a watershed for bodybuilding. This "sport" bears following as does its impact on bodybuilding and relationship to Figure and Fitness competitions. Due to its newness, this chapter does not discuss the Bikini Division.

5 Niall Richardson (personal communication) has suggested that Lenda Murray's racialized otherness is an important consideration in pushing the boundaries of muscularity in women's bodybuilding. Likewise Schippert (2007: 165) has also noted the absence of race in scholarly discussions of women's bodybuilding. Whereas Schippert argues that Carla Dunlap's body is iconographically contained in the documentary *Pumping Iron II: the Women*, because she is dangerously other as an African American built and strong woman; it could also be convincing argued that it is precisely because Lenda Murray is dangerously other she was able to continue to push the perimeters of muscularity in the Ms. Olympia and escape containment. I wholeheartedly agree that research on the nexus of race and gender in women's bodybuilding bears further scrutiny and would benefit from extensive systematic research. The complexities of interrogating this issue require attention to the cultural and historical context of women's bodybuilding. For example, Murray did indeed outmuscle Frances in 1990, but this was not the case in 1991. In the 1991 Ms. Olympia, Francis came in a close second to Murray because she was too muscular, although she actually lost in the posing round (Bolin 1992: 201). In the media and bodybuilding sub-cultural circles, this particular Ms. Olympia is nuanced by the subtleties of bodybuilding judging criteria. It may well be that Murray's symmetry is what trumped Francis' muscle density in 1992. Although Frances could excel in muscle excess she was bedeviled by a blocky physique that did not embody the wasp waist of iconic X of bodybuilding (Bolin 1996: 132, 1997: 189). Whether Murray's subsequent Olympia domination until the even more muscular and white Kim Chizevsky claimed the Olympia title in 1998 can be understood in terms of racial otherness remains to be explored and detailed with evidence. I would suggest that symmetry itself may be interrogated as a discourse at the nexus of race, gender, and embodiment.

6 See NPC Rule Changes for 2004, http://www.npcnewsonline.com/new/npcrules_changes2004.html (accessed 21 September 2010) and NPC 2009 Rule Changes, http://www.npcnewsonline.com/new/2009BOGMeeting.html (accessed 25 July 2010).

2 Outside and Inside the Gym

Exploring the Identity of the Female Bodybuilder

Tanya Bunsell and Chris Shilling

This chapter explores how female bodybuilders seek to maintain a viable sense of self despite being stigmatized by the gendered 'interaction order', the unavoidable presentational context in which identities are forged during social life (Goffman 1983). In examining their attempts to avoid the detrimental effects of these interactional norms, we draw on a two-year ethnographic study of British female bodybuilders and focus upon the *workout*: a ritualized activity-space central to the identity affirming activities of these women. Drawing on Victor Turner's (1992) analysis of liminality, we argue that while the workout is key to the creation of female bodybuilders' identities, and is relatively autonomous from wider interactional norms, the experiences associated with, and the social consequences of, this activity remain phenomenologically and culturally ambivalent. Immersion in the rituals and routines of weight lifting provide female bodybuilders with a temporary, "liminoid," escape from daily life, but offer no permanent solution to the "spoilt" identities attributed to these women.

PRESENTABLE BODIES

The manner in which people *present* their bodies to others has been central to sociological analyses of individuals' identities in the West. Presentational concerns were central to Cooley's (1922) notion of the 'looking glass self'; for example, Mead's (1962) analysis of 'generalised others,' and subsequent studies informed by symbolic interactionism (e.g. Waskul and Vannini 2006). In establishing links between individual public presentation and sustainable forms of self-identity, however, the work of Erving Goffman provides us with some of the most insightful formulations of this relationship.

Goffman (1983) identified the 'interaction order' as the ritualized, constraining domain of face-to-face relations that formed the presentational context in which identities are forged during social life. While some demands of this interactional sphere stem from the universal preconditions of human life, including the irreducible bodily components of co-presence, the interaction order also reinforces gendered cultural meanings (Goffman 1979, 1987). As Kessler and McKenna (1978) argue, dominant Western norms admit of *two* genders only, and the status of being male *and* masculine or female *and* feminine is one of the first things individuals attribute to each other in encounters. The significance of these gendered attributions are more than nominal, furthermore, having long informed views of the *acceptability* of the interacting self (Beauvoir 1993 [1949]). Contemporarily, with certain context-based exceptions, the gendered interaction order remains the place where men are expected to display their capacity for physical dominance – as a counterpart to their (aspirations for) social and cultural dominance – even if this has become increasingly subtle in recent times (Goffman 1974: 196–197; Goffman 1979: 9; Bartky 1988: 68).

The gendered interaction order does not *compel* men and women to present themselves in a particular way, though disrespecting this order can result in aggression, but does provide strong incentives to conform. For Goffman (1983: 2–8), as for Mead (1962), these derive from the fact that our ability to experience ourselves positively is structured by the responses of *others*. If we transgress gendered norms, stigmatizing feedback makes it difficult for us to see ourselves in anything other than a negative light, though individuals may seek to manage and mediate such negativity (Goffman 1963). The social consequences of transgression, furthermore, can result in exclusion from the 'order' of respectful interaction as a morally 'discredited' individual (Goffman 1963: 31, 43, 112).

In this interactional context, female bodybuilders are particularly vulnerable to stigmatization as women who challenge normative gendered performances through their pursuit of *muscle* (Bartky 1988; St. Martin and Gavey 1996).[1] Muscular size, strength, and definition have traditionally been associated with *men* as correlates of social power, and with the maintenance of masculine/feminine identities as binary opposites (Connell 1987). Yet it is the pursuit of this "male attribute" that lies at the core of female bodybuilding identities irrespective of the differences otherwise separating these women. It is not simply that their bodies transgress gendered presentational norms, but that they have made the *choice* to transgress this order: a choice that constitutes for many "normals" a statement of disrespect for core social values. This choice poses a considerable challenge in relation to the task of sustaining a viable sense of self-identity. It also raises questions about what identity-affirming resources or, to use Mills' (1940) term, 'vocabularies of motive' exist for female bodybuilders. How do they maintain a viable sense of self within a society that perceives them to be "oddballs," "deviants" or "freaks"?

"DEVIANT" FEMALE MUSCLE

The challenges women face should they express an interest in female bodybuilding are illustrated in the two-year ethnographic study, conducted by Tanya Bunsell, on which this paper is based.[2] The study focused on one site – a gym located in a city in the South of England. It included interviews with 26 female bodybuilders in the study supplemented by 76 interviews with friends and family members of these women and other gym users. In this chapter, we analyze this data on the basis of the insights it provides into the processes involved in acquiring and maintaining an identity as a female bodybuilder. All these women were concerned to maximize muscular size and definition; they were not involved in 'softer' versions of toning or figure-fitness activities.[3] While several of the female bodybuilders worked out in "hard core" bodybuilders' gyms, most trained in health and fitness gyms closer to home and adequate to their needs. Hard core gyms are distinguished from the latter by their sole focus on weight training – either for bodybuilding or power-lifting purposes. These gyms, also referred to as "spit and sawdust" gyms, consist of basic facilities and do not endorse the range of cardiovascular equipment, luxuries of nice changing rooms or attractive décor that health and fitness gyms like to offer. In the analysis that follows, we focus on experiences generally common to these women as bodybuilders. We begin by exploring the reactions of "significant others" to them, and analyzing the wider consequences that followed their muscle-building activities.

The following comments made by families, friends, work colleagues, and partners are typical of those directed to, and remembered by, these women when they first became interested in and developed their musculatures through bodybuilding. They contribute to the sense that female bodybuilders are deviant, a deviance that manifests itself in terms of their *motivations*, their pursuit of a *masculine* aesthetic, and a *disgust* directed toward their existence.

> Why are you doing this? What are you trying to prove?
>
> (Question asked of Lucie, bodybuilder
> of eight years, by her mother)

> Why do you want to look like a man?
>
> (Question asked of Rachel, bodybuilder
> of two years, by a work colleague)

> She looks so unfeminine and unladylike . . . Her walk is slow and pronounced, she even walks like a man . . . I don't like it, I don't like it at all.
>
> (A mother talking about her daughter, Christine,
> a bodybuilder of five years)

Bodybuilding competitions are disgusting. Those women are sick, disgusting, repulsive.

(Comment directed to Debbie, a bodybuilder
of seven and a half years, by her father)

Such remarks reveal the significance of gendered norms and convey the sense that any woman interested in building muscle must be psychologically or sexually deviant. At the extreme, male bodybuilders are also stigmatized for going beyond hegemonic ideals of masculinity. However, this is a *hyper*-masculinity and a body project that does not threaten their identities as *men* in the same way as bodybuilding threatens the maintenance of an identity as a *woman* (Fisher 1997; Shilling 2003). In this context, female bodybuilders run risks in their personal relationships and stand to be excluded from the privacy and respectful recognition enjoyed by others within the interaction order.

In terms of their *personal* lives, for example, Monica (a bodybuilder of two years) broke up from her boyfriend after being told by him 'I don't want you to train anymore ... Having sex with you from ... [behind] is like having sex with a man.' In terms of their interactions in the *public* sphere, Sharon (a bodybuilder of 12 years) was refused money in a bank because the teller did not believe she was a woman. More generally, Caroline (a bodybuilder of 17 years) reflects the experiences of many female bodybuilders when talking about unprovoked comments (from people in cars or on the street) questioning her feminine identity by asking 'Are you a man or a woman?'

These responses support the conclusion of Lowe's (1998: 44) study, conducted in the United States, that female bodybuilders have to live with unsolicited, negative remarks about their physiques. They also raise the issue of how female bodybuilders maintain a positive sense of identity, and it is in this context that we investigate the ritual that lies at the heart of bodybuilding culture – the workout. The workout constitutes a highly ritualized activity-space key to the construction/maintenance of bodybuilding identities. In what follows, we explore two questions. First, does the workout and the milieu in which it occurs constitute a hospitable back-region for these women, shielding them from gendered interactional norms and allowing them to engage in identity-constructing routines unhindered by external prejudices (Goffman 1969)?[4] Second, can the workout function as more than a temporary break from the gendered interaction order, providing a context in which female bodybuilders prepare for more permanent identity-affirming status-passages? We begin by drawing on Victor Turner's conception of ritual in presenting the workout in ideal-type terms, emphasizing its positive features for female bodybuilders, before complicating this picture by identifying the constraints that bear upon this activity-space. Turner's analysis is useful as it complements Goffman's concerns with the structured character of social regions, enabling us to focus on the transformative potential of the workout as a ritual event.

THE WORKOUT AS RITUAL

Turner (1957, 1977, 1974), developing Arnold van Gennep's explorations of status transitions, analyzed ritual as involving the individual in: 1) a break from the conditions of their previous existence (pre-liminal phase); 2) a liminal period in which they were emotionally, psychologically and physically separated from their previous selves (liminal phase); and 3) a re-emergence into society (post-liminal phase). Liminality promoted communitas (during which initiands experienced a collective effervescence, an emotional merging with others, that took them beyond their old selves), and ended with the re-emergence of the individual as a new self, occupying a new social role. Turner's depiction of ritual serves as useful heuristic means of exploring how women in this sub-culture develop new identities, as bodybuilders, that impact upon their status outside the gym. It could be argued that Turner's analysis applies equally to men's bodybuilding, but his concern with status transition makes it particularly relevant to women. It is they who confront the largest gap between the gendered foundations of the interaction order, on the one hand, and their appearances and identities, on the other.

In contrast to the challenges female bodybuilders experience in the formal interaction order, the workout constitutes for many a ritualized activity-space *separating* them from their previous existence and enabling them to pursue their goals less hindered by gendered conventions. The workout is central to *the* goal of bodybuilders, the goal of increasing muscle mass, density, and definition. The space in which this is pursued, the gym, is supported by a highly structured day in which muscle-increasing exercise is complemented by regular meals/snacks (most bodybuilders eat every two to three hours), supplements, and rest. As Becky (bodybuilder of two years) put it, bodybuilders 'wake up, eat, medicate, work out, eat, work out, eat, medicate, sleep.'

The distance between the ritual of the workout and normative existence is evident in the pre-liminal efforts female bodybuilders make to keep gym life separate from the profane world of muscular stasis. Preparation for the workout usually involves carefully planned meals, a workout kit (which may include straps, a weights belt, gloves, and chalk), and particular drinks. Some take stimulants (e.g. ephedrine, caffeine, etc.), but most prepare a post-workout protein drink. In contrast to the conventional feminine relation with food, these women are concerned with their *own* nourishment and *own* needs. Some female bodybuilders also watch training videos prior to their workout, for motivation, and engage in visualization techniques to assist concentration. These activities help women *leave behind* any other roles they may have, prior to entering the gym.

These rituals not only prepare female bodybuilders for the workout, then, but also separate them from anything external to this "world" of muscularity. They are reinforced by these women's efforts to maintain "purity" *within* the activity-space of the workout. These include visiting the gym when it is not, to use Douglas' (1966) term, 'polluted' by the presence of casual users. Most female bodybuilders use public gyms during times when the presence of "ordinary" gym members (those less committed to, and appreciative of, the commitment to muscularity as a goal in itself) is least evident. As Barbara (bodybuilder of seven years) put it:

> I don't want to train when its busy and there is some clown touching the barbell or something – ruins my focus . . . I'm in the zone of lifting weights – so any interruptions get me annoyed.

Many male bodybuilders also seek out such training times and spaces but female bodybuilders may be more vulnerable to interference, especially from men who 'feel they have a right to look and get in our way just because we are women' (Pauline, bodybuilder for six months). As Monica (bodybuilder for two years) confirmed 'men definitely dominate the space . . . a lot of their mentality is that girls are just playing at it . . .'

These ritual preparations for entry into the sacred space of the gym – what Durkheim (1995 [1912]) refers to as 'positive rites' which facilitate contact with the sacred – provide the basis on which female bodybuilders leave behind the gendered interaction order in favour of *phenomenological transformations* and *collective encounters* based around the pursuit of muscle and reminiscent of Turner's liminal stage of ritual.

In terms of phenomenological changes, Merleau-Ponty (1962) highlights what is at stake by observing that our bodies constitute our 'vehicle in' and 'viewpoint on' the world as our senses 'unfold' onto their surroundings. This is the background against which female bodybuilders undergo a metamorphosis that shapes their sensory experience of themselves/others/their environment. As Heywood (1998: 3) notes, the gym is 'a place of incarnations where our bodies inflate and we shuffle off our out-of-gym bodies like discarded skins and walk about transformed.' To begin with, the workout facilitates *undivided* focus on the body. As Rachel (bodybuilder of two years) comments, 'training time is me time. I can just forget about my worries and just focus on my body.' This attention develops through a *physical immersion* in repetitive lifting that allows these women to 'release any internal anguish, stress, anger and numbness.' As the workout progresses, the heart rate increases, muscles are "pumped" with blood, and the brain releases endorphins: the phenomenological experience of inhabiting a body undergoes a sensory and sensual change (see also Monaghan 2001). Debbie (bodybuilder of seven and a half years) describes this as an 'amazing feeling' accompanying the sense that 'your muscles are bursting out of your skin,' while Heywood captures such changes using the following terms:

> [O]ur muscles fill up with blood. Here, in this space, we begin to grow, to change . . . we pick up our shoulders, elevating our chins, shaking ugliness from our torsos with a series of strokes, the glistening dumbbells, listening to the blood's rush . . . Our breathing is quick, our skin is flushed, our hearts are pounding thickly.
>
> (Heywood 1998: 3)

Female bodybuilders associate this with a *heightened sense of being alive*. As this occurs, the boundaries between pleasure and pain weaken within the bodybuilding "high." What was previously uncomfortable becomes transformed as a 'beautiful and pleasurable' product of pushing the limits (Tate 1999: 38). Like Becker's (1997) marijuana users, there is a 'learning how' to interpret the feeling of being 'high,' a process developing through symbolic and emotional interaction with others. While the experience of pain is generally viewed as prompting interoception, and associated with the dysfunctional intrusion of the body into the lifeworld (Leder 1990), female bodybuilders engage positively with discomfort/fatigue; transforming it into a meaningful and welcomed experience. This reconfiguration of sensual experience is clear in the comments of Samantha (bodybuilder of three years) who explains how the bodybuilding high touches something 'beyond pain,' including an 'adrenaline buzz, the satisfaction of working to the max . . . Post workout . . . my body feels strange, almost sick, but at the same time everything appears heightened, I feel euphoric.' Similarly, for Mary (bodybuilder of 12 years), aches and pain are to be enjoyed and embraced even when leaving her 'unable to walk down the gym stairs.'

This euphoria can extend to a feeling of erotic potency as illustrated by the comments of Frueh and her friends when they admit to 'swaggering to the drinking fountain, radiating sex' and feeling 'horniest' when 'working out' (Frueh 2001: 71). Here, the gym is a pleasure zone that provides 'challenge' and 'sensual transformation' (ibid.), descriptors that resonate strongly with Monaghan's (2001) comments on the eroticism of the gym, but that provide an interesting contrast to Crossley's (2006: 38) identification of sexual motivations for gym use. While the motives of some gym users are to meet attractive others, the sensuality discussed here is more an autoeroticism in which female bodybuilders revel in the experience of their *own* flesh.

Against the background of these comments, it is not surprising that female bodybuilders talk of being 'reborn' in the gym, a description that bears a tantalizing, if ultimately partial, affinity with Turner's focus on liminality as preparation for re-emergence within the post-liminal stage of ritual. This rebirth extends beyond the body, furthermore, enveloping others joined in corporeal transformation. In contrast to the hostility these women experience outside the gym in the daily interaction order, encounters inside the gym can involve a 'camaraderie among all body-builders' (Jacqui, bodybuilder of 11 years). As Jacqui continues, this camaraderie is based on the mutual recognition of the efforts they make in relation to 'intense training and dieting.'

In this milieu, female bodybuilders do not have to be concerned about their "unfeminine" postures and movements. To begin with they often train with a partner, thus forming a dyadic, intimate space in which attention is directed to the task at hand. More generally, in this activity-space of the workout, serious weight trainers are 'supportive' and frequently 'offer to spot' for those without a partner and 'share training tips' (Corina, bodybuilder of four years). People may ask for advice and it is not unusual for female bodybuilders to receive compliments on their physiques from admiring others (those Goffman (1963) would call 'their own') embarked on the same quest for physical perfection. For some, this camaraderie culminates in the experience of an incomparable collectivity (see Fisher 1997). As Becky (bodybuilder of two years) claimed, 'Bodybuilders are a unique group of people. I have found more compassion, thoughtfulness, encouragement and sense of community in my short time of being a bodybuilder than anywhere else.' This is reinforced by the fact that these women occupy the same 'social field' and recognize, and pursue, the same form of physical capital (Bourdieu 1978). Male bodybuilders are not radically different from their female counterparts in this respect or, indeed, in some of the phenomenological changes they undergo (Paris 1997; Monaghan 2001). Again, however, the contrast for women is greater given the ostracism they risk in the wider interaction order as a result of their more radical transgression of gender norms (Young 1990).

As mentioned above, the bodily experiences and relational contexts associated with the rebirth talked of by female bodybuilders bear important resemblances to Turner's depiction of ritual liminality as removal from status and relationships *past*, and as a preparation for a *new* self. In this context, the workout does appear to constitute a positive activity-space for female bodybuilders in which their desires can be expressed in a context protected from the criticism and abuse they risk elsewhere.

To leave analysis here, however, would be to present an incomplete picture of the reality of the gym. The above description represents gym life as an ideal type, but also in certain respects at its most ideal. There are occasions during which the gym stops being a back-region (albeit a highly ritualized back-region) in which female bodybuilders can be themselves away from the gendered interaction order. Furthermore, there remains a question about the social consequences, or the post-liminal stage, of the workout. Key to the significance of ritual for Turner was the enduring personal *and* status changes effected by liminality, but are the liminal-like experiences of female bodybuilders contained within this ritual activity-space of the workout associated with permanent changes? We deal with these issues in turn.

CULTURE CLASH IN THE GYM: THE INTRUSION OF THE INTERACTION ORDER

Despite the identity-affirming experiences and interactions reported above, gym life is not unambiguously positive for female bodybuilders. It is possible for the workout to be interrupted by looks and comments that ask these women to reflect back on what they are doing in the gendered terms of the interaction order and to experience as internally divided their sense of self (Goffman 1963: 12).

The fact that these women's bodies are "on display" forms the basis on which this can occur even during the workout. Bodies are being worked on, body parts are being toned and shaped, and inter-corporeal comparisons are made frequently, often by casual users in relation to idealized, normative visions of masculinity and femininity. Hard core gyms might provide some insulation from this, although even then female bodybuilders are not protected completely. Several of those using hard core gyms in this study reported having to deal with 'incidents' involving male bodybuilders. None of these was as disturbing as Marcia Ian's story of how a huge male bodybuilder who was working out close by turned to her and said 'One of these days I'm gonna knock you on the floor and fuck your brains out' (1995: 89). Nevertheless, they still interrupted the flow of the workout. Elsewhere, in the milieu of ordinary gyms, casual exercisers sometimes looked, stared, commented, and pointed at muscular women in the free weights area, and this sometimes filtered through into the experiences of female bodybuilders. The following reflect the experiences of female bodybuilders in ordinary gyms.

> I've had strangers come right up to me in the gym and just say 'You're a woman, women shouldn't be muscular' . . . 'She looks like a man.'
>
> (Gemma, bodybuilding for six months)

> Guys have put down their weights and left when I'm training. People tend to be quite horrified to see a small woman lifting heavy weights.
>
> (Lucie, bodybuilding for eight years)

> Several friends at the gym commented on how big my biceps had got: 'show him your bicep,' 'you big lesbian you.'
>
> (Laura, bodybuilding for ten months)

Boys and girls learn early that female strength and size is unattractive to men (Nelson 1994: 45), that being attractive to men is a cultural imperative, and that voluntaristic transgressions of this norm give people a license to comment that does not always stop at the doors of the gym. Female bodybuilders are aware of this, which is why they generally workout at a time when few casual weight trainers are around, and do their best to ignore comments.

> I don't particularly notice other people's comments. Sometimes they piss me off, but most of the time I don't really care.
> (Christine, bodybuilder of five years)

> I love the gym . . . Apart from the twats . . . silly little boys with their sideways looks and stares . . .
> (Barbara, bodybuilder of seven years)

> I didn't come here to look pretty . . . And I sure as hell didn't come here to talk to boys . . . I came here to lift. So put your book down, pick a weight up, or move aside and GET OUT OF MY WAY.
> (Pauline, bodybuilder of six months – email communication)

These vocabularies of motive exhibit a determination on the part of female bodybuilders to ignore negative feedback, and also illustrate the manner in which they neutralize criticism by condemning those that condemn them, and the courage and boldness they exhibit in staking a claim to their "own" space (see Koskela 1997). Nevertheless, they also illustrate that not even the gym is immune from the wider interaction order or the disapproval directed to those who transgress gendered norms. There are also other ways in which the gendered foundations of the interaction order impinge on these women's action and identities. Indeed, female bodybuilders sometimes judge *each other* through a metric of heterosexual femininity. Alice (bodybuilder of one and a half years) referred to another female bodybuilder, for example, as 'butch' and suggested 'she doesn't help herself, she wears vests to train in. It's like she's trying to compete with the men.' Furthermore, despite the determination of these women to "be different," it is common for them to feminize their appearance in various ways. While only one of those in this study worked out in an ostentatiously feminine combination of hot pants and crop top lycra set, half these women involved themselves in such activities as dying their hair blond, acquiring hair extensions, and undergoing breast augmentation.

These actions were frequently undertaken in response to the effects that training regularly with heavy weights, and taking steroids/estrogen blockers, had in distancing their bodies from gendered norms. Regular intense exercise increases muscle, drug regimes and pre-competition dieting are responsible for the loss of fat/breast tissue, while steroid use often results in loss of head hair. Additional consequences of steroids, such as acne and the growth of facial hair, prompted women into other measures. One female bodybuilder interviewed, who was adamant that she would not involve herself in such measures, decided after two years of training to undergo breast augmentation when she became fed up of being mistaken for a man. Female bodybuilders would also sometimes self-consciously alter their demeanor and carriage in order to maintain a non-masculine presentational self outside the gym. As Charlie (body-builder for four years) noted, 'occasionally when I have trained my upper body, I'll be pumped up and have to stop myself walking like a man . . . [and also] you know, take my hair down.'

These actions suggest there are limits to the transformations many female bodybuilders are prepared to display. The transcendence enjoyed by these women as they became one with the weights around them, and as they experience alignment between their desires and the opportunities the gym provides for the expression of these desires, does not appear to result in a full-blown re-formation of their embodied self. Instead, actions that compensate for a loss of femininity compromise with the 'dull compulsion' of gender norms. These female bodybuilders pursue muscle, but also pay respect to presentational norms by donning some accoutrements of femininity. Felshin (1974) refers to this as the 'feminine apologetic.'

These compromises, if compromises they are, may not be unreasonable if they enable female bodybuilders to pursue their primary goal, but illustrate the efficacy of wider presentational norms. Of course, it is also important to consider the possibility that these women *want* to maintain a feminized muscularity, that the combination of muscle *and* hair extensions, physical bulk *and* make-up, and refined vascularity *and* prominent breasts are all expressions of a single coherent identity. As one professional competitor (and UK female judge) noted:

> I think I look like a woman (though I know other people don't always perceive me in this way). Femininity is very important – your skin tone, the way you look, walk, your posture, the way you act. Make-up, hair, nails (even the way you pose on stage needs to be feminine). Femininity can be destroyed if people abuse drugs rather than use them – go overboard and develop masculine characteristics.

The concerns expressed here can also, however, be interpreted as suggesting that this balancing act involves, at least for some, a degree of compensatory femininity incongruent with the identities they would ideally like to develop. This is evident in the comments of those who acknowledged making reluctant compromises.

I prefer the way my body looks now muscularity wise, but I know to most people I look 'too big' . . . So as much as I hate to admit it, I guess I compromise and probably make more of an effort with my clothes and hair than I used to.'

(Corina, bodybuilder of four years)

My breasts just looked like saggy socks when I had dieted down for competition . . . and I don't think I placed very high because I didn't have the whole package.

(Charlie, bodybuilder of four years, on deciding to undergo breast augmentation)

[In terms of the competitions] you need to play the game at the end of the day. If they want me to look 'feminine,' by wearing make-up, getting my nails done, and so on, then I'll do it.

(Christine, bodybuilder of five years)

These comments support the analyses of those who conclude that these women 'perform femininity during [bodybuilding] contests' (St. Martin and Gavey 1996: 53); a context in which 'lipstick and blonde locks are as necessary for the woman bodybuilder as they are for the female impersonator' (Mansfield and McGinn 1993: 64). Indeed, in 2005 female bodybuilders were instructed by their governing body to reduce their muscularity by some 20 percent.[5]

The extent to which gendered norms intrude on female bodybuilders raises important questions about the *social significance* and the postliminal consequences of the workout. Female bodybuilders may hope to experience their time in the gym as a carefully demarcated ritualized time away from normal prejudices, a time in which they experience the embodied pleasures of vibrant physicality away from the limits of workaday existence, but their lives are not without compromises.

THE SOCIAL LIMITS OF FEMALE BODYBUILDING

If the workout is not protected completely from the interaction order, neither is it a milieu in which female bodybuilders live all their lives. Indeed, the spatial and temporal specificity of the gym raises questions about the social consequences of female body builders' actions and experience in relation to the third, post-liminal stage in Turner's conceptualization of ritual. Turner (1992) associated the liminal stage of ritual activity and experience as an 'in-between' period which prepared its subjects for a *transfer* from one form of identity and social role to another. In traditional societies, such liminality would typically accompany the transition of a child to full adult status, or the elevation of an adult to a leadership position. Here, the limen is a threshold, and the subjects of ritual are on the threshold of a new status with corresponding rights and obligations (Turner 1977, 1992: 49). Rituals involved change for the individual, but were also integral to general processes of *social reproduction*.

The significance of ritual for social reproduction in Turner's model contrasts with the ritual features of female bodybuilding. Indeed, it seems that the ritualized activity-space of the workout is inevitably curtailed in its social consequences by the continued influence of the gendered interaction order. Far from female bodybuilding offering the means to develop a socially legitimate identity, women bodybuilders continue to be stigmatized. The public view of them is still one of "gender freaks." As a report in the *Independent* newspaper entitled 'Bulked-up Barbie girl waging war on her body' raged, 'she sounds like a bloke and she's got a five o'clock shadow . . . She's put through her paces by her friend Debbie, who looks like Sly Stallone and sounds like Tom Jones' (Thomas 2005).

So, where does this leave the identity of the female bodybuilder, concerned with developing a self centered upon corporeal transformation? What we suggest in the light of the above is that there is *no* full transformation: the activities/role associated with female bodybuilding result in no post-liminal realignment of social roles or norms. Female bodybuilding is not a vocation that results in a neatly defined career. Indeed, the most influential bodybuilding organization in the world (the International Federation of Body Builders) refuses professional status to British women, and there is no prize money on offer to women in British bodybuilding contests. While it is extremely rare for even male body-builders to be fully professional, it is not possible to conclude that a formal, structurally induced, occupational transformation awaits women committed to the pursuit of muscle.[6] In fact, UK female bodybuilders cannot support themselves from earnings or sponsorships, relying instead on such activities as personal training, working in shops, managing a pub, and office work, and by occasional opportunities in the realm of muscle worship (see Chare, Chapter 10, this volume). Furthermore, there is no resolution to the problems female bodybuilders confront in the gendered interaction order.

It is important not to overlook the experiences of empowerment reported here, however, nor to dismiss them as false consciousness. In making these points, it is useful to return to Turner's writings on rituals, but this time to his suggestion that the optional nature of ritual in the modern world makes it more realistic to talk of *liminoid* experiences. The experience of the liminal and the liminoid are similar, but while the former is associated with individual transformation *and* social reproduc-tion, the latter simply provides a temporary vacation from societal norms. Thus, liminoid experiences such as those reported by female bodybuilders occur 'outside the central economic and political process, along their margins, on their interfaces' (Turner 1992: 57).

The workout provides an activity-space that does at times provide a ritualized back-region, and a rest from social norms. It is also associated with the development of female size and strength that may be interpreted as prefiguring symbolically an existence apart from traditional femininity. As such, it is no wonder that female bodybuilders seek to dwell in the workout. In seeking identity with this activity-space, despite those occasions in which the gendered foundations of the interaction order intrude into the gym, female bodybuilders are explicit in the priority they attribute to their training over personal relationships, holidays, social and even working-life:

> My partner knew what I was like when she took me on, she knew first and foremost that I was a bodybuilder and that that would take first place above everything else including her.
>
> (Christine, bodybuilder of five years)

> I haven't had a holiday for several years . . . I don't feel comfortable not knowing whether I can find a gym . . . I hate the idea of taking time off from training.
>
> (Emma, bodybuilder of 19 years)

Turner (1992: 161) recognizes the allure of living away from structure, of subsisting in a comfort zone or 'womb' away from 'the responsibilities and obligations' of formal social roles. Ultimately, however, his analysis implies that these liminoid activities and experiences effect no permanent changes for these women. There are no 'rites of re-aggregation' for them through which they return from temporary escape to respectable roles in the social structure (ibid.: 133). In stretching the space and time occupied by the workout, however, the female bodybuilder is on a mission to invert the relationship between the gendered foundations of the interaction order and the phenomenological world of muscle in which she feels at home.

CONCLUSION

We have analyzed how female bodybuilders seek to maintain a viable sense of self-identity despite being stigmatized by the gendered foundations of the interaction order. While the gym has been examined before in terms of its interactional procedures, patterns and rituals (Sassatelli 1999), we have highlighted here the significance of this site in relation to female bodybuilders as they seek to maintain their identities amidst the gendered foundations of the wider interaction order. Our focus has been on the workout as both central to the primary goal of muscle building pursued by these women and as an activity-space that offers at least a partial break from the criticism and abuse experienced by female bodybuilders in their public and private lives. Despite the phenomeno-logical transformations and collective encounters they experience in this milieu, however, the wider interaction order constrains this activity-space and its social consequences. In this context, we suggest that the identities of female bodybuilders possess at their core an ambivalence insofar as this sub-culture provides its members with no ritual passage to a new, socially validated self. Against this background, it is not surpris-ing that female bodybuilders seek to expand the time in which they inhabit and experience the liminoid; the space which effects for them a *partial* escape from the profane world of the interaction order.

Notes

1 There are, of course, other groups who could be placed in the same corpore-ally deviant category as women bodybuilders. What distinguishes female bodybuilders from many other groups, however, is the extent to which they embrace and take pride in their transgressions.

2 For more details of the overall study on which this chapter draws, including its research methods, see Shilling and Bunsell (2009).

3 As the pursuit of muscle was articulated by all the women in this study as the central feature of their self-identities, we have identified them exclusively in terms of the time they have spent pursuing this goal. All names are pseudonyms.

4 Goffman's notion of back-region is ordinarily used to indicate an unstructured arena away from the front stages of life, but we use it to denote how spaces may sometimes be structured according to norms and expectations that nonetheless provide individuals with a break from dominant presentational standards.

5 This took place following a memo dated December 6, 2004, in which IFBB Chairman Jim Manion instructed female athletes in bodybuilding competi-tions to decrease their muscularity by 20 percent. It would be wrong to present this as a determining pressure, however, as several women who reached the British finals in 2008, for example, refused this "feminine imperative." Two clearly had facial hair and no make-up, and neither was knocked out in the first round of competition. This supports the view that whatever else divides female bodybuilders, and whatever compromises they make, the pursuit of muscle remains central to their identities.

6 This is not to rule out the exceptions to this situation in the USA, nor to sug-gest that female bodybuilders are unable to earn money from their bodies in a number of ways (for example, product endorsements, websites for fans). However, these exceptions do nothing to compromise the conclusion that there is no general socially legitimated role awaiting the female bodybuilder in wider society.

3   Accounting for Illicit Steroid Use
Bodybuilders' Justifications

Lee F. Monaghan

The media was able to demonize steroids with their uninformed reportage of steroid-related cases. Now and then, steroid users are being portrayed as angry, aggressive, and paranoid individuals. No wonder the public have misconceptions about steroids. Many people don't know that steroids do have good effects on the body.

(www.bodybuilding.com 2010)

INTRODUCTION

Many bodybuilders take anabolic-androgenic steroids (hereafter abbreviated to steroids) illicitly in order to enhance their performance and physiques. This practice is not confined to elite competitors. Recreational gym members and (non-)competition bodybuilders, with little hope of financial gain or fame, also supplement their exercise and dietary regimens with oral and injectable steroids. This occurs on a global scale despite legal sanctions in some countries, health warnings from clinicians and others (e.g. the media, friends, and family), commonly reported steroid side effects (Korkia and Stimson 1993) and the risk of social stigmatization (Monaghan 2001a). In short, a gap exists between illicit steroid users' actions and societal expectations.

Sociologists have long described the various ways in which illicit drug users verbally bridge the gap between actions and expectations. Weinstein (1980), for example, draws from C. Wright Mills (1940) and Scott and Lyman (1968) to explore illicit drug users' 'vocabularies of motive,' or phraseologies, for interpreting and accounting for their 'untoward' actions. Aligned with Weber's (1947: 98, cited by Scott and Lyman 1968: 46) definition of motives as 'a complex of subjective meaning which seems to the actor himself [sic] or to the observer as an adequate ground for the conduct in question,' Weinstein (1980) adopts a sociological rather than psychological approach to motives for illicit drug use. Here attention is focused on '[t]he symbolic meanings users plac[e] on drugs in connection with interactional strategies to assuage the negative implications of their actions' (Weinstein 1980: 578).

Such strategies take many forms. In the twenty-first century, the imbrications of bodies with multiple technologies mean that the internet, for example, provides fertile terrain for exploring bodybuilders' globally circulating symbolic meanings. However, in what follows I will use rich qualitative data that I generated face to face during a study of bodybuilding, drugs, and risk funded by the Economic and Social Research Council (ESRC). This ethnography was undertaken in South Wales and published as a monograph (Monaghan 2001a; also, see Monaghan 1999, 2001b, 2002; Monaghan et al. 2000). The study prioritized members' meanings and entailed following the Chicago School of Sociology's precept of 'getting the seat of one's pants dirty in real research' (for a reflexive account of the research process, comprising 67 in-depth interviews and 16 months participant observation in "hard core" bodybuilding gyms, see Monaghan 2001a).[1] In this chapter I will report members' vocabularies of motive, or accounts, for illicit steroid use. As an aside, such data from the field resonate with various postings on pro-steroid internet bodybuilding forums that I have since browsed and my embodied understanding of bodybuilding as a regular gym member who has some ongoing contact with male steroid users outside of Wales.

Regarding the broader context of the South Wales research, the possession of steroids for personal use was legal and usage was normalized among dedicated bodybuilders and their peers but the activity was stigmatized outside of their subculture. This stigma was compounded by a media-fuelled moral panic concerning the putative link between bodybuilding, steroids and violence or "Roid-Rage" (a concern that periodically resurfaces in different media within and outside the UK). Hence, South Wales bodybuilders usually only admitted to taking steroids when among people whom Goffman (1968) would term 'the own and the wise' – that is, people of like body and/or mind who understand the social situation of pro-steroid bodybuilders. For those bodybuilding contacts I established rapport with and learnt from, justifications, rather than excuses, were the predominant type of account for illicit steroid use. With justificatory accounts, social actors accept responsibility for a questioned act but deny or challenge its pejorative status. Justifications differ from excuses. Excuses are socially approved accounts in which the actor 'admits that the act in question is bad, wrong, or inappropriate but denies full responsibility' (Scott and Lyman 1968: 47).

In defending the fundamental tenets of bodybuilding as a drug subculture, respondents claimed steroid use (as opposed to abuse) was an appropriate and relatively innocuous practice for dedicated muscle enthusiasts. Three main types of justification, which were integrally related to the social construction of "appropriate" bodies and identities, are explored below: self-fulfilment, condemnation of condemners, and a denial of injury (also, see Scott and Lyman 1968; Sykes and Matza 1957; Weinstein 1980).

SELF-FULFILLMENT ACCOUNTS OR CONSTRUCTIVE RATIONALES

Weinstein (1980: 583) defines self-fulfillment as 'an account by those who stress they turn on [use drugs] for the personal satisfaction derived from a drug's psychological or somatic effects. These users do not find anything wrong with their behaviour and they tend to champion the drug's advantages as well.' Bodybuilders I talked with often voiced self-fulfillment accounts for steroid use by emphasizing the drugs' physique-enhancing effects. Here steroid use, in contrast to the "recreational" use of intoxicating (il)legal drugs, was considered a legitimate means to an end rather than an end in itself. A successful junior competition body-builder who used steroids and, similar to other dedicated bodybuilders, eschewed alcohol, said:

> Steroid users use steroids just as a tool to reach their goals, and they are taken for a reason as opposed to Speed or cocaine which are taken for no purpose, no end purpose. At least there is a purpose achieved by taking steroids as opposed to just taking them for recreational purposes, which to me is a total waste of time. If there is nothing to be gained in taking drugs why take them? It's the same with alcohol really. There's nothing to be gained in getting drunk really.
>
> (Respondent 22)

A former competition bodybuilder and drugs counselor, who reported using steroids to maintain muscle mass while dieting for physique shows, voiced a similar justification. Although this bodybuilder sharply contrasted himself with other types of illicit drug-taker, recreational drug users have also expressed 'constructive rationales' (Schaps and Sanders 1970). In the following excerpt, where a sharp sense of drug ownership and division is evidenced, steroids are claimed to be a (relatively safe) means to attain some "higher" objective than pleasure:

> With our drugs, the end justifies the means. Whereas if you're using recreational drugs like coke or H [heroin] or something like that, there's no end to it is there? The end is probably, you know, death perhaps. With steroids it tends to be, it's not a negative drug as such, it's a plus drug. You're trying to do something constructive. You're trying to build a body – whether you call it art or sport – you're trying to build something and there is an end product. With other

drugs there just seems to be tonight, today – live for today and tonight.

(Respondent 24)

These constructive rationales may be particularly significant for competition bodybuilders who are the largest consumers of steroids and who also adhere to monastic lifestyles during lengthy pre-contest preparation. A world championship standard competitor, whose steroid regimens exceeded subcultural parameters for "safer" usage (Monaghan 2001a: 107–119), said:

> I don't class steroids as being a drug. You only use [steroids] to help push more weight, gain extra weight, whereas with other drugs they're just taking them to, you know, get high. They're taking ecstasy when they go to raves just to help give them a buzz and you just don't need any of that like.

(Respondent 35)

Similar words were voiced by non-competition bodybuilders, who generally used lower dosages, over shorter periods with longer breaks between courses (a "course" is defined as a period of usage usually lasting several weeks). A "recreational" bodybuilder, who reported using one course of steroids, remarked:

> I wouldn't put them [steroid users] in the same category [as other drug users]. I mean, I know it's a drug when it boils down to it but the thing is, as I said, it's a conscious decision to improve yourself. I mean, if you get people who use heroin and people like that, they do it for a buzz first of all like. In the end it's habitual. They've got to have it to survive basically.

(Respondent 16)

In their study of a campus drug-using community, Schaps and Sanders (1970) explain how students ingesting recreational drugs differed from drug-using musicians and others because they stressed "lofty" motives. Explicitly drawing from Wright Mills (1940), these researchers state that the students' motivational structures and the patterns of their purposes were relative to societal frames. In contrast to musicians, students are 'more involved in the larger society and are therefore more accountable to it [they] can be expected to offer, both to themselves and to others, more compelling arguments than sheer pleasure for their violations of societal standards' (Schaps and Sanders 1970: 141). Certainly, in contrast to opiate injectors observed in more recent ethnographies (e.g. McKeganey and Barnard 1992), steroid-using bodybuilders I encountered were more often involved in the "straight" world of production and consumption: most bodybuilders frequenting commercial gyms in South Wales were in full-time formal employment, unlike many heroin injectors from deprived British inner cities. Bodybuilders voicing constructive rationales distanced themselves from stereotypical "drug takers" by claiming they were not fatalistically seeking to escape a depressing reality. A former competition bodybuilder, who reported taking steroids once but discontinued after an adverse reaction, said: 'Bodybuilders take drugs to enhance themselves, not to bloody induce some kind of catatonic state away from reality' (Respondent 29). Another, who regularly used steroids, similarly argued:

> There's no high to be got off it [steroids]. I mean, people wouldn't take cocaine if they didn't get a rush. If you take steroids you don't get a rush, you don't get any buzz. You know? There's no highness [sic] about it, so, they're not doing it for that reason. They're not trying to get away from reality, are they?
>
> (Respondent 23)

This does not mean pleasure is irrelevant in bodybuilding settings. After all, bodybuilders derive aesthetic pleasure from their own and other members' body modification practices. Steroid-related pleasures are also linked to what Mansfield and McGinn (1993) term the 'erotics of the gym,' that is, the sensuous bodily pleasures associated with intense anaerobic exercise and which are enhanced through steroid use (see Monaghan 2001b). However, in avoiding pharmacological reductionism, the national physique champion and gym owner quoted below stressed that the "highs" associated with steroids are self-achieved through dedication to ascetic bodybuilding regimens and disciplined, productive action in the world:

> The buzz [high] off it is like a self-achieved buzz. You couldn't take gear [steroids] sitting in your armchair and just sit there and start glowing and start laughing your head off. To be honest the only way I think steroids work is if you go into the gym. You attack the weights. You go home. You take your rest. You take everything into consideration that makes a bodybuilder. And this is where the achievement and goals come from really. It's the hard work that you put into it, and it's not just the drug itself. The drug only assists the bodybuilder to make his goals really. Look at say cocaine or heroin. You can just take that, sit in your chair and imagine yourself being on the moon if you wanted to. But whereas, when it comes down to bodybuilding, unless you go out and achieve these goals yourself physically, then it's not going to come to you.
>
> (Respondent 18)

Stylized or 'ideal typical' bodybuilders embody a subcultural system of relevances and typifications that is accepted beyond question by members (Monaghan 2001a: 45–72). Parameters for successful bodybuilding – knowledge, dedication, finance and genetic potential – constitute members' common-sense understandings of their shared reality. Here, individuals as bodybuilders are 'at home' (Schutz 1964: 252). In this context, bodybuilders' 'background expectancies' or 'sets of taken-for-granted ideas that permit the interactants to interpret remarks as accounts in the first place' (Scott and Lyman 1968: 53) render constructive rationales acceptable. Such talk is likely to be honored by other members because they "know" steroids are simply an *adjunct* to the demanding bodybuilding lifestyle. As stated by non-competitors who used subcultural typifications to justify accomplished bodybuilders' steroid use:

> Just taking steroids, growth hormones or whatever isn't going to produce a good physique. I mean, there's a lot of training and dieting and intelligence that goes into producing a good physique as well. Dedication, a lot of things which people would recognise as being in common with other sports, you know, like training and skill, strength and endurance and all sorts of psychological qualities as well that go into being a top bodybuilder. So, they aren't steroid freaks or drug abusers. There's a lot more to it than that.
>
> (Respondent 25; non-steroid user)

> People get this fucking wild imagination and say: 'he's a big boy.' And say straight away: 'he's on steroids.' They think you take steroids or a jab [injection] and they think you are going to grow overnight. No, you've got to work at it. Just because you take steroids doesn't mean you are going to grow overnight. You've got to do your half of it, or even do ninety percent of it. You've got to train and eat properly.
>
> (Respondent 48; steroid user)

According to such reasoning, people who take steroids in the absence of a proper exercise program and sound nutrition "abuse" rather than "use" these substances. Steroid abuse was widely disparaged by dedicated bodybuilders – it could not be justified through constructive rationales – just as taking LSD, without realizing its higher meditative potential, was disparaged by 1960s "heads" (Davis and Munoz 1968; also, see Bloor et al. 1998). Interestingly, nobody contacted during this research claimed they currently abused steroids, though some admitted they made this mistake in the past when they were less knowledgeable about bodybuilding and steroids.

In summary, self-fulfillment accounts or constructive rationales enabled members of bodybuilding subculture to justify illicit steroid use.

These vocabularies, for those expressing and honoring such talk, bridged the gap between (potential) actions and societal expectations. Embodying powerful ascetic ideologies, similar to Weber's (1930) early Protestant capitalists, muscle enthusiasts collectivity legitimated their own and/or other bodybuilders' instrumental use of steroids. In short, such accounts enabled narrators to resist accusations of opprobrium, negotiate potentially deviant identities and defend the fundamental tenets of their drug subculture. Here dedicated bodybuilders were sharply differentiated from people taking recreational and illegal "street" drugs and those taking steroids in the absence of hard training and proper nutrition. Other types of account also often buttressed such talk.

CONDEMNATION OF CONDEMNERS

This justification is comparable to those 'techniques of neutralization' first discussed by Sykes and Matza (1957) when studying 'juvenile delinquency.' In condemning their condemners, "transgressors" shift the focus of attention away from their own censured acts to the motives and behavior of disapproving others. In Sykes and Matza's (1957: 668) words, the 'validity' of such talk is secondary to its 'function in turning back or deflecting the negative sanctions attached to violations of the norms.'

During interviewing, I asked respondents: 'What would you say to someone who claimed bodybuilders were a bunch of drug abusers?' Whereas weight trainers, who were marginal to bodybuilding subculture, were likely to agree, those integrated into bodybuilding subculture often condemned (imagined) condemners. Evaluations of bodily appearance and lifestyle were central in such talk. In visually oriented consumer culture, where the body is an index of the self and the consequences of bodily neglect are a lowering of one's acceptability as a person and an indication of low self-esteem (Featherstone 1991), bodybuilders understandably felt physically (if not morally) superior to potential condemners. A steroid user retorted:

> The people that normally think like that have a pint in one hand and a big fat stomach hanging over their trousers and a bag of chips in the other hand. What you find, you can't even educate half the people like that anyway. They're just totally blind. All they can see is their point of view.
>
> (Respondent 32)

Such talk gained credence for respondents in a larger healthist culture where health and individual behavior are frequently linked. The pursuit of health through regular physical activity and the avoidance of harmful commodities (e.g. tobacco, alcohol, fat-laden food) is an imperative in contemporary Western society (Lupton 1997). In the next excerpt a "health conscious" steroid-using bodybuilder, besides denying injury, condemned imagined condemners by calling them hypocrites:

> If they were stood there with a fag in their hand and a pint of beer, I'd say: 'it's no different to what you're doing is it?' If not, it's probably a lot worse what they're doing. A lot of people are hypocrites without realising what they're saying. They're talking about what I'm putting in my body. They're probably going to have chicken curry afterwards, twenty fags, ten pints of Guinness, and tell me injecting steroids is a bad thing, which it isn't compared to some things people do, but there you go.
>
> (Respondent 31)

As can be seen, members easily bolstered their "condemnation of condemner" accounts with reference to what was imagined to be other people's unfounded and unreflective criticism. The social distribution of knowledge was significant in that respect. Interestingly, a sophisticated ethnopharmacological stock of knowledge is identifiable within bodybuilding subculture, comprising: a taxonomy of different steroids, theories of usage, methods of administration, and awareness of effects, possible side effects and strategies to avoid or attenuate these.[2] Many respondents claimed competent steroid-using bodybuilders are more educated on this topic than the typical doctor (Monaghan 1999). A weight trainer and former professional bodybuilding judge, who said he never used steroids, offered this account before criticizing people outside of bodybuilding for their mistaken beliefs. In short, he condemned condemners by claiming the public are ignorant:

> I mean, if you have a bottle of aspirin, a bottle of painkillers, a bottle of sleeping tablets, and a bottle of steroids, the only one that wouldn't kill you is the steroids. I think it's all overemphasised. I think there's so much bullshit about it. I think people get the wrong idea about it. They don't understand it.
>
> (Respondent 13)

Others condemned the media and the law. The bodybuilder below, as well as legitimating his personal use of steroids, justified the illegal act of steroid dealing and expressed a general sense of injustice against the unenlightened establishment:

> The thing is, we're carrying the can. Because the media have given such an adverse publicity and the people outside think 'drugs are

drugs' – irrelevant of whether it's a steroid or whether it's cocaine, Crack. They think a drug is a drug. They don't see the difference between one and the other. So therefore they see us as drug users. This is the biggest problem. The media think 'yes,' they catch a steroid dealer. But he's not dealing in anything really that's harmful to a person. Compared to cocaine, to Crack, to heroin, this is Mickey Mouse stuff. So I just feel we're being very harshly dealt with.

(Respondent 21)

The possibility of future legal sanctions against those possessing steroids for personal use (as opposed to those illegally dealing in steroids) also prompted some to mount a verbal attack against the government and the police. By condemning the authorities, the steroid-using gym owner and steroid dealer quoted below was able to neutralize the moral bind of conventional society:

At the moment the police can't cope with the ordinary drugs out there. So what'll happen is, when they get to the stage where they can't arrest people, because if they say arrested a druggie, he's probably on the bones of his arse, got no money, right. He's probably robbing anything anyway. So, they'd take him off the streets and it'd probably cost £300 a week to keep him in a secure prison and treat him as well, right. If you get someone taking steroids, then they arrest him, he's probably got a job because he trains at a gym and he can pay a fine. So, they'll get them in the end. Because, all they do is look for a way of making revenue. And I think it's the only way they'll go about it. The government will say: 'look, drop the hard drugs, because half the blokes you're catching haven't got any money anyway. Let's start hitting the people with the steroids because they're working and we can get some bloody money.' That's all it is. They just won't admit it.

(Respondent 10)

In summary, condemnation of condemners constituted another justification for steroid use among bodybuilders. Moral, legal or health-related objections raised by real or imagined people were easily neutralized. Respondents justifying their own or other bodybuilders' steroid use were able to reject accusations of opprobrium by claiming condemners are likely to be in poor physical shape, hypocritically engage in more common risk practices (e.g. smoking, eating fat-laden food, excessive alcohol consumption) and are ignorant about steroids. Institutions were also criticized, including: medicine, the media and the law. Of course, the validity or otherwise of such accounts is of secondary importance. According to Sykes and Matza, this and other techniques of neutralization are 'critical in lessening the effectiveness of social controls'

(1957: 669). Such talk may have increasing significance for steroid-using bodybuilders in the UK given the "expansion" of Steroid Laws in the run up to the 2012 Olympic Games in London, and the expectation in body-building media that representatives of the International Olympic Committee will 'continue to lobby the U.K. government to adopt legislation that criminalizes mere use and possession of anabolic steroids' (Baker 2009).

DENIAL OF INJURY

Weinstein (1980: 582) writes: 'with a denial of injury it is maintained that drug use is permissible on the grounds that it is not injurious to health.' Although this justification was broached above, it perhaps stretches credulity to believe illicit steroid users honor this type of account. Medicine, a powerful institution of social control despite mounting public skepticism (Gabe et al. 1994), warns against the hazards of steroids. Steroid contraindications and 'injury' associated with 'long-term abuse' (Herlitz et al. 2010), as reported in the medical and behavioral science literature (Kashkin 1992; Uzych 1992), include: acne, loss of scalp hair, oedema (water retention), hypertension, cardio-vascular disease and other damage to internal organs (e.g. scarring of the liver), aggression, and violence. Other side effects are gender specific. Male steroid users risk gynaecomastia (development of breast tissue), impotence, and testicular atrophy. Female illicit steroid users may suffer irreversible masculinizing effects such as excessive facial and body hair and deepening of the voice (Elliot and Goldberg 2000). Reference is also made in the literature to the risk of HIV infection and hepatitis among those injecting steroids (Grogan et al. 2006), though this risk is dependent on injecting with a previously used needle from an infected user and South Wales bodybuilders routinely reported using sterile equipment which was available free of charge from needle-exchange facilities.

According to bodybuilding ethnopharmacology, steroid use (as opposed to abuse) is conducted within certain parameters with the goal of minimizing harm while maximizing benefits. Thus, while steroid users often report side effects – particularly short-term and reversible side effects such as testicular atrophy, water retention, and acne (Korkia and Stimson 1993: 90) – many steroid-using bodybuilders seem able to resist the claim that they are simply abandoning their health. Experienced steroid users I talked with claimed that it is possible to avoid or reduce immediate and cumulative side effects. Ethnopharmacological risk management strategies included abstaining from particularly toxic compounds, cycling steroids (using for a specified period following by a period of abstinence), tailoring dosages in response to observed (side) effects and administering other compounds to combat steroid side effects.

Steroid users practicing these, and other (gender specific) harm reduction techniques, often used 'denial of injury' as a vocabulary of motive. An experienced steroid user, who reported suffering no ill effects, said:

> I just take to everything. Do you know what I mean? Some guys don't, but I don't get spots, trouble with the old dick, none of that. Never lost no hair. No problems at all. Never had a side effect. I started getting itchy nipples [possible gynaecomastia]. I take two Nolvadex [anti-oestrogen] tablets and that's gone. No problems at all.
>
> (Respondent 23)

A steroid-using competition bodybuilder, who attributed his nosebleeds and hypertension to a steroid accessory drug (Clenbuterol), claimed all physique enhancing drugs are relatively safe provided they are not taken in excess: 'Everything's OK in moderation. If people want to take stupid amounts, let them take stupid amounts. They are the ones that are damaging their health. So, let them get on with it' (Respondent 22). A particularly knowledgeable bodybuilder reflected upon the relativity of steroid "use" and "abuse" by stating 'a very fine line' divides these practices. Even so, he reasoned that long-term steroid use could probably be maintained with minimal risk to health. After emphasizing the importance of avoiding particularly androgenic (strong, toxic) compounds, reading indigenous pharmacopoeia and other harm minimization strategies, he stated: 'I think that steroid use can probably go on for years and years and years if done sensibly, if done in moderation, and taking the other precautions I talked about' (Respondent 24). One ethnopharmacological precaution is abstinence from alcohol while using steroids. A high-level competition bodybuilder, who told me his steroid courses could last up to 12 months (lengthy even by subcultural standards), proclaimed a position of responsibility and denied serious injury when he said:

> Alcohol and drugs, it's a fact that they both put stresses on the liver. In my case, you're gonna take steroids which causes a certain amount of stress on the liver so avoid alcohol which, as everybody knows, can cause cirrhosis of the liver. So I think you're just shortening the odds if you don't combine both. That was a major factor in why I stopped drinking initially.
>
> (Respondent 21)

Bodybuilders also appealed to various modalities of embodiment – including, but not limited to, bodily appearance – when denying injury. Within postmodern culture, health is often conceived in representational rather than instrumental terms: according to Glassner (1990), in postmodernity the image of healthiness has almost become more real than the "real" thing it references. Certainly, bodybuilding, similar to fitness more generally, may be accounted for on "health" grounds despite being associated with physiologically detrimental practices (see Bailey and Gillett, Chapter 4, this volume). Many bodybuilders present an image of vibrant physicality and also experience well-being in the gym which may have benefits for everyday pragmatic embodiment (Monaghan 2001b). A bodybuilder, who reported never using steroids, legitimated others' steroid use when he said: 'You've only got to take one look at their physique. They don't look ill do they? They don't look ill' (Respondent 41). Bodybuilders' adherence to low fat diets and regular exercise supported their view that they were far 'healthier than the average person' (Respondent 19, female steroid user).

As documented within the sociology of illicit drug use, a denial of injury seems to be particularly salient when 'mouthed with a personal reference; that is, [when] users affirm that a particular drug has not harmed their mind or body [and] has not addicted them' (Weinstein 1980: 582). Bodybuilders, while accepting some people may become psychologically dependent upon steroids, consistently rejected the idea that steroids are addictive in the same way that opiates are physiologically addictive (also, see Monaghan 2009). The following account, mouthed with a personal reference and extended to other steroid users, was typical:

> I've never craved a tablet or an injection. When I've come off them I can't say that I missed them or needed to have them. Like with hard drugs you have the craving, you've got to have it. You don't feel well or whatever it is until you have it, so you have to have it. But with steroids, no, it's not a problem like that. If someone can't afford their injections then they go without and it doesn't really lead to a big change in attitude.
>
> (Field Diary)

In elaborating upon this particular type of account, Weinstein adds: 'Users also offer this justification in a general sense . . . by holding that drug use is not socially disruptive, destructive, or detrimental to individuals' (1980: 582). In attempting to counter the dominant view in society that steroid users are like other maligned drug takers, a female bodybuilder who reported abstaining from steroids stated: 'No, it's not the same thing, is it? They're not going around thieving, beating people up to get money for their addiction. It's not like that. It's not a social disease like heroin takers. That's a disease' (Respondent 11). Male steroid-using bodybuilders agreed:

> I don't think steroids cause that much threat, you know, to society and that. You know, it's not like cocaine or heroin and that where

people do sort of, they're sort of addicted to the drug that they have to well, burgle or whatever to get money for the drug. I can't see steroids doing that to anyone like.

(Respondent 42)

I've never met anyone who has taken steroids who was driven to poverty to be on the streets, to doing robberies. Do you think? At the end of the day, you train better in the gym. But when you're taking a lot of the anti-social drugs, they're going to slip off and just do their own thing under a bridge or just crash out in houses.

(Respondent 10)

Interestingly, a former heroin addict turned steroid-using competition bodybuilder also denied injury to others. He justified his current steroid assisted bodybuilding by sharply contrasting it with his previous "junkie" outlook and behavior, and that of "boozers" or alcoholics who were seen to lack compassion or concern for others:

When I was on heroin I could cut someone's face from one side of it to the other, and think nothing of it. I couldn't possibly do that now. It's not in my heart. Heroin makes you emotionless, makes you feel-ingless [sic] and you can do anything and feel no way about it. Some of the things I gets told I done when I was a junkie. I look back at them and it scares me to be honest with you. It disgusts me. You know what I mean? I could have killed my own kids. I'm not joking! That's how emotionless it can make you, heroin. It takes you, gives you no heart. It's like people who go on the booze for years and years, they become emotionless. They can hurt anyone and can do anything. As long as they're getting their drink they don't care. It's the same with heroin. As long as you get your heroin, you don't give a shit who you hurt or what you do. So, coming from that to steroids. Bloody hell! Like I say, now I sit in most nights with my family and kids and I'm not interested in any trouble. I think it's telling you a completely opposite story.

(Respondent 43)

As above, "innocuous" steroids were not only contrasted with highly addictive illegal drugs. Bodybuilders also claimed steroids were less problematic than drugs taken by the majority of the British population, and which, according to sociologists, might be implicated in a 'de-civilizing process' in ways that go beyond the "alcoholic" as a minority deviant type (Dunning and Waddington 2003: 362). This justification was even maintained despite widespread media claims that steroids cause violence:

Probably sixty or seventy percent of people drink alcohol on a regular basis. Obviously the figures are probably greater . . . I'd like to say steroids are not in the same [league]. Well, they're not. You don't get people singing, dancing, falling around the streets when taking steroids, but then you're supposed to get the so-called 'Roid-Rages which manifest themselves in bodybuilders. Again, I don't believe ... it's a media thing, isn't it? 'Roid-Rage.

(Respondent 24)

A high-level competition bodybuilder, whose steroid regimens were lengthy, acknowledged personal harm but denied injury to others. Similar to other bodybuilders contacted during this study, he was loath to accept steroids as an exculpatory discourse for violence (see Monaghan 2001a: 156–80):

R35: You can't class steroids as a drug like. You don't get high on it. You still know what you're doing while you're taking it. All right, they can harm you but like you know the effect. Like where you would take marihuana or anything like that, or ecstasy, where you didn't even have a clue what you were doing. And they're going out and they'd kill someone and they wouldn't know they'd done it. Steroids can't do nothing like that to you so I don't really look at them as a drug 'cause you don't get no side effects off them in that sort of way like.

LM: But there's been some steroid users in the courts who've been violent or whatever and said 'the steroids made me do it.'

R35: Ah, they're just using that as an excuse. Help them get off with it. That's all. 'Cause, like, ever since I've used them I've always known what I've been doing.

Another user, when denying injury to others, buttressed his argument by citing the legality of steroids. Like others, he contrasted steroids with illegal drugs *and* alcohol:

R36: Well, yes they [steroids] are classed as drugs. Are they as bad as Speed or heroin? I don't think so. I have never known anybody yet to smash hotels in a fit of frenzy, to stab people or shoot people and cause fights. I don't think it's a bad drug. If it was a bad drug why aren't steroids at this moment illegal to take? Steroids, you can still take them and they [the police] can't touch it. It's only illegal to sell and make a profit out of it, so it can't be that bad.

LM: So, in your view, steroid users aren't like drug abusers?

R36: Far from it. Drinking is a drug. How many fights have you seen through drink abuse and marriage break-ups through drink abuse? I think drink is a worse drug than steroids ever will be. Drink's ruined many a life.

Finally, for the public and many official sports councils, illicit steroid use contravenes the spirit of good competition. So-called "doping" is said to injure the ethic of fair play (Waddington 2000), a topical concern, as noted above with reference to the 2012 London Olympics. Yet competition bodybuilding is a domain where steroid taking is often accepted and expected.[3] Within many bodybuilding federations, competitors are not drug tested and there is a widely shared assumption that steroids have been used. There is also a common understanding among "in-group" members that if "doping tests" are administered (in some high-level events, for example), this is merely a public relations exercise. A female steroid-using bodybuilder, of world amateur standard, denied injury to the ethic of fair play as such:

> Well, I don't think it's cheating. I cannot see that it's anymore cheating than if you were to have a personal dietician or a personal trainer who would write you out or give you the ideal diet or the ideal training plan. I can't see that having, well, an artificial substance, is any more cheating than that. If you are competing against somebody who has not got his own nutritionist or has not got his own personal trainer, then they are still at a disadvantage.
>
> (Respondent 19)

In summary, members of the bodybuilding subculture voiced various accounts which justified (rather than excused) steroid use. As well as offering constructive rationales and condemning condemners, respondents denied (serious) injury to themselves and to others, and the ethic of fair competition. Steroids, relative to other legal and illegal drugs, were considered fairly innocuous. This type of account was also mouthed by those reportedly abstaining from steroids, thus supporting the fundamental tenets of bodybuilding as a drug subculture. When "healthy-looking" steroid users denied injury, their talk was buttressed with a personal reference that steroids had not harmed or addicted them. To be sure, (tolerable) side effects are often associated with illicit steroid taking and my bodybuilding contacts were discursively aware of potentially serious health problems (e.g. harm to internal bodily organs). However, users expressed faith in bodybuilding ethnopharmacology: they claimed if steroids were used rather than abused, cumulative and long-term damage could be minimized. Even if respondents exceeded ethnopharmacological parameters for "correct" usage (Monaghan 2001a: 107–119), and admitted to jeopardizing their own health, they were still able to deny injury to others. This vocabulary of motive again served to legitimate (potential) steroid use and preserve competent social identities within a demonized drug subculture.

CONCLUSION

For people outside of the bodybuilding world it is largely taken for granted that illicit steroid use is unnecessary, wrong, and dangerous. For sociologists such as Dunning and Waddington (2003), such reactions may be theorized in terms of 'established-outsider configurations' where drug users are perceived by dominant social groups as unclean, unhealthy, criminal, and threatening. Hence, the public is likely to reject accounts for steroid use as verbalized by those supporting the activity. Unsurprisingly, members of bodybuilding subculture, who use or have used steroids for physique enhancement, often engage in strategies for avoiding drug accounts when interacting with non-participants. The likelihood of disapproval, or legal sanctions in some countries, mean illicit steroid users often find it situationally appropriate to conceal their "deviant" acts from non-members. Even non-users affiliated to body-building subculture, who may otherwise justify steroid taking, may find it expedient at certain times and in certain contexts to denounce illicit steroid use.

Understandably, other researchers have reported difficulties accessing steroid users' understandings in the field (Pates and Barry 1996). Also, other sociologists studying bodybuilding and steroid use tend to account for (excuse) the activity through appeals to antecedent predispositions, that is, psycho-social forces and gender anxieties (Klein 1995). Correspondingly, gaps remain in the social scientific knowledge on what legitimates and sustains this potentially risky practice. During my study I adopted a physically demanding active membership role (Adler and Adler 1987), which enabled me to generate ethnographic insights and further sociological knowledge on an under-researched and easily misunderstood topic. As with others undertaking 'sensual ethnographies in sport and exercise sciences' (Sparkes 2009: 26), this entailed sustained engagement with 'lived bodies' in an embodied social world.

Critically, while illicit drug use may be excused on the grounds that it is "wrong" and damaging to minds, bodies, and society, my contacts inside the bodybuilding subculture voiced different vocabularies of motive. They largely justified their own and/or other members' instrumental use of steroids and many steroid accessory drugs as part of their commitment to bodybuilding (on bodybuilders' use of these other drugs see Monaghan 2001a: 129–155). To be clear, members' accounts are situated (Wright Mills 1940); hence, other vocabularies of motive may have been offered to different audiences for purposes of presenting a moral self-image. Also, in providing morally adequate accounts, South Wales bodybuilders often denigrated certain types of steroid and other "physique enhancing" drugs (e.g. Nubain), which were constructed as 'risk boundaries' (Monaghan et al. 2000). However, and overwhelmingly, bodybuilders and other group members contacted during this research – irrespective of their own reported status as a steroid user – supported a norm of steroid use. Their subculturally acquired vocabularies of motive emphasized the drugs' "positive" effects and minimized or denied self-other related harm. In a subculture comprising a sophisticated ethnopharmacological stock of knowledge, and where "excessively" muscular bodies were valorized, risk perceptions were socially organized by social norms and context (also, see Rhodes 1997: 216).

In closing this chapter it should be recognized that the illicit use of steroids and other ergogenic drugs may be subjected to different types of social scientific analysis. Waddington (2000), for example, develops a critical sociological understanding of doping by exploring the medicalization and "de-amateurization" (commercialization, politicization) of sport. Such processes, which may be less salient for non-professional steroid-using bodybuilders and recreational gym members, warrant social scientific attention alongside the role of steroid taking in the construction of masculinity (Klein 1993). While the accounts framework, as used here, has much to offer concerning the analysis of (potential) steroid users' perspectives as social constructions, such analyses have been criticized for being unreflexive about differences between members vis-à-vis gender, class, and ethnicity (Davis 1995). Nonetheless, as stressed by other sociologists researching illicit drug use, it is imperative to explore the shared meanings which participants attach to medically defined 'risk behaviours' (Rhodes 1997). In the absence of these understandings, researchers may struggle to appreciate fully why illicit drug takers behave as they do. None of the sociological analyses mentioned above adequately account for illicit steroid use among (non-) competition athletes as understood by users themselves and their peers. It should be added that qualitative research on illicit drug use, and voluntarily risk taking more generally, may also be of practical value. Clearly, experienced steroid-using bodybuilders are unlikely to be dissuaded from their "hazardous" practices by clinicians who are perceived to be less knowledgeable (Monaghan 1999). However, as suggested by Hart and Carter (2000: 236), health promotion will be more adequate if it connects with the meanings shaping people's identities, practices and, I would add, their lived bodies.

ACKNOWLEDGEMENTS

I am grateful to the ESRC for funding this research, my ethnographic contacts for sharing their insights, as well as Michael Bloor, Russell Dobash, and Rebecca Dobash for supervising the 'steroids and violence' project.

Notes

1 In noting some general characteristics of the interview sample (N=67), 40 reported using or ever using steroids (60 percent) and 27 claimed to have never used. Bodybuilders comprised a significant proportion of the sample (N=40 or 60 percent). Three-quarters of all bodybuilders interviewed (N=30) said they used or had used steroids. Regarding the competition status of bodybuilders, 60 percent (N=24) had entered a physique show. These competitions ranged from the local level to world championship standard. Most interviewees were male, though six women were recruited. The mean age of the interview sample was 30. Only four bodybuilders were officially unemployed, though they received an income as door supervisors (bouncers). There was a wide range of occupations, including: television researcher, fire fighter, youth and community worker, fitness instructor, police officer. Most were in skilled manual or clerical positions (mechanic, architectural technician) and a few in the professions (solicitor, computer programmer).

2 The exponential rise in internet usage in the past decade means that bodybuilding ethnopharmacology is now also discussed in considerable detail in virtual communities. Advice about chemical bodybuilding is often sought online, freely given, and perhaps dissected by other contributors. Various "online pharmacies" also dispense steroids to muscle enthusiasts for a fee. These sites are often presented as the antithesis of "shady" underground outfits. Rather, they construct the image of an established and successful business offering discerning customers a highly professional service. I am aware of one customer, with access to laboratory facilities, who has tested his purchases and was happy with the results. Many of the steroids I purchased legally as part of the ESRC study were also analyzed in a laboratory and contained active ingredients.

3 An exception often cited by my contacts was the Association of Natural Bodybuilders. This federation was considered marginal. Muscle cognoscenti generally agree that "natural" physiques are unimpressive compared to "freaky" drug-enhanced bodybuilding physiques (see Locks, Chapter 8, and Richardson, Chapter 9, this volume).

4   Bodybuilding and Health Work
A Life Course Perspective

Brian Bailey and James Gillett

On the covers of magazines such as *Flex* and *Muscle & Fitness*, body-builders are commonly depicted as men possessing extremely muscular, nearly fat-free bodies. This figure of the bodybuilder emerged in the 1980s when subcultures of men, such as those described by Klein (1981, 1985) in his studies set in southern California, sought to push the limits of muscularity and to advance 'professional competitive' bodybuilding. Thirty years later, bodybuilding is a more generalized and normative practice, a trend described by Monaghan (1999a) as the plurality of the muscular body. A more diverse range of men are pursuing muscularity as a component of their gender identity.

In this chapter we examine the health dimensions of bodybuilding for men who are at different points of their life course. We build upon existing social scientific research on the meaning of bodybuilding practices for men who work out regularly but do not compete professionally. A prominent theme in studies of bodybuilding is the connection between muscularity and the construction of hegemonic masculinity (Klein 1986, 1992, 1993; Gillett and White 1992; White and Gillett 1994). The practice of bodybuilding is seen as linked to a broader crisis of masculinity in which men turn to the muscular body as a means of reasserting dominance as traditional sources of authority for men recede with transformations in the gender order. This premise continues in more recent studies of male bodybuilding. Bridges (2009), for instance, introduces the idea of gender capital to describe the process by which male bodybuilders use muscularity to negotiate their masculine identity, which may but not necessarily reproduce broader hegemonic social relations in different and contingent social settings. We build upon this work by examining the place of gender capital among men involved in bodybuilding at moments in their life course when their masculine identity is renegotiated and transformed.

Along with masculinity, the health dimensions of bodybuilding is another predominate theme in social research on men involved in the sport. This literature tends toward questions regarding the health benefits and risks of bodybuilding. The use and misuse of steroids among men involved in weight training and bodybuilding is a central concern in this research (see also Monaghan, Chapter 3, this volume). Keane (2005) highlights the extensive number of studies that link bodybuilding with steroid abuse as a public health threat. Steroid use among bodybuilders is framed either as a form of elicit drug use or as a result of men suffering from a 'disorder' or problematic masculine identity (Keane 2005). Not all research on health and bodybuilding attend only to the rise of steroid abuse among men. Monaghan (2001a and Chapter 3 this volume), for instance, expands this frame of reference to include an analysis of the lay knowledge that bodybuilders acquire and use in weight training and participation. Understanding the pharmacological knowledge that body-builders acquire and use to manage the risk of steroid and supplement use suggest that bodybuilding is work that men do in pursuit of muscu-larity and also undertake in pursuit of what they define as health.

The discourses of muscularity and health are becoming increasingly intertwined. Studies indicate that understandings of health in the body-building community are closely associated with descriptions of ideal masculine physiques (Monaghan 2001b; Grogan 1999; Gill et al. 2005). This trend is evident in the titles of popular magazines such as *Muscle & Fitness* and *Men's Health* that promote and twin a relationship between hegemonic masculinity and the muscular male body. Yet, few studies examine the meanings of health for men who participate in bodybuild-ing. In a preliminary study, Gillett (1995) indicated that many young men think about bodybuilding as a means to health, albeit an under-standing of health that is closely twinned with conventional understand-ing of masculinity (strength, power, control, invulnerability). There is a need for further research on the intersection between the meanings of health and the meanings of masculinity for men who are involved in bodybuilding.

The purpose of this chapter is to move in this direction by exploring bodybuilding as a form of health work that is carried out by men at different stages of their life course. We explore questions such as: How is health negotiated by male bodybuilders as they pass from one stage in the masculine life course to the next? How is health expressed in terms of bodily aesthetics and function as men age? How do the forms of health work performed by men change as they grow older?

In this chapter we begin by describing the sample of male bodybuilders and the context in which interviews took place. Participants shared expe-riences that followed a heteronormative life trajectory while conversing about the health dimensions of bodybuilding. The dimensions are struc-tured in relation to two broad understandings of health: aesthetic and functional. We then move to examining the constructions of masculinity through the health work of bodybuilding at three distinct moments in the life course: youth, middle age, and elderly. To conclude, in looking at the health dimensions of bodybuilding across the life course, we make the point that, for men, the importance of the body's ability to function takes precedence over achieving an aesthetically pleasing physique as men age.

INTERVIEWS WITH BODYBUILDERS

A total of 32 digitally recorded interviews were conducted with predominantly Caucasian male bodybuilders between the ages of 18 and 68. They took place between September 2007 and June 2008 most often in local coffee shops or in residences' homes; five interviews were conducted over the telephone. An interview guide containing questions around the topics of bodybuilding experience, aesthetics and functionality of the body, and sources of trusted knowledge was created; the order in which these topics were addressed often depended on how pre-interview conversations progressed. The interviews lasted an average of 52 minutes. While all men participating in this study identified, in some way, with being a bodybuilder, few identified as being "hard core." The participants who most strongly identified with being serious or "hard core" had won provincial or national level bodybuilding competitions, one of whom shared aspirations of competing professionally.

Participants were recruited from gyms to represent a bodybuilding continuum: from recreational bodybuilders to winners of national-level amateur bodybuilding competitions. As such, purposive sampling techniques were used in order to obtain a sample that would be diverse in terms of age and in bodybuilding experience. All participants understood their bodybuilding practices as a means to enhance health yet the kinds of work done to achieve health varied by age. The study used an inductive approach that began with the meanings participants attached to bodybuilding activities and their health, and we sought a greater understanding of those meanings.

Bodybuilders interviewed for this study were mainly recruited either through pre-established contacts made by one researcher (BB) in local gyms, or through recruitment posters placed in these facilities. These two gyms, both part of a national chain, are located in a large suburban area in middle-class neighborhoods. Both gyms were much busier in late afternoon and early evening than in the early morning hours (i.e. prior to 7 a.m.); a markedly younger demographic populated these facilities later in the day than in the morning. One site was more commercial than the other and has an open concept design to house its combination of free weights and machines. Amenities include several fitness classes (e.g. spinning, "boot camp" style, and such) as well as towel and child-minding services. The other gym has fewer amenities and the closed concept design avails itself to different workout atmospheres. The primary basement weight room, a low-ceiling and dimly lit room, lends itself to a rather "hard core" feel. Groups of young men performing sets of bench presses, barbell curls and deadlifts dominate the weight room floor in the evening. The upper level contained cardiovascular equipment and weight machines in a less intimidating atmosphere.

HEALTH DIMENSIONS OF BODYBUILDING

Male bodybuilders in this study led a seemingly heteronormative lifestyle. The vast majority of men spoke of being career-oriented and having a desire to raise and provide for a family as a natural life course trajectory. Questions focusing on sexual orientation were not explicitly asked of participants, but through conversation, most revealed their sexual interest in females or in being involved in monogamous, heterosexual relationships.

Men in this study closely associated bodybuilding with the pursuit of health. Western culture embraces and promotes the concept of healthism, which calls for individuals to be responsible for their own health (Goldstein 2000; Pawluch et al. 2000). Healthism, according to Crawford, 'is the preoccupation with personal health as a primary – often *the* primary – focus for the definition and achievement of well-being' (1980: 365). He posits elsewhere that 'health must be achieved. It is dependent on health-promoting behaviors. As the goal of health acquires a new-found importance, priorities must be reordered, a commitment made' (1984: 67). Participating in bodybuilding activities, then, can be viewed as the health work done by men to achieve positive health.

The health work done by participants went beyond just lifting weights. Many men described living a bodybuilding lifestyle that included being dedicated to working out regularly and to eating nutritious foods. It also requires discipline and self-control by foregoing temptations (Crawford 1980, 1984). One participant explains:

> When I think of bodybuilding I think of someone that makes the lifestyle choice of bodybuilding. It's not just going to the gym 3 to 5 times a week and training. They alter other aspects of their lives to conform to their bodybuilding lifestyle. They eat a certain way, they exercise a certain way, they're not heavy drinkers, heavy partiers, they eat healthy. The whole lifestyle is thought towards being healthier and building their body the best they can.

Throughout our interview, this man shared his beliefs on the positive benefits of living a bodybuilding lifestyle. These included relieving stress and having a positive mental outlook on life. Of importance to him was that by living this lifestyle, he developed a good work ethic that transcended the gym to other areas of his life, such as his occupation.

His experiences were shared by other male bodybuilders. There were several health dimensions that emerged during this research. Similar to other findings (Monaghan 2001b; Robertson 2006), when asked what being in good health meant to them, many participants proclaimed they 'looked good and felt good.' Others felt they were in good health precisely because they were not experiencing symptoms of illness, injury or disease. Dimensions of health, however diverse, tended to be organized around two tendencies: aesthetics and functionality. Each of these tendencies plays a role in shaping the health work conducted by men of all ages, albeit to varying degrees of importance throughout the masculine life course.

HEALTH AND THE AESTHETIC

Men of all ages cared how they looked. There is great social significance placed on the aesthetic desirability of the body, which is often the reason that males engage in bodybuilding activities. Possessing a lean, muscular body aligns with Western social ideals of physical attractiveness for men (White et al. 1995). To deviate from this ideal is to risk being socially stigmatized as lacking self-control, discipline, and will power (Crawford 1984) as bodily indulgence is a sign of 'immortality, irrationality, decadence, and weakness' (Gruneau 1997: 198).

There is no single masculine ideal type. Images of ideal masculine physiques are disseminated through various forms of media, and how a man *should look* is, of course, historically and contextually specific. Contemporary media representations of men vary in shape and size, but what commonly appears are nearly fat-free bodies with, in the least, a modicum of muscularity. Hardcore bodybuilding magazines would represent the very extreme in images of hyper muscularity. Very few participants in this study identified the physiques of professional bodybuilders specifically when discussing their aesthetic goals. The goals of younger men, however, seemed to align with such extremely muscular images as they stated, in the most general and non-specific terms, a desire to get "huge" and "ripped." When it was discussed, a couple of younger bodybuilders aspired to look like cartoon superheroes or action movie stars. Older bodybuilders, in contrast, generally wanted to avoid getting fat with less concern on developing exaggerated muscularity.

The peer group provided a relational context for men to evaluate their physique. Compliments and positive reinforcement received from peers on the appearance of their body served as a source of pride for participants. Men wanted to look better than their peers at all phases of the life course. In turn, how they felt about the appearance of their bodies had a profound impact on their masculine identity construction. Our findings also support that 'bodybuilders are united in the ongoing project of enhancing bodily aesthetics' (Monaghan 1999a: 268).

HEALTH AND FUNCTION

The functioning dimension of health refers to the body's ability to *do something*. Men lift weights to better prepare their bodies to undertake an activity. What that something tended to be was contingent on one's place in the life course. Younger men, and men reflecting back on their younger years, disclosed their desire to improve their performance in sport through bodybuilding health work. Older men, conversely, wanted to maintain the ability to perform daily activities.

It is during the period in between these life course phases that the functional dimension of health recedes in importance to identity (re)construction. The body, during this phase, becomes an absent present (Leder 1990; Sparkes and Smith 2002). When not experiencing injury, illness or disability, the ability of the body to function becomes taken for granted and disappears from conscious awareness (Leder 1990; cited in Sparkes and Smith 2002: 266). As men age, we argue that the preservation of this functioning body re-emerges to serve as a health work goal for male bodybuilders.

The aesthetic and functional dimensions of health exist on a continuum for male bodybuilders. These dimensions are not dichotomous in that males are ever only concerned with aesthetics *or* functionality, but rather the importance they place on them changes over time and in response to life experiences. The interplay of these dimensions of health is prominent in masculine identity construction throughout the life course.

MASCULINE LIFE COURSE AND IDENTITY CONSTRUCTION

Bodybuilders place varying degrees of importance on the symbolic and pragmatic representations of health as they progress in their life course. Lawton states '. . . within popular culture, health is increasingly being conceived and evaluated in representational rather than instrumental terms, the *appearance* of health (achieved through the cultivation of strong-looking, fat-free body) often being regarded as more important than the attainment of health *per se*' (2003: 33). While the lived experiences of younger bodybuilders in this study align with this reasoning, older participants challenge this notion as their health work is performed with pragmatic bodybuilding goals in mind. The interplay between the aesthetic and functional dimensions of health influenced masculine identity construction during various phases of the life course.

Health work was organized to develop muscular physiques that were the literal and symbolic embodiment of power, a characteristic of traditional hegemonic masculinity (Connell 1987; Connell and Messerschmidt 2005). For others, we found the truth game of masculine identity construction through bodybuilding was more centrally tied to developing a functional body. These men tended to be older and worked toward maintaining good health and independence. Although still influential, the importance afforded to physical appearance at this stage in the life course for identity construction had lessened.

We categorized men in this study to occupy positions in one or more phases in the masculine life course, namely younger, middle-aged, and older years. Chronological age alone does not differentiate between these phases. Blaxter argues that 'A real lifetime is measured subjectively in social periods – infancy, schooldays, family formation, work, retirement – rather than calendar years; periods of life which may be determined by social roles, but are particular to individuals' (2000: 41). We compare the health work done throughout the masculine life course at these phases, as has been done elsewhere (Oliffe 2009), but acknowledge that they are temporal in nature, being neither fixed, nor self-evident (James and Hockey 2007: 136). They are not clearly defined or mutually exclusive as men, arguably, could be part of more than one phase.

"THE SEXY BEAST" IMAGE: YOUNGER MEN

An important component of masculine identity construction for younger males is tied into the appearance of their bodies. The body can be developed as a resource to gain gender capital. Bridges defines gender capital to be the 'knowledge, resources and aspects of identity available – within a given context – that permit access to regime-specific gendered identities' (2009: 92). These men wanted to portray a muscular, sexualized body image that would be accepted and admired by their peers. Notions of what it meant to be a "real man" for them – someone that same-sex peers respected and that females would find sexually attractive – encompassed the display of a physically strong and lean body. One bodybuilder recalls an experience he had while in high school.

> You know, the motivation when I was bodybuilding was that if I could get my arms a little bigger, get my chest a little bigger, get a little leaner and get my abs popping out, I'd feel better. You want to be the guy that the girls look at . . . I remember one incident in high school in particular where a girl made a comment to me: "Oh, you look like you've been working out" and right there, that was all the incentive I needed to keep going to the gym. It was like wow, like this hot chick just noticed that I got a little bigger. You know, I went from 154 pounds at 6'1 to 164 pounds at 6'1.

Cooley's (1964) concept of the 'looking glass self' can be applied to understand the process of masculine identity construction for younger men.

He identifies three components to the 'looking glass self': the imagination of our appearance to the other person; the imagination of judgment of that appearance; and some sort of self-feeling, such as pride or mortification (Cooley 1964: 184). One participant recalls his desire to develop a muscular body that, in this particular context, would not only be admired and envied by other males, but would also receive approval from females.

> I had it in my head that, I wanted to be a big guy with big arms – and I wanted other guys to notice. Yeah, it kind of got overblown because I wanted chicks to think the same thing. I remember I was showering once in university, it was night-time in the dorm and everyone was running around drunk, and when I opened the shower, they looked at me. I then heard a couple of my buddies say "the girls looked at you and they loved your body" and I thought I could eat this up. It was a good thing.

At the time, this male was in his early twenties. He had a masculine ideal type in mind that he idolized and thus the health work he did was intended to align his physique closer to this ideal. He projected an identity of being "the big guy" to his same-sex peers, and that of "the sexy beast" to interested females. In receiving positive feedback from others – either real or imagined – his body image was reinforced.

Once reinforced, the bodybuilder internalizes his masculine identity which becomes his master status (Becker 1963). He becomes known to others by the aesthetic image he projects. This identity becomes a self-fulfilling prophecy (ibid.) insofar as he continues to organize his bodybuilding health work to maintaining it. The following exchange with a participant exemplifies how once established, he worked to maintain (or continually re-construct) his masculine identity.

> Interviewer: So, when people start recognizing you that way [big, muscular], do you feel pressure to maintain that identity?
>
> Participant: Definitely, yeah. It's like you almost feel like you have to be the big guy, you have to be the strongest. And it's like you start – sad to say – sizing up the people around you because you want to have that edge over them. You want to be a little bigger than them, you want to be a little stronger than them because you know the minute someone stronger and bigger comes along, you wonder who you are. Who am I? If he's the big guy, what am I?

Ideal masculine images for younger bodybuilders tend to focus on extremely muscular or hypermasculine bodies (Gillett and White 1992; White et al. 1995). Such ideal types are representative of superheroes or embodied by iconic professional bodybuilders that are commonly reproduced in popular culture. The mass media is an important source of images of masculinity for youth (Connell 2008: 133) and plays a role on youths' identity formation. We argue that younger men might be more susceptible to such images than middle-aged or older men. One participant recalls:

> You know, I always liked watching Arnold Schwarzenegger and action stars [as they] are always, like, ripped and built. I thought that's cool, you know what I mean? So I was always, like, I wanted to look like that.

Developing muscular physiques were of interest to young men who participated in sports. A strong body was perceived as being functionally beneficial to improving performance. Being successful in organized high school sports allowed young bodybuilders to integrate and identify with a group (Elling and Knoppers 2005) that endorses traditional masculine scripts (Miller et al. 1999). Connell (2008) argues that sport serves as a site for peer group interactions where definitions of masculinities are created and adopted in adolescence. Constructing bodies that would facilitate success in sport provided motivation for young men to begin undertaking bodybuilding practices.

> All through high school I played every sport like football, basketball, rugby, hockey, tennis . . . like every sport. That was my first motivation to start working out. I was really skinny and scrawny and you notice that all the bigger, more muscular guys are better at certain sports. So, like I say, I didn't want to be an average guy on the team. I wanted to be one of the studs you know, one of the guys that was playing.

It was not uncommon for males to organize health work in order to build strength and muscularity in the body even apart from playing sports. Muscles were desired and considered to be manly, while being skinny, conversely, was viewed as problematic for young bodybuilders.

> Well in high school I was, you know, I was kind of a skinny kid. I guess more or less people do it [body build] to find an area to fit in. You know, maybe they're kind of bookish or they're kind of a nerd if you will. You know I would qualify myself as possibly being a nerd at that age but bodybuilding is just a way to fit in, to feel a little bit more accepted with your peers, girls and your buddies.

Another male found that developing physical capital in his body through increased musculature held social currency with older peers.

I got big pretty quickly at that time and I got more respect for being bigger in the gym. Bigger guys – older guys, started talking to me more because I was bigger even though they were 20 and I was 16. They wouldn't normally talk to 16 year old little skinny guys in the gym. They'd talk to guys who were just as big as them and they would teach me stuff.

Younger men personify the "sexy beast" image in the social contexts in which they find themselves. An integral part in performing this gender identity is presenting a muscular and lean physique. Health work for them incorporated bodybuilding activities in the pursuit of obtaining this type of gender capital. As men aged, however, the embodied goals of approaching bodybuilding changed.

AVOIDING "THE POT BELLY" IMAGE: MIDDLE-AGED MEN

The men in this study expressed that they experienced different events as they aged that competed for their time. Events such as starting a career, a marriage, a family or purchasing a house were seen as part of a normative life trajectory and challenged the amount of time that they could dedicate to bodybuilding health work. In turn, these life occurrences also offered men ways to re-construct their masculine identities apart from their body image. We consider these life events to be biological transitions that may signify a male moving toward the next phase in the life course.

At the time of the interview, a 29-year-old male was married and purchased a house within a year. He also provided the bulk of the family income and was studying for a new career. He explains how as he encountered more demands for his time and resources, the meaning he attached to bodybuilding changed.

You get older and then your career starts kicking in. You're doing school or you have a baby or you buy a new house – like I just bought a new house – or getting married you know. Before it [bodybuilding] was more of seeing how big I could get. Now I don't have the time for that anymore.

At 68 years old, an older bodybuilder recalls how bodybuilding health work changed in significance during his middle-age years.

As you age and, you know, you get married and you have kids and you have a house and you got a career, you have to fit all the training into your lifestyle. For a while there I was obsessed with the training.

I started to realize at that time that bodybuilding had to be part of my life but not all of my life.

The health work that middle-age men engage in develops gender capital that is significant across different contexts. As Bridges states, 'the value of bodies is dictated largely by the contexts in which they are presented' (2009: 93). For middle-age men in this study who are trying to balance a family, career, and social life, certain traditional hegemonic masculine characteristics such as having a successful career and being a good provider gain importance. Such identity-forming and gender-performing avenues were not present in the lives of younger men.

One participant, a man in his mid-thirties who owns a business in the bodybuilding industry, explains how changes in his life circumstances altered his health work goals. The construction of his masculine identity, implicitly, was influenced by more than just the appearance of his body.

> In your 20s you could do whatever, hang in the sun and drink until 3 in the morning; do whatever you want to your body and you're sort of invincible, right? As you get to your mid to late 30s, you know, I get injured a little bit more, I need more sleep; you know I have a business and a family to take care of – I have a son. These things start playing in your mind saying you know what, is it worth doing those extra things to benefit my appearance . . . as opposed to making wise choices and trying to prolong life? I'm here for the benefit of my family and my business.

This is not to say that the appearance of the body lacks social value in this phase of the life course. The demarcation of status within the aesthetic dimension of health, however, rests more in the comparison against same-aged peers as opposed to masculine ideal types.

> [After working out] I just feel better you know because I don't want to be like the guys at my office who're sitting there and it looks like there's a beach ball in their shirts.

> If I take a snapshot of the average 50 year old, I don't see me, I see a guy that's overweight whose going to have heart problems. He's going to have problems in the future possibly. And I see myself as probably looking better, you know, than the average guy my age.

It is during this phase of the life course that age becomes an important category in and of itself. Middle-age men were far more likely to qualify their health experiences by their age than their younger counterparts. More specifically, the pursuit of gender capital by these men tended to center on looking younger than their chronological age.

Receiving compliments from others on their appearance also shapes, in part, their masculine identities. A 48-year-old participant describes how engaging in bodybuilding health work helps him feel younger and has resulted in the admiration of others.

> After weight training, you feel like you're pumped and you feel strong. Yeah, you feel good, you feel strong and athletic and you don't feel like a 50 year old. I feel like a 30 year old. And it's important too, when people tell me that I don't look my age or that they can't believe how fit I am for my age. It just gives me a lot of satisfaction. I feel great about it, I feel like I'm doing something that nobody else is doing.

We contend that the body during middle life becomes an absent present (Leder 1990; Sparkes and Smith 2002) where a presumption exists that the body will function as desired. In other words, men in this phase of the life course largely didn't think about their body's ability to do daily tasks. The body returns to consciousness when one is experiencing illness or disease (Leder 1990, cited in Sparkes and Smith 2002: 266). It is precisely the experience of living with colitis for five years that prompted one bodybuilder to say: 'I don't think you appreciate your health until you're sick.' Middle-aged men, in turn, tended to organize their bodybuilding health work toward achieving non-specific and conceptually imprecise goals such as 'being healthy,' 'feeling good,' or 'not getting fat.'

The intersection of the aesthetic and functional dimensions of health plays an interesting role in developing gender capital and in the construction of masculine identities in this phase of the life course. Physiological indicators of vulnerability were experienced by men, yet they were able to concurrently realize good health based on a positive aesthetic self-image. When asked how he would describe his health, one male bodybuilder shared how even though he was facing physical ailments – arguably symbolic of poor health – his better-than-average appearance allowed him to construct a healthful masculine identity.

> You know what? I'm 37 and I feel like I hit a bit of a wall. I feel like I'm like running to stand still. I was just at massage and I feel like I'm falling apart. I've had two knee surgeries. My rotator cuff in one shoulder is bugging me and then I got some wrist problems and stuff. As I get older I don't recover as well . . . But my health yeah, I still think if you looked at every 37 year old you know and did an average I'd probably be better than average I think. Yeah, I'm still in pretty good shape.

As men in this study aged, they experienced greater demands for time which limited opportunities for engaging in bodybuilding health work.

These demands, however, also provided ways in which they could construct their gender identities in ways apart from their physical appearance. Achieving status through career progression and providing for their families, for example, gain importance in shaping their sense of heteronormative masculinity. The preservation of being able to live an enjoyable, independent lifestyle into later life was acknowledged, and the types of bodybuilding health work undertaken were adjusted to align with these goals.

THE "INDEPENDENT" IMAGE: OLDER MEN

Experiences at different points during their lives challenged and shaped understandings of health and health work for male bodybuilders. Men develop more pragmatic health goals as they transition into the last phase in the life course. For older men in this study, the bodybuilding health work they performed focused on maintaining a high standard of living after retirement. Retirement, for these men, signified a stage in the life course characterized by less stress and fewer demands on their time than while they were employed. They engaged in bodybuilding health practices in order to maintain physical fitness, mobility, and independence. Part of leading a quality life and developing gender capital was being able to perform daily tasks.

Implicit in the health experiences of these men was a vulnerability of becoming dependent on others and losing a part of their masculine identity. Engaging in bodybuilding activities was a means for older men in this study to maintain their independence which, as Smith and colleagues (2007) found, was a central component to successful aging. One bodybuilder articulated how he became reflexive of his bodybuilding health work goals as he aged.

> Look around in the gym. There aren't many guys my age around. I'm 68. That means I'm 2 years away from 70 and 12 years away from 80. Twelve years away from 80! Think about that. I've re-evaluated why I train, like "What am I doing this for?" As you age you tend to train for just day-to-day routine things like being able to do the things you enjoy. In my case, I like to go hiking and you might want to hike for 10, 15 kilometres. You also want to be able to do the day-to-day routine things that you've got to do like cut your grass. I've moved away from just bodybuilding and lifting heavy weights to work on more endurance. It's balancing these.

Part of being masculine at this phase of the life course was developing a body that enabled men to perform their daily tasks. Another participant, 57, illustrates how being physically fit serves as a source of pride and is essential to enjoying an independent life in the years following retirement.

> You go out shopping or do any of your daily activities and just feel good about yourself. To take out the garbage, you're not struggling; you know you could shovel snow and everything would be right. Usually when a person retires at 65, he's not in any shape to do anything and he can't enjoy his retirement. This is where physical fitness comes in because now you see people, you know, who have worked out and have stayed in shape. They can be 65 or 70 and you see them out working out and they're in great shape, you know, they're jogging. You may live to be 100 but if between 60 and 100 you are in bed and basically vegetating and people have to feed you and care for you, well that's not a good quality of life. If you can maintain that fitness, you can be very independent and have a good enjoyable retirement for 20 or 30 years which is basically what life is about.

In this phase of the life course, the body re-emerges from being an absent present in middle life to occupy a more central role in masculine identity (re)construction. Older bodybuilders participating in this study directed their health work, in part, to preventing health problems. Of particular concern to older bodybuilders was prostate health. According to Gray and his colleagues (1997), 'The vast majority of men with prostate cancer are diagnosed after age 60, and as many as half have no observable symptoms at the time of diagnosis' (cited in Gray et al. 2002: 44). Preventative health practices, as a component of the functional dimension of health, became primary (as opposed to tertiary) foci for older bodybuilders.

> Apparently selenium is helpful for your prostate. As you age, that's the thing [prostate] that can get men in the end. You get a lot of, you know, problems with the prostate so I'm just trying to keep mine healthy. In addition to that I take vitamin E and I take One A Day vitamins. The reason I take the One A Day is I heard on the radio how it has lutein. I think it's something like lutein, which is to stop [prevent] cataracts. I've heard that so I decided well that's got to be a good thing so now I take One A Day.

In marked contrast to the "sexy beast" image pursued by their younger counterparts, older men placed more importance on the functional, rather than the aesthetic, dimension of health. This is not to say that older men were not concerned with their physical appearance, but as one participant, 68, explains, 'When you get to my age, you're not working out to look pretty for the girls anymore, I can tell you that much.'

Conway and Hockey (1998) found that if older people 'did not actually feel ill, they found it hard to identify themselves as elderly' (cited in James and Hockey 2007: 150). One participant, 57, began participating in bodybuilding in his early fifties because he did not like the changes in his physical appearance. Further, he did not want his physical appearance and ability to function to decline to the point where he felt old like some of his same-aged peers.

> I thought "Okay, I've got to get into the gym as I'm starting to get fat (laugh)." Basically I got into bodybuilding just to get back into shape because I've got a lot of buddies that are 210 pounds, [have] pot bellies, sit around, eat whatever, and watch TV. Good friends of mine of the same age and they can't do anything. They'll say, "I'm too old, my body won't do it" and I just don't want that to happen to me.

Male bodybuilders in the later phase of the life course organized their health work through bodybuilding with pragmatic goals in mind. Maintaining independence and self-reliance became a central component in masculine identity construction for men in the years after retirement. Men expressed the desire to live a good quality of life during their later years and engaged in bodybuilding in order to keep physically fit and to prevent health problems.

CONCLUSION

Men engage in bodybuilding activities as part of the health work they perform. While the men in this study ranged in age from 18 to 68 and provided various reasons for working out, the organization of health work through bodybuilding tended to have two recurring dimensions: aesthetics and functionality.

Characteristics of traditional hegemonic masculinity situated in heteronormative lifestyles were shown by men throughout the life course, but how they were performed differed over time. The "sexy beast" image performed by younger men transitioned into a masculine image that revolved around self-reliance later in life. A muscular and lean body has currency with younger men and their peer group: in this context, a powerful body is aesthetically desirable and helps facilitate achievement in sports, which leads them to gain social and gender capital. For middle-aged men, to look good was to avoid getting fat and to look better than their peers. Middle-aged bodybuilders seemed to take their physical ability to perform daily tasks for granted, and the body, when not ill or injured, became an absent present (Leder 1990; Sparkes and Smith 2002). Masculine identity construction in this phase had roots in career success, and being providers for their families. The body re-emerged in the post-retirement years as older men organized their bodybuilding health work with the goal of maintaining their independence. The construction and performance of a masculine identity was represented by having the ability to do daily tasks (e.g. taking out the garbage, shoveling snow) and to maintain a high quality of life.

The ways in which men develop masculine identities differs over time and context, which supports the notion that a plurality of hegemonic masculinities exists. On one hand, men in this study aligned with traditional heteronormative and hegemonic ideals by desiring physical strength, by being breadwinners for their families, and by being self-reliant. On the other hand, men in this study were also expressive in sharing health concerns and vulnerabilities, and displayed nurturing tendencies in discussing the importance of their spouses and children.

Future research could expand upon the health work that men performed at each phase of the life course, and how they managed perceived risk. Similar to other studies, the majority of male bodybuilders participating in this research stated that they used performance-enhancing substances such as dietary supplements (Atkinson 2007) and/or steroids (Monaghan 1999b, 2001, 2002, Chapter 3 this volume) as part of their bodybuilding health work. Not surprisingly, younger males consumed dietary supplements in order to improve their muscular strength or physical appearance. Older bodybuilders, conversely, consumed dietary supplements such as multivitamins and preventative health products in order to maintain mobility and to thwart disease.

5 The Shame–Pride–Shame of the Muscled Self in Bodybuilding

A Life History Study

Andrew C. Sparkes, Joanne Batey and Gareth J. Owen

Emotions are enormously complex, and difficult to define. Shame can be seen as the entwinement of negative self-evaluations and the fear of this being made public. These social dimensions are acknowledged in Scheff's analysis of shame that leads him to view this as 'the large family of emotions that include many cognates and variants, most notable embarrassment, guilt, humiliation, and related feelings such as shyness that originate in *threats to the social bond*' (2003: 255). He suggests that the maintenance of social bonds is fundamental to human motivation, and threats to these bonds, however slight (for example, arising out of failure, criticism, sarcasm, inadequacy, misunderstanding or rejection), give rise to feelings of shame. Given the central position of shame in social interaction, Scheff names it the "master emotion" of everyday life. It is a painful experience of the self by the self, and one which, momentarily at least, "affects" our self-esteem. By exposing ourselves to ourselves, it is the affect most central to the development of our identities. It is like a 'looking-glass' (Cooley 1922) in which we imagine how we are seen by other people and, therein, how we might be judged.

Munt acknowledges that shame is a very sticky emotion. When it brushes a person it tends to 'leave a residue to which other emotions are easily attached, namely envy, hate, contempt, apathy, painful self-absorption, humiliation, rage, mortification and disgust, the inventory of related subsequent feelings is substantial. Shame becomes embodied, and the body begins to speak for itself, in specific ways' (Munt 2007: 2). Thus, emotions are self-feelings as an embodied form of consciousness, they are always felt physically and bodily sensation is an eradicable aspect of emotion. Linked to this, Probyn notes that shame can comment on the body, awakening the recognition that several bodies may inhabit an individual. She believes 'shame refigures the body and its conceptual possibilities' (2000: 24). Clearly, shame and pride are intense emotions and can be experienced in a variety of contexts. This intensity is likely to be heightened when the body is on view to others in the pursuit of specific performance outcomes. Accordingly, Probyn notes the salience of shame and pride for sporting bodies that compete, win, and fail, so that they can be either covered in shame or beam with pride.

> In general terms, sport reveals commonplace connections between pride and shame . . . it is clear that shame as a very bodily affect has the potential to focus attention on the body as a vehicle of connection. As a frequently shamed entity, the sporting body fundamentally connects with class and race matter in ways that may embarrass white middle-class sensibilities. Sporting bodies also compete, and remind us of the visceral dynamics of pride, shame and bodily affect in ways that have been notably missing within much feminist and cultural analysis.
>
> (Probyn 2000: 13–14)

Against this backdrop, it is interesting to note the relative neglect of the emotions in sports-related research. Recent work seeking to rectify this situation includes that of Davidson (2006) who focuses on the Gay Games to explore the notion of 'queer shame for gay pride,' and Owen (2006) who utilizes reflexive ethnography to show how his body and the emotions of pride and shame are inseparable from understanding gender and sexual identities in competitive rowing. Both these scholars identify shame and pride as the emotions of competition.

In what follows, we seek to develop this work on shame and pride by exploring the dynamic cycles of these emotions in the life history of a male, black, heterosexual, elite bodybuilder called Jessenka (a pseudonym) (for details of methodology see Sparkes et al., 2005). His story illuminates the embodied dynamics of pride and shame in certain sets of circumstance that are framed by issues of gender, social class, and race.

THE SHAMEFUL BODY: YOUNG, SMALL AND BLACK

Jessenka was raised in a working-class, black family in a large city in England. He was a very small, shy child, who was no good at sports, and weighed less than seven-and-a-half stone at secondary school. In contrast, his two brothers were good at sport and "very rough customers" with a stature and attitude more appreciated by their father.

> I do believe to this day that my Dad always looked at me as sort of a wimpy person. He'd always been quite rough, a man's man. He boxed for [name of club] . . . My other brothers get on better with him because I believe they were shown to be rough or harder than

I was. From very young [brother] was just a brilliant sportsman . . . so it left the little one who wasn't particularly bright and couldn't do any sport . . . I felt the odd one out from quite early on . . . A couple of incidents, we were playing cricket one day and my Dad decided . . . he was going to teach me to play cricket properly. He bowled this particularly fastball damn hard and nearly took my fucking head off, bashed me in the face and I ran off. And then he came in to give me a hard time, "Don't cry you big sissy, you will get back out here and play cricket."

With regard to boys, sport, masculinity, and schooling, Bramham (2003) designates physical education (PE) as *the* site for the construction and display of hegemonic masculinity in which boys must be competitive, tough, physically aggressive, brave, and so on. He emphasizes that this involves embodied power, and competence, that is exercised over others in ways that generate status, pride, and identity at the expense of others. Wellard (2006) supports this view, pointing out that boys who cannot display such characteristics through their bodies via sport learn to define themselves as weak, inferior, and "unable." Similarly, Drummond (2003), in his study of school-based adolescent males, illustrates how muscularity is a highly prized feature among this age group. Those boys who have muscular and mesomorphic bodies are often held in high esteem, are led to feel good about themselves, often developing a healthy body image and positive self-esteem. The same cannot be said for boys who are small and frail. Such boys often develop a poor body image and low self-esteem. During their period of schooling, boys quickly learn in relation to size and shape what is a "successful" and "unsuccessful" body and then define their own bodies in relation to these categories in ways that have consequences for masculine identity construction. Drummond notes, those with unsuccessful bodies perceive their identity as 'flawed within a social and cultural context that upholds and vindicates specific forms of physicality as a masculinized virtue' (2003: 138).

From an early age, sporting prowess, physical size, muscularity, and strength emerged as defining features of a "successful" body and a respected masculinity for Jessenka. These features were prominent at his school where racial tensions ran high. Here, because he was black *and* small Jessenka was bullied: 'There was a lot of racism there . . . I got fairly beat up as you can imagine, being small and the rest of it.' However, due to their physical size and prowess, he was "protected" by his two elder brothers. There was a period where his elder brother "ruled the roost" and the bullying subsided. But, once his brothers left school the bullying erupted again: 'They left. That year was fucking open season. It was like a shooting season it really was. They weren't there, everybody who had been upset by my brother, or had grief with him, came after me. I had a full year to swallow it all.'

Jessenka remembers other racist-fueled incidents during his adolescent years. He recollects being very scared and frightened because of his small stature. Against this, he recalls the pride and admiration he had for the qualities displayed by his brother in the face of racist threat, 'He's just a hard bloke. Sometimes I envy him because he is as rough as he is. Sometimes I wish I had that sort of air about me that people sort of knew I was hard.' This racist atmosphere eventually led to Jessenka leaving the neighborhood when he was 16 years old. The backdrop was a simmering feud with a group of older white men that was escalating with regard to the violence used: 'I saw this [white] man one particular day on the road walking . . . I was just in shock because he went "You're next nigger" and he was a big grown man . . . I was just scared. I haven't been that scared before . . . The truth is that I was quite happy to get away. I was frightened to fucking death.'

Shaped by the powerful psychological impact of racism, Jessenka's fearful experiences were truly embodied via his smallness in relation to his peers, his elder brothers, and his father. Jessenka was simultaneously impressed, protected, and frightened by black, male, hard, muscular bodies and a specific form of masculine subjectivity and performance that enabled self-survival plus an element of control in a threatening and hostile environment. Equally, he was terrorized and frightened by white, hard, male, racist bodies that posed a potential and actual threat to him on a regular basis. Issues of "hardness" and "softness" are significant because as Sabo points out 'Some men strive to be hard as a way of building self-esteem, garnering the respect of others . . . The hard man sends a message that he is not a pushover, not someone to "fuck with"' (1994: 166).

Within the matrix of emotions experienced by Jessenka during his adolescent years, the feeling of shame in relation to his own body was paramount. This shame was to act as a powerful motivator for him to adopt a bodybuilding lifestyle when the opportunity presented itself. In this regard he is not alone. Similar motivations, rooted in dominant social constructions of gender, are identified in a study by Wesley. Here, young men began bodybuilding because 'as children they were sickly, teased by peers, or felt otherwise insecure and powerless; what they saw or imagined on the muscled male body conjured feelings of being powerful' (2001: 170). Of course, as Wesley points out, this is not to suggest that all male bodybuilders were sickly as children, nor is it to say that all weak boys become bodybuilders. However, within her study, 'the more powerless a boy or adolescent felt, the more appealing the muscular body became as he matured' (ibid.: 170).

More recently, Wolke and Sapouna explored the childhood bullying experience and its relationship to muscle dysmorphia and other mental health problems in bodybuilders. Interestingly, 21 percent of their sample of 100 bodybuilders reported that they had been regular victims of bullying during childhood. Their analysis revealed that victimization was negatively related to self-esteem, 'indicating that bodybuilders who had experienced bullying victimization were more likely to report lower levels of self-esteem' (2008: 598). Their findings suggest that early experiences of victimization increases high muscle dysmorphia tendencies and in conjunction has a particularly adverse impact on global psychopathology. They add that 'autobiographical accounts of successful bodybuilders and spontaneous reports of bodybuilders in this study suggest that being a victim of bulling as a schoolboy and feeling weak and pushed around can lead to taking up bodybuilding' (ibid.: 602).

THE PROUD BODY: BUILDING THE MUSCLED SELF

After leaving school, Jessenka had a chance meeting with a bodybuilder, and then visited the gym where this man trained with his brother. When asked why he decided to do this, Jessenka commented, 'I needed to be stronger for what I was doing, being as small as I was, and just the way this guy was walking and the way he approached me. The way he stood and the way he walked, he looked good.' On entering the gym, Jessenka began the journey that took him from the outside to the inside of hardcore bodybuilding.

After five months of regular training, Jessenka recalls getting a "real taste" for bodybuilding when, at the end of a session, the two brothers, both weighing about 17 stone, took off their tops and began flexing their muscles and checking out their poses in the mirror. They then looked across at Jessenka:

> And they made me take my top off and flex, and I'd never done flexing up like that before. So I had a little flex. I saw them look at each other, and one of them said, 'You got a good little shape there'. I said 'really?' That made me smile and want to flex some more. I got a little bite of it then.

This episode signaled the beginning of a sense of pride in an emerging muscular body that was to stand in direct opposition to the shameful body that he had entered the gym with previously.

Gradually, Jessenka adopted the bodybuilding lifestyle described by Monaghan (2001). For a period of years, he disciplined his body in the pursuit of muscle: 'I trained, I ate, I trained, I ate and trained and trained, and watched videos and ate.' Jessenka attributes his rapid progress and willingness to endure the bodybuilding lifestyle in the quest for muscle to his feelings of insecurity in his youth:

> I knew if I went back home I've gotta be able to take a hit. I could give out a hit but I still wasn't strong enough, nobody was going to

fall down . . . I was the little one and couldn't really participate.
I couldn't do my piece and so because I couldn't do my piece for
my brothers . . . I had a lot of anger then, and all that went into my
training over the years.

Jessenka's desire and willingness to make sacrifices in order to gain
muscular mass might be interpreted by Klein in the following manner,
'The more insignificant he feels on the inside, the more significant the
bodybuilder strives to appear on the outside. In bodybuilding this trans-
lates into an obsession with appearing large' (1995: 114). Thus, the
hyper-muscular body becomes a mask or wall between low self-esteem
and a potentially threatening world. That is, a muscular wall between
pride and shame. For Jessenka, this process was clearly working. All his
training and sacrifice eventually led to him becoming a British Champion.
On the morning before he won the title he recalls his body with an
unapologetic sense of intense pride:

> I was about to get showered, I looked in the mirror and I have never
> looked so good in all my life. I had a big smile just come across my
> face, and I flexed my abdominals and my obliques in the mirror and
> they all stood out like three or four fingers. All of my abdominals are
> like chocolate biscuits and I just smiled at me in the mirror . . . I felt
> confident, I looked fucking tremendous. That sounds really arrogant
> doesn't it? But I did. I felt tremendous, I felt full, I'd got my carbing
> right, literally spot on the bone. I was ripped to the bone and hard
> and full . . . I felt like I'd won it before going on stage.

Winning a British title was a peak moment in Jessenka's life and he
remembers the emotions he felt on stage:

> I felt my eyes almost burst out of my head and my mouth dropped
> open. All these really bright lights are in my face. And it's, 'got the
> fucker it's mine.' Then they say it 'And first place Mister Jessenka . . .
> the new.' I love that word 'and the NEW (weight category) British
> Champion.' That was just incredible and then they play the music
> again and the lights flash on and off. It's just too much, and they
> hand you the trophy, and put a medal around your neck. I picked
> this trophy up.

At this moment, Jessenka bathed in the admiring glances and raptur-
ous applause of others. He rightly took pride in his achievement and
felt extremely proud of his hard, cut, ripped and hyper-muscular body.
At this moment he epitomized the triumphant *mirroring* body in
action. This kind of body, according to Frank (1991), seeks to recreate
the body in the image of other bodies that are more muscular than itself.

The primary sense is visual. The body sees a hyper-muscular image, idealizes it, and then seeks to become the image of that image by many hours of intense training each day over a number of years. Importantly, the mirroring body is judged by its appearance and feelings of pride and shame are associated with these judgments.

Winning a championship confirmed an overwhelming identification with the bodybuilding role at this period in his life. As he put it, 'Life was bodybuilding. Jessenka *was* bodybuilding. If you looked it up in the dictionary you'd see me and my name right in front of it . . . It was my whole identity because it has to be your life. It was my whole life. I can't say any more on it than that. It was *everything*.' At this stage of his career, Jessenka felt 'fairly invincible' and began making plans to win the forthcoming World Championships in his weight category because, in his words, he was now an invulnerable 'monster.' Thus, it could be argued that, quite literally, Jessenka's muscles had assisted him develop a positive and proud sense of self in relation to the fragile and shameful self he had prior to his involvement in bodybuilding. In Giddens' (1991) terms, the development of muscle for Jessenka might be seen as a defensive carapace or protective cocoon that provided emotional support and protected him against previous feelings of inadequacy and the ontological insecurities that permeated his childhood as described earlier.

Becoming a British Champion also heralded the start of a new lifestyle for Jessenka, as his physical capital was exchanged for economic and social capital. Along with a new car came free entry into nightclubs, guest appearances at bodybuilding competitions, and feature articles in magazines. He was now sponsored by a leading supplements company who provided all his dietary requirements and was making good money as a personal trainer who was in big demand due to his newfound fame and celebrity status.

All this came to an end two years after winning the British Championship when Jessenka was involved in a car accident causing an injury that terminated his bodybuilding career. According to Giddens (1991), fateful moments have major implications not just for the circumstances of an individual's future, but also for self-identity. Such moments, he argues, threatens the protective cocoon which defends the individual's ontological security because the "business as usual" attitude that is so important to that cocoon is broken through. The sense of invulnerability provided by the cocoon is threatened and the bodily and psychological integrity of the individual is challenged.

Reflecting on the impact of this injury on his life, Jessenka states, 'It was like one minute being in Buckingham Palace and the next minute being a pauper. It just rocked my world completely . . . In the bat of an eyelid that day you [the driver] decided you was late getting to where you was going and you fucked up my life.' Unable to continue with bodybuilding, Jessenka entered a period of depression that involved drug and alcohol abuse, 'I just didn't care. My World Championship dream had gone. Life didn't matter any more . . . I was at the lowest that I'd ever been.' Indeed, at the time of interview, four years after this event, Jessenka acknowledged that he had yet to find a replacement for the sense of self he lost as a bodybuilder, 'Replaced it? I haven't if I be honest . . . Every so often I try to believe, or I try to tell myself to believe that I've got over it and I'm really kidding myself. I don't know how long it's going to take and I thought I would have got over it by now.' A key issue for Jessenka revolved around the erosion of pride he felt about his body as it gradually lost its muscle mass, propelling him back toward a shameful body-self relationship.

THE SHAMED BODY (AGAIN): LOSING THE MUSCLED SELF

According to Nathanson, 'There is an infinitude of possible patterns that can be made into reasons for pride or shame. If the possession of an attribute can make us proud, the sudden "loss" of that possession will cause shame, no matter what the nature of the attribute' (1992: 165). Jessenka's car accident and resulting injury meant that he had to endure chronic pain and experience his body as something alien and foreign to the proud muscled self. In the first instance, he could no longer control the body and it became an oppositional force preventing him from hardcore bodybuilding. Unable to train intensively with heavy weights, even though he could continue to operate as a personal trainer (with the assistance of large doses of pain killers), Jessenka's changing body came under his own critical gaze and the gaze of others in a process of mirroring that made direct comparisons between his "Championship" body and his current body.

> I was really depressed one morning. I got up, looked in the mirror and my legs were like sticks. Two people had recently told me 'Oh Jessenka haven't your legs disappeared' and that was like such a blow to me because I was really well known for having great legs. I was so ashamed.

For Giddens (1991), feelings of shame have a direct bearing on self-identity, and the experience of shame often focuses on the body as the "visible" aspect of self. Over time, as the loss of muscle mass and definition has become more evident, Jessenka appears to have grown increasingly ashamed of his body's aesthetic appeal. This may be because the body he is on the verge of becoming is a reminder of a past body-self that was deemed by him and significant others as inadequate and inferior. Jessenka is fearful of returning to this body that was itself fearful. Indeed, his sporadic attempts to train again with heavy weights are fueled by this fear of losing muscle and the desired self that goes with this. As he stated, 'I just feel like I'm fucking fading away, just fading away.'

Given that muscularity is associated with masculinity, any loss of muscle would appear to have ramifications for the masculine self. Thus, Jessenka's hyper-muscular and masculine sense of self, a self that he has invested in heavily to construct is, quite literally, disappearing in front of his eyes. Having transformed himself over a number of years from a frail, small body into a "short monster," his body is now metamorphosing back to whence it came. In this process, Jessenka's body is once again becoming an embarrassment to him, a reminder of his inadequacies, and a deep source of shame. As muscles waste, Jessenka avoids looking into mirrors which once reflected back his proud muscled self and hides in shame behind cars when he sees old bodybuilding friends coming his way down the street. At times, however, he cannot hide his body from view nor can he protect himself from the reactions of others. On visiting a friend he recalls the following incident.

> His wife proceeded to tell me how skinny I looked. That was very difficult for me, but I have to tell myself that I was always a very small person. It's like someone who was this thin becoming very, very, fat and then becoming very thin again. It's difficult looking at this body in the mirror. It's very difficult. You get up and look in the mirror and you think 'Yuck!' . . . And people turn up in the funniest of places and catch you by surprise. People have turned up in supermarkets and stared at me. Sometimes they don't want to say it but they'll do this [makes shocked face looking someone up and down] almost in shock. I see the look on their face and I feel a sadness and it's almost as if to say 'please don't ask,' and I just feel as though I need to be somewhere else.

Other key events heightened Jessenka's dissatisfaction with his body and diminishing masculine sense of self. One such occasion was when he made a trip abroad to visit a close bodybuilding friend and perform a guest pose down in his gym. The trip was a disaster and he returned home feeling humiliated and undeserving of his British Championship title.

> He was expecting me coming to [country], big bodybuilder and everything, and I wasn't this short monster that he'd expected . . . He'd shown the [old] photos and videos of me to them . . . I'd let everybody down. They were expecting an elephant and I brought them a mouse. That was very hard to take because I could see the

disappointment in him . . . I didn't look nothing like my former self and I even felt bad because there's mirrors all over the damn place, and I wore my England shirt because it is *my* England shirt, and it's the shirt I'm most proud of. But, it was very difficult wearing it because I wasn't in the condition to deserve to wear an England shirt . . . But I didn't know which was the worst of two evils. Do I not wear it at all? I came to him with nothing and the least I can do is wear my fucking England shirt, but I didn't feel right wearing it.

Besides not feeling right about wearing his England shirt, Jessenka does not "feel right" in the body he currently inhabits. Just like he let his friend down with his smaller body, so Jessenka feels his body has let him down. Like many other male athletes who have experienced a serious injury there is a sense of bodily betrayal and heightened feelings of alienation.

As you get up in the morning and you wash your face and you wash your body, you feel your body and it doesn't feel like it's my body. You know someone borrowed mine and they gave me this, and I don't want this, I want mine back. It's like you've driven round in a Rolls Royce for twenty years and then someone takes it away and gives you a Mini. This isn't fair, this isn't right, this isn't mine. Where's mine?

The sense of loss and shame associated with losing muscle as described above are intimately connected to racial dimensions within Jessenka's life story. This issue will now be explored.

LOSING MUSCLE AND BECOMING BLACK AGAIN

Issues of race, while vitally important in contemporary life and politics, are not separate from other factors (class, gender, sexuality, disability), nor is it always the most important characteristic in human experience and action. Sewell notes, 'Race may be more or less important to the same person at different times in different contexts' (1997: xiii). For Jessenka, as for many other black athletes, success in sport takes on a specifically racial and ethnic dimensions (Carrington 2000; Hylton 2009). Being a black British champion was something he was immensely proud of and he gained a lot of attention once in this position: 'I'm here and I'm British champion, and I'm from England. I've got an English accent, and just to speak in an English accent to foreign people with a black face and my look, it was just different so I caused a lot of attention.' Despite being aware of the racism that pervades British society, Jessenka felt his success in bodybuilding could help break down racial barriers and allow black people to gain acceptance. Indeed, he acknowledged how issues of race and ethnicity often "disappeared" or became blurred when he was a British champion.

> Being black and in Britain is very difficult. Someone said the other day, 'because a dog is born in a stable that doesn't make it a horse' and that really opened my eyes to what I already knew was true. If you look at any black people in Britain in sport they're known and respected but only because they represent their country. We are then classed as British and they are proud of us, we are British. Being black doesn't occur then, but in the other 99 percent of your life you are a black person and you're in Britain, you shouldn't be here. So to become British champion, to be black, British and proud, and representing my country gave me belonging. Jamaicans still class you as British, British class you as West Indian or Afro-Caribbean as they like to call it these days, but nobody wants to accept you. It's the same as mixed race children, it's like being in the middle and nobody wants to accept you on that side or on the other . . . so to be British champion, the belonging, the pride, the pride of competing for my country, representing your country all over the world was great.

For Jessenka, being a British champion, resolved a number of contradictions and tensions he felt regarding his ethnic identity by foregrounding his national identity through success in bodybuilding. By doing so, he gained a sense of belonging and pride that had been denied to him previously. However, as Carrington (2000) and Hylton (2009) note, such acceptance for the black athlete is normally conditional on the athlete renouncing claims to their own cultural history and dissolving themselves within the notion of nationhood and "Britishness." Jessenka appears to have been willing to adopt such a position. As a consequence, he remains resentful of the woman who caused his injury because he believes this act robbed him of his newly gained national identity, his "Britishness," accentuating his race and ethnicity once again. In short, Jessenka feels he is no longer regarded as British but just another young black man on the streets having to deal with the racist stereotypes imposed on him.

> It goes all the way back to what I said at the beginning about being black and being British and belonging. She's taken away my belonging and made life difficult for me on so many other fronts to be accepted. If Linford Christie walked into a sports shop everybody knows who he is. Everybody is happy to see him in their shop and he's British and he's black, yes? Now you walk into a shop and the assistant comes and looks at something beside you to see if you're gonna nick something. You see what I'm saying? There's that anger.

Yes, there's the anger of me being in constant pain but there's also the anger of her taking away my British passport, she put me back floating in the river of not belonging to either side.

The comments made by Jessenka are testimony to the manner in which the social meaning of muscle and masculinity are infused by issues relating to race, ethnicity, social class, and national identity. Here, it is interesting to note how his experiences parallel those of other black athletes (Hylton 2009) who, as long as they are successful and conform to the role of the wholesome, non-threatening, hard-bodied hero, they are deified and lauded as "one of Us." Their athletic identity is foregrounded and the importance of their racial identity slips into the background. However, should the black athlete not be successful, or not conform to their expected role, then they are quickly redefined as the racial Other. As Mercer commented with regard to the situation in the United Kingdom, 'On the front page headlines black males become highly visible as a threat to white society . . . But turn to the back pages, the sports pages, and the black man's body is heroized and lionized . . . they're not Other, they're OK because they're our boys' (1994: 179). Indeed, examining the processes of racialization and mediated racial identities, whitecentrism, and mimetic representation, Hylton (2009) notes that even when successful in sport and beyond in business, black and white athletes are constructed very differently in the media in ways that undermine the achievements of the former and reinforce the image of the negative Other.

Against such a backdrop, as a national champion bodybuilder Jessenka's racial identity was effectively displaced and neutered. He was not located as the shameful and feared Other. In contrast, following his injury, the loss of his athletic identity, and the loss of a champion hypermuscular body, Jessenka experiences the "twist of race" that brings into sharp relief his racial identity reminding him that in the eyes of many he is the Other once again.

REFLECTIONS

The moments presented from Jessenka's life illuminate the dynamics of pride and shame associated with differing forms of embodiment over time and in specific circumstances. These moments, as they are woven into the tapestry of his life, also reveal the stickiness and power of shame as an emotion and how it begins to speak for itself in different ways. This is not to suggest that all men who take up bodybuilding are motivated in the same way as Jessenka, or that they experience the interaction of pride and shame in the same ways. As Monaghan (2001) rightly points out, bodybuilding as an activity is characterized by heterogeneity and there are many reasons why men choose to engage in it. Bearing this in mind, we proceed with some caution in providing the following reflections on Jessenka's life history.

It would seem that for Jessenka, as shame avoidance became increasingly linked to bodybuilding, the pride experienced in the "successful" muscular body through the looking-glass self became reinforcing. But body projects are always vulnerable to interruption (e.g. through injury) and as "hard" muscles waste and become "soft" so pride returns to shame. In this regard, perhaps there is an "inevitable" cycle of shame–pride–shame in bodybuilding if self-esteem is too closely invested in body image and muscularity.

Although speculative, the notion of an inevitable cycle of shame–pride–shame in bodybuilding under certain circumstances challenges the promise, reflected in numerous advertisements in bodybuilding magazines, of a permanent, positive, self-transformation that the muscled body can bring. Analyzing such advertisements, White and Gillett (1994) suggest that in constructing muscular bodies, men seek to pursue and construct what they perceive to be their true, real selves. That is – the man's true self, a masculine self, possessing power and self-confidence – is one that is encased in a hard, defined muscular physique. What is required, the advertisements suggest, is the transformation or metamorphosis through the consumption of bodybuilding commodities and involvement in disciplinary regimes (diet and bodywork), from the non-muscular, passive, weak, and shameful self via bodybuilding into a muscular, hyper-masculine, body that represents the new, better, powerful, and proud self.

Clearly, as his comments indicate, for a while this promise came true for Jessenka and he felt 'fairly invincible.' But, with injury, the body broke this promise and left him feeling betrayed and back where he started with regard to his experiences of shame. The speed and intensity of this demise might suggest that despite building up a muscular body, Jessenka's core sense of self did not change. That is, the hard muscular exterior he developed encased a fragile and vulnerable self that remained continuous with his former self. From this perspective, while Jessenka believed that by building muscle he could transcend his former self, this was evidently not true because this self remained, lying dormant within his hyper-muscular frame. As the muscles disappeared so did the *illusion* of the powerful, transformed, new, and proud self, as the fragile, and in many ways the feared and shameful self, announced itself once again.

This illusion with regard to ideals of masculinity raises a number of identity dilemmas that foreground the issue of gender. However, as Jessenka's comments reveal, his trajectory into the world of hyper-muscularity is also shaped by his social class position. As Shilling (1993), points out, the body bears the indisputable imprint of an individual's social class. Thus, working-class individuals, via their habitus, tend to develop an instrumental relationship to their body that becomes a means to an end. Accordingly, it might be argued that, given his lack of ability in conventional sports, Jessenka's "choice" of bodybuilding as a means to the end of bolstering his insecure and shameful sense of self is classed as well as gendered.

Jessenka's social class position is also connected to issues surrounding his race and ethnicity in terms of the ways in which he comes to understand the multiple meanings of muscle and physical size in relation to his own body and the bodies of others within a racist society that has historically objectified, sensualized, and sexualized the black body. Such bodies have also encountered a limited structure of opportunity in terms of access to education, employment, and institutional power. Against this backdrop, Majors (1990) suggests, the dominant goals of hegemonic masculinity have been sold to black males, but access to the legitimate means to achieve these goals has largely been denied. As a consequence, he argues, many black males seek to prove their manliness to themselves and others via sporting activities. Likewise, Messner (1992) notes the role of sport in allowing subaltern groups to realize a masculine identity and to resist (at least symbolically) racist, colonial, and class domination. In this sense, Jessenka's choice of bodybuilding and his use of this sport to develop one of the defining features of masculinity – muscularity – are understandable. His commitment to bodybuilding can also be seen as an attempt to recuperate some degree of power or active influence over the objective conditions of powerlessness created by institutionalized and individual racism. Thus, becoming and being a successful bodybuilder and developing an empowered sense of self, even if this is short-lived and precarious, can be interpreted as an act of resistance by Jessenka.

If, however, as Barbalet argues, 'emotions link structure and agency' (2002: 3), how might the "affects" of shame and pride link the structures of race, gender, and social class to the agency of Jessenka's body? Hochschild (1983) observes that people in positions of power have 'status shields' which protect against ontological insecurity, and Freund (1990) argues that 'emotional modes of well-being' are influenced by the experience of empowerment and disempowerment in both structural and personal relationships. Working on the idea of the emotionally expressive body Freund found that, '"External" social structural factors such as one's position in different systems of hierarchy or various forms of social control can influence the conditions of our existence, how we respond and apprehend these conditions of existence and our sense of embodied self' (1990: 461).

Applying these ideas to Jessenka's bodybuilding life history, the resources Jessenka had at his disposal to experience 'emotional modes of well-being' were strongly influenced by his social status. As his comments suggest, the feelings of empowerment and disempowerment triggered by social status correspond emotionally to pride and shame. The embodied experience of being small, black, and working class created feelings of shame and disempowerment while bodybuilding proved to be a resource which eventually became a 'status shield' which Jessenka could use to defend against racism and to experience pride in his Britishness. But once the muscular status shield was down, Jessenka was no longer protected from the shame of powerlessness, and was returned to the status of diminutive "racial Other," while facing the difficult task of finding an alternative identity narrative from the structurally limited sociocultural resources at his disposal.

Clearly, the ways in which the dynamics of pride and shame interact with issues of gender, social class, ethnicity, and race to shape the story told, and lived, by Jessenka and other men like him, are complex and warrant further consideration. We hope his story as we have represented it will act as a resource and encourage further exploration of the shame/pride axis in the embodiment of masculine identities.

6 Building Otherwise
Bodybuilding as Immersive Practice

Leslie Heywood

Once, a long time ago, I was in love: iron, muscles, veins, the incredible rush of the pump, the exhilaration of the 350 squat, the 225 bench. This, I thought, was the great equalizer, some precious, off-the-beaten track place where gender assumptions and restrictions fell away at the first lift and every vestige of historical constructions of female weakness floated away like San Francisco fog. Here, in the gym, I fit in. Here, in the gym, I had a place. A validation of my deepest longings, convictions, an unwavering sense of my own gold.

'Bodybuilders call it "the disease,"' Sam Fussell says, writing in the early 1990s about that cultural moment and the decade that had preceded it. 'Symptoms include a complete commitment to all matters pertaining to iron ... You find "the diseased" in bookstores hovering by the rack containing the muscle magazines (invariably adjacent to the pornography). You overhear them in vitamin stores, discussing the merits of branch-chain amino acids and protein powders. You scan the on the subway, their hypertrophied bodies a silent, raging, scream of dissent' (Fussell 1991: 19). Bodybuilders, the defiant exception, had become, briefly, a normative rule: bodybuilders as an iconic American cultural ideal. 'Bodybuilders in commercials, in sitcoms, even in game shows,' Fussell writes. 'Every beer advertisement seemed to have one of the diseased pumping weights in the background ... It had gone as far as the White House, where President Reagan was photographed pumping out a few bicep reps on his chrome dumbbells just before a briefing ... Clearly, this whole muscle thing was no longer just *my* problem' (ibid.: 146).

Once, right about this time, I was one of 'the diseased,' though I never competed, not in bodybuilding. I never did steroids. But I *did* mainline on creatine, energy drinks, and protein powder in 10 lb containers. My everyday wardrobe included lifting straps, a thick leather weight belt stained with 20 years worth of sweat, and funky, thick-striped tights made by a now-defunct company called *Hotskins* featuring in-your-face shades of red, purple, and black. The way people reacted to my body made it clear that they understood it was a 'silent, raging, scream of dissent': down the hallways near the English Department I'd stride in my muscle shirts, lats flared, biceps on display, my wolf hybrid in tow, and the hallway would clear, office doors discretely shut. But I didn't just work on my body. I wrote about it, continually, in books and articles that spanned the first ten years of my career. When I wasn't spending six hours doing 100-repetition "Arnold Squats," I was at my computer writing about doing them. I'd go from one activity, to the other, then back again. There was nothing else. I was in love. And then. . .

Bill Lowenburg, an art photographer who did a series of portraits of bodybuilders in the early 1990s and whose work I often wrote about, took me to a local bodybuilding show in 1997.[1] He was a little concerned that I was so focused on *representations* of bodybuilding (but I had a Ph.D. in critical theory, isn't representation reality? – see introduction to next section), that my only experience with the iron world was my own obsessive gym training. He knew I needed to see the thing itself, to confront bodybuilding's semiotic indicators in the flesh. So we met at a show in a tiny rust-belt Pennsylvania town with weathered buildings, shut-up shops, and crumbling highways – so unlike when, in the privacy of my own home, I lingered over images of bodybuilders in *Flex* and *Muscle and Fitness* and *Women's Physique World,* so unlike the safe space of my gym where everyone had known and supported me for years. Here, on a cold, gray evening, a vanished world creaking through the rusted signs lining the boarded-up windows of Main Street, the distance between what bodybuilding signifies, the fantasy structures it sustains, and what it actually *is,* the actual place that it has in the world and the audiences it serves, was simply too great for me to deny. The women in black stilettos or clear platforms backstage in that high school gym, their red press-on nails, hair in big curlers, clutching a dumbbell to pump themselves up, the audience with its Carhartt jackets and gold chains, the air outside so cold you could barely breathe, the old-model Chevys in the parking lot with their sagging mufflers and mismatched doors, a high-school auditorium never refurbished, dirty carpet, seats torn, splinters of wood shearing off of a well-worn stage – this was the staging area for all my bodybuilding dreams. Yet even given the starkness of this scene, my impressions of impoverishment took years to sink in. Instead, I tried to give these impressions a philosophical justification: bodybuilding as a defiant performance in the face of the abyss, a brave acceptance of non-meaning, a disavowal in which you knew all the limitations and myths, but did it anyway. In *Bodymakers,* for instance, I describe Lowenburg's portraits of bodybuilders as revealing 'how much our poses – detached from them though we may be – mean to those who strike them, a sense of how those poses, though ontologically meaningless, are nonetheless all we have and create complicated patterns that join us' (Heywood 1998: 119). As if the meanings we impose create a world all their own. Like the bodybuilders, like my postmodern academic compatriots, I was a big believer in the power of self-creation. Postmodern narratives, and perhaps maybe especially the American postmodern, with its roots in the mythology of American exceptionalism (the idea that America is special, exceptional, because of its history as a nation built upon the strength and individuality of freedom fighters and frontiersmen), could make anything seem grand. But on that dark Pennsylvania night, bad lighting casting shadows on a rickety stage, the doubts began to creep in.

In *Iron Maidens: The Celebration of the Most Awesome Female Muscle in the World*, Kristin Kay describes experiencing a similar sensation in the aftermath of her foray into women's bodybuilding subculture, in her case as the playwright/director for the New York City-based show called *The Celebration of the Most Awesome Female Muscle in the World* which took place in 1993. Following the frenzied, much-hyped build-up to the show, and then the disappointment of the show itself and its post-celebration party, she writes, 'I took my place among the sea of bobbing heads and shuffled toward the underground corridor to meet my train home feeling unsettled by the notion that the stories we tell ourselves and others are often only partly true' (2005: 226). The female bodybuilders, Kaye found, signified a mythological power that was only mythic. Much like the ideology of American exceptionalism that was beginning to fray around the edges at this time (see Pease 2009) – the idea that America was an unconquerable superpower whose hegemony knew no boundaries and whose reign was immeasurable, extending indefinitely across time (Hardt and Negri 2000), everything Kaye told herself about her position as playwright/director, as well as everything Laurie Fierstein – the bodybuilder who was the show's conceptualizer and organizer – told herself about her position as creative visionary body artist, and everything the female bodybuilders told themselves about what their lives and bodies and activities meant, were revealing themselves as palpably shabby, hollow.

Outside of bodybuilding's insular subculture, bodybuilders, perhaps particularly female bodybuilders, can seem like the bewildered and beguiled practitioners of a much broader philosophic world-view and economic practice. In this light they might seem to function much like the remainder, what Derrida called *le reste*, of American exceptionalism, that thing that the system just can't accommodate or swallow, the thing that reveals the workings of the system itself.[2] Their distorted jaws, their deepened voices, their fake nails, breasts, tans and frizzy hair, and, worst of all, their eyes like children who have been hurt and disappointed one too many times, all reminders of the relentlessness of this fantasy machine, so powerful it persuades you to give up absolutely everything, your very flesh, to its flim-flam stories and car-barker whims. Working with the female bodybuilders, Kaye writes, 'you saw mythic images of strength . . . Literally larger than life, they seemed untouchable, powerful in being exceptions to the rule. Yet look again, and you saw the hint of nervous girlishness that lingered in their ever-ready smiles and eyes that quickly scanned each other's bodies; you could have mistaken the scene for a high school bathroom on prom night' (Kaye 2005: 134). Here Kaye marks the distance between mythic image and lived actuality that I began to experience backstage at that Pennsylvania high school, the dawning realization that the broad liberatory claims I'd been making for the practice of female bodybuilding were as much imagined as real (of course, my training in postmodern theory contributed to my thinking that the two are or can be one and the same).[3] Kaye's hands-on experience was one I never had before that night. When she observes that 'despite the pride they took in their personal transformation, you couldn't help but feel a kind of loneliness when they described their muscles as shields or armor; when they admitted to childhood sexual abuse or noted that most other competitors they knew had been abused and that their muscles had been built as a kind of protection and isolation; when they recounted that the world thought of them as freaks and competitions as freak shows' (ibid.: 137), she has an experience of the distance between the imaginary and the real that I had been trained to theoretically dismiss. But I could only do so in theory – I had yet to observe that while the bodybuilding memoirs such as Samuel Fussell's *Muscle* and Paul Solotaroff's much more recent *The Body Shop* (2010) show males becoming bodybuilders partially to overcome a sense of physical inadequacy and masculinity and "get laid," female bodybuilders often take up weight training as a protection against "getting laid" – in the sense of being seen as insubstantial "chicks" whose only worth or purpose is to "get laid" and thereby boost the male ego.[4] Bodybuilding, the thinking goes, makes one substantial, something more than a female sexuality that exists to support male fantasies of prowess, but the bodybuilding industry itself then does everything it can to resexualize female bodybuilders and make them precisely into the emptiness they are building themselves to avoid. My experience of this "real" that night was enough to make me turn away from female bodybuilding as a source of liberatory potential for women and girls, and instead turn to women's sports more generally.[5]

Looked at in this kind of doubting light, from a perspective of one who has begun to recover from 'the disease,' bodybuilding began to appear very different. Indeed, as the years wore on and the world horizon shifted from the glorification of dot.coms and the so-called "information economy" to a focus on ecological crisis and the externalities produced by the very companies that serve as its infrastructure, in this context bodybuilding begins to look even more absurd, even more excessive than it did in its heyday, when it more closely matched the goals of "grow or die" economics. From this skeptical perspective, one informed by the logic of 'the disease' but also outside it, one might ask, for instance, what Monsanto, British Petroleum, and competitive, steroid-based bodybuilding have in common, and be able to come up with a convining answer. It might be said that the practices of all three institutions (factory farming, the petroleum industry, and bodybuilding) involve externalities of blatant damage and waste, that their practices are unsustainable, and that the specific ways in which they're unsustainable are rapidly converting them into historical anachronisms.

In this narrative, then, I wish to make three central claims: 1) that competitive, steroid-based bodybuilding and its long-term detrimental health effects can be read as a synecdoche for globalization and its "grow or die" imperatives that ignore externalities such as long-term environmental damages; 2) that bodybuilding was more fully part of the mainstream in the late 1980s/early 1990s than it is now for specific economic and cultural reasons, and that, as a strangely literal embodiment of the economic global fetish with capital growth, bodybuilders now seem like a historical anachronism, out of step with more austere times; 3) the "New Austerity" emphasis allows us to explore the potentiality of bodybuilding in a different modality: that of immersive practice.

BUT BEFORE THE 'GOODBYE TO ALL THAT:' POSTMODERN FANTASY, AMERICAN EXCEPTIONALISM, AND THE TRANSCENDENCE OF THE FLESH

Postmodernism was the word that aspired to describe the era of surfaces, the elision of content, the "image is everything" rush of consumerism that characterized the deregulated 1980s, a deregulation that ushered in the era of "globalization," and that preached an equality of image if nothing else. Every day was a form of theater, people playing with signifiers to make their look present the message of the day, image of the day, "self" of the day. A carnival of surfaces, a "be-all-that-you-can-be" free for all. Postmodern theory pronounced the death of the self, the author, and that everything was text – that is, an endlessly re-arrangeable collection of signs that had no fixed, pre-determinate pattern or shape, and this was the true nature of reality according to this mode of conception. The perfect world for the emergence of the bodybuilder as a dominant cultural image, and bodybuilding as a mainstream practice.

'That's when it hit me,' Fussell writes, describing his reactions to his fellow bodybuilders as he ate and lifted and dieted down with the best of them.

> Bad theater. Every word they uttered, every move they made seemed rehearsed – as rehearsed, in fact, as any performance I'd seen on stage. That explained the pregnant pauses before delivering the lines I knew from the magazines. Lines like 'You gotta stay hungry,' or

'you work hard, good things will happen.' Much of being a body-builder, I gathered, meant playing at being a bodybuilder.

(Fussell 1991: 48)

A very literal form of "play" in which your own body is the construction site, the bodybuilder's dream is the dream of endlessly re-arrangeable flesh, the manipulation of the material without limits, the ultimate victory over "nature": 'while my legs spasmed through the night,' writes Fussell, 'I'd dream of Tom Platz, the so-called "Golden Eagle."' Precisely describing the way a postmodern sensibility informs bodybuilding, he writes that

> more than any other bodybuilder, [Platz had] given up everything to reverse the course of nature. He had been born with a miserable structure, his hips wider than a yardstick, his shoulders narrower than a ruler. But through sheer industry, through set after set of 315-pound squats for 50 straight reps, through training sessions interspersed with vomit and blood, Tom hurdled these obstacles and became Mr. Universe.
>
> (ibid.: 77)

You don't like the body you were born with? You don't like the shape to which your genetics have contributed? That's ok, that's just fine, because you can physically remake yourself however you'd like. Here Fussell gets at the way the concept of postmodern plasticity combines with earlier ideologies of self-determination – ideologies intrinsic to the larger cultural dream of American exceptionalism – to create a cultural context in which bodybuilding could flourish for a time.

In a brilliant analysis of the ideology of American exceptionalism, liter-ary cultural critic Donald Pease defines that 'exceptionalism' as 'a fantasy through which U.S. citizens bring contradictory political and cultural descriptions into correlation with one another through the desires that make them meaningful' (Pease 2009: 8). Those desires are connected to the desire for autonomy, the celebration of the individual (and America as a nation of unique individuals), and the desire to start fresh, unencum-bered by the past or one's origins. Those correlations have a long history related to the United State's foundation as a colony that rebelled against its sovereign to create alternative political, social, and cultural structures:

> American exceptionalism has been taking to mean that America is 'distinct' (meaning merely different) or 'unique' (meaning anoma-lous), or 'exemplary' (meaning a model for other nations to follow), or that it is 'exempt' from the laws of historical progress (meaning that it is an 'exception' to the laws and rules governing the develop-ment of other nations).
>
> (ibid.: 8)

Perhaps most influential to the American psyche is 'the belief that the U.S. was unencumbered by Europe's historical traditions' (ibid.: 11). While the desire for a sense of personal sovereignty and power seen in bodybuilders may have universal inflections, there may be a particular "Americanness" for bodybuilding in that the ideology/fantasy of American exceptionalism has parallels with a bodybuilder's preoccupation with difference from "the masses." Like the bodybuilder who seeks to escape the his genetic somatotype and remake himself to a better purpose and image, the ideology of American exceptionalism sought to excise the political, social, and individual body from its European and particularly British antecedents and start again a new foundation, the earlier foundation razed clean. The preoccupation with breaking free from the past, forgetting and ignoring the past, and starting to build anew is one that has been directly imported into bodybuilding psychology and subculture.

Anomalous, exemplary, and unencumbered – these three adjectives are key descriptors of bodybuilding lore, absolutely central to beliefs about the fundamental project bodybuilding becomes. As Fussell describes the attitude he and his fellow builders share: 'I want to look like something you've never seen before.' I understood. The shock value is all. It's saying, or rather screaming, 'More than anything else in the world, whatever it takes, I don't want to be like you. I don't want to look like you, I don't want to talk like you, I don't want to *be* you' (Fussell 1991: 137). This uniqueness is something that is worked hard for, achieved, an undeniable difference encoded in the flesh. A difference worth, apparently, compromising one's long-term health, and even dying for: 'I told myself that taking steroids was a Faustian bargain. I was selling my soul to the devil in exchange for transcending what was permitted to ordinary mortals. I was my own alchemist, I said, transmuting the base metal of myself, the dross, into gold' (ibid.: 122). Transmuting the dross into gold, building a physique that is valued for its difference, exempt from the physical laws that limit the development of others, providing a physical ideal to which others could or should aspire, Fussell enacts the fundamental exceptionalist drama of the bodybuilder, neatly combining its different strands into a living, breathing work of transformed flesh.

Historically speaking, bodybuilding began at the turn of the twentieth century, was mainstreamed in the 1980s when Arnold Schwarzenegger as The Terminator became the masculine ideal, and began to fall out of favor at the end of the 1990s, when on a mass scale gyms converted themselves to "fitness centers" and "no grunting" became a fitness center rule. At my own gym, my training partners and I were reprimanded by the gym owner for letting the local newspaper take a picture of us training for a fitness article – we were 'too big,' he said. He was running a fitness center, not a gym, and he didn't want to intimidate anyone. We talked about it indignantly for days, but we knew our days were numbered. Now, chains such as *Planet Fitness* market a "no judgment zone" where supposedly everyone can train without being evaluated for the quality of their physique, and grunting from the strain of lifting heavy weights is explicitly forbidden in gym rules. The brief moment of bodybuilding hegemony was dead.

'GROW OR DIE': ECONOMIC AND BODILY IMPERATIVES IN THE LATE TWENTIETH CENTURY

This trajectory wasn't random, rather neatly following the expansion of the global economy and deregulation and the relentless emphasis on economic growth despite externalities. Like a global economy gone wild in an excess of production and consumption, not considering any of the environmental costs, the clear-cut forests, destruction of marshlands, dammed-up streams, many bodybuilders – especially competitive but also non-competitive – ingested various kinds of steroids and all kinds pharmaceuticals in the effort to pump themselves up. And pump they did – bodybuilders in the 1990s and through to today became almost impossibly big, starting with Dorian Yates and running through to Ronnie Coleman, who is more than 300 lbs in contest shape. Even bodybuilders themselves are questioning this direction:

> Notice how ESPN showed a lot of bodybuilding shows back in the 80's and early 90's. Turn the TV on right now and you will see water polo, chess, hot dog eating contests and poker. But not bodybuilding. Our sport has always been a sub-culture, but with the mass monsters of today we took out every chance we had to succeed and make bodybuilding mainstream. I look at this as neutral, because bodybuilding is not a normal activity, and that's a part of why I love it and it's special to me. It's not for everyone. Personally I like the mass monsters because it sets out new goals in which me or you could go after [sic]. It shows that it's possible to achieve. I believe that for bodybuilding fans the turn around to size is somewhat good, but when it comes to general public we are taking ten steps back.
> (bigcalves, "In the World of Bodybuilding, How Big is Too Big?" http://www.bodybuilding.com/fun/topicoftheweek130.htm, accessed June 10, 2010)

"The general public", which may have embraced extreme muscularity as an ideal more in the mid-1980s through mid-1990s than it does today, seems to have reverted to its characterization of bodybuilders as excessive narcissists. Aware of and sympathetic to the kind of stigmatization bodybuilders face, Lee Monaghan's study of the knowledge specific to bodybuilding subculture attempts to put bodybuilding drug use into perspective:

> the reported global 'abuse' of steroids among gym members – anomalous with the supposed healthism of exercise and widely considered dangerous and polluting – renders 'bodybuilder' synonymous with the pejorative label 'risk taker' in many people's minds. Within Western scientific and popular discourse such deviancy is claimed to manifest in the materialty of the body. A possible long-term hazard of drug-assisted bodybuilding, not immediately apparent but instead dependent upon the probing of biomedical science, is damage to internal bodily organs such as the liver, kidneys and cardiovascular system. Moreover, the marking of deviancy on 'excessively' muscular fe/male bodies is in a more recognizable fashion – the inscription and projection of powerful cultural meanings – represents another possible risk for those bodybuilders who transgress the normative ideal of the 'fit-looking' body.
>
> (Monaghan 2000: 1–2; see also Monaghan, Chapter 3, this volume)

As Monaghan so convincingly shows, bodybuilders are well aware of public perceptions and exist in perpetual dialogue with them even as they take pride in their difference from dominant standards. Monaghan's study 'explores the sustainability of the "risky" practice of bodybuilding as participants endeavor to construct and maintain "appropriate" bodies and identities' (Monaghan 2000: 2). While Monaghan never comes to specific conclusions about whether bodybuilding is sustainable as a lifestyle, in the next section I will argue that bodybuilding, if it is performed as an immersive practice (what many call "weight training"), is sustainable over the life course, while competitive bodybuilding is anything but.

As Monaghan points out, "bodybuilders" are far from a monolithic category, with variability informing the overall conceptions of the "ideal" body in terms of location, individuals within a specific location, and variability of that conception over a bodybuilder's lifespan. My analysis, while allowing that there are a wide range of reasons why people bodybuild, and very different understandings and formulations of its meaning, focuses largely on the underlying premise – that growth (in this case physical growth of the already-mature body, facilitated by the (over) consumption of food, supplements, and in some cases, steroids) is good. Whatever meaning an individual bodybuilder may assign to his/her growth, I'm interested in exploring the symbolic connections between over-consumption as an individual practice related to bodybuilding, and over-consumption as an externality produced by the global economic fetish with growth. Just as the growth mandate in the global economy produces externalized environmental damage that results in phenomena such as climate change, the extinction of species, over-utilization of resources and destruction of habitat, the growth mandate in a body-builder's individual life is often similarly externalized. Moreover, the ideological shift from a blind emphasis on growth to a more moderate emphasis is paralleled by a similar shift in the mainstream fitness industry from the hypermuscularity of bodybuilders as an ideal to the more general category of "fitness" as an ideal. While no one has the right to prescribe for any individual what is "too big," it can be observed that the "greening" of marketing and its emphasis on avoiding wastefulness has had the effect of further stigmatizing bodybuilders and their growth projects. My further point is that, as in all sports, bodybuilding in its competitive modality tends to incur externalities in a way that training in an immersive modality does not.

Of any sport, bodybuilding marks the ultimate postmodern dream, the transcendence of genetics, of the non-conforming flesh, and for American builders, at least, that dream is shot through with the residues of ideologies of American exceptionalism – America is different, and it is its "duty" to grow and dominate and show everyone else the way, just as bodybuilders see themselves as exceptional and greater forms of humanity than others. Mr. Universe and all that sign implies, the body-builder's dream of surfaces is the drama of size, and the drama of size has its shadow side, its barely concealed externalities of excess and waste:

> EAT BIG, SLEEP BIG, TRAIN BIG was the iron edict obeyed by all of us. In our muscle stable, we averaged 5,000 calories a day. The stove was constantly burning, the oven baking, the refrigerator cooling, the cupboards storing . . . Nimrod injected himself on a daily basis with Vitamin B12 in order to maintain his extraordinary appetite. Vinnie could be heard throwing up every afternoon from an excess of food even his body couldn't take . . . to us, food represented fuel for the future. Every chicken breast and beef flank we ate was consumed in the hope that it would help make us into the giants we dreamed of being.
>
> (Fussell 1991: 132, emphasis in text)

Eating to the point of excess, consuming more than the body can process, bodybuilding's primary drama is first one of scale – of continual, unlimited growth – and it shares this aspect with the global economy, whose "grow or die" imperatives have 'taken place without reference to environmental consequences such as global warming, ozone layer depletion and the loss or irreplaceable scarce resources' (Brown 2005: 565). Like the global economy blind to the externalities its fetish with consumption and thereby economic growth entail, and the permanent damage those externalities produce, bodybuilder sacrifice everything, including their long-term health, for size. As sport sociologist Alan M. Klein writes in *Little Big Men,* his groundbreaking study of bodybuilding, 'the physiological effects of steroid use are increasingly clear. A variety of health risks are associated with taking them, ranging from increased risks of heart disease and liver disorders to shrinkage of testicles, the development of breast tissue, and acne . . . steroid use can adversely affect the . . . normal function . . . of liver and kidneys' (Klein 1993: 150–1). The use of Human Growth Hormone (HGH) can permanently enlarge the bones of the face, and in women, steroid use is also associated with permanent changes in voice. These externalities to the process of bodybuilding are simply ignored by most builders, who continue to practice and compete even though, in the words of one of Klein's research subjects, 'When we're up there [on the posing platform], we're closer to death than we are to life' (ibid.: 153). Any attribution of "health" to the world of bodybuilding is purely specious.

Another aspect shared with the global economy is an emphasis on image – the final "package" rather than the production process itself. The image of the bodybuilder that most people remember are those in the muscle magazines, which represent a contest state that, because pre-contest dieting and water restriction is so severe, can only last for at most a few hours. The work that goes into building the contest-ready physique has fleeting results, so fleeting that even in the grip of 'the disease,' Fussell writes that:

> it had begun to dawn on me that the whole building thing might be merely a parody of labor, and I myself a well-muscled dilettante. . . . the iron we lifted didn't help build a bridge or a battleship or a skyscraper. It enlarged our biceps and spread the sweep of our thighs. The labor of farmers and factory workers and longshoremen had a kind of dignity and purpose ours didn't.
>
> (Fussell 1991: 148)

Of course, Fussell writes at precisely the time 'farmers and factory workers and longshoremen' were being downsized, replaced by corporate factory farms, or outsourced to Third World countries where people would work for pennies on the dollar. In the so-called "information economy" or "dot.com economy," labor was supposed to have transcended its material base, and all that was left was a "parody of labor," a profound disconnection – like bodybuilding – from what it signified, and what it *was.* The post-industrial information economy signified a freedom from the dirt and grit of industrial production, when in actuality that production was merely outsourced to continents where the environmental restrictions were not so strict and labor was cheap. Bodybuilding signifies an escape from the self, from "natural" limitations, a signifier of potentially unlimited growth and power. What it *is,* however, is a kind of subordination of the self (as well as all one's expendable income) to the brutal routine of excess steroids, excess food, excess supplements, excess training, and, finally, excess flesh. 'Between my clients and my own workouts, I was now spending twelve hours a day at the gym . . . I saw nothing but iron casualties' (Fussell 1991: 153). Concerned about the poor, broken, down-on-their-luck builders he saw around him, physical wrecks doggedly returning to the gym each day with, over years, diminishing paybacks, he mentions his concerns to his friend. 'What, do you think this has anything to do with health?' Nimrod asked, shaking in mirth at the idea' (Fussell 1991: 193).

Always a highly individual practice, bodybuilding, despite its subcultural aspects, has been seen, and perhaps largely experienced as a departure and disconnection from others: 'I loved iron not for its offering of a community', Fussell writes, 'but for its promise of solitude, for the chance to escape from everyone and everything' (Fussell 1991: 155). James Howard Kuntsler and many others diagnose one of the most pernicious problems related to globalization as precisely the erosion of community, the retreat of individuals into the enclaves of their McMansions, silent neighborhoods where no one speaks and no one knows each other's names (Kuntsler 1994, 2005). The future, he insists, will depend on the reestablishment of local production economies and vital communities who share goods and services on a daily basis. In such a future, bodybuilding would have no place – unless it is practiced otherwise, in an immersive mode.

'THE NON-NEGOTIABLE NEEDS OF THE BODY': SPORT AS IMMERSIVE PRACTICE

So what, then, is an "immersive practice"? If the competitive model of sport tended to see transcendence of the body and its limitations as a goal, its reshaping as the only desirable end, and the body as the raw material for transformation into something better, and that model of sport is a subset of a globalized economy that approaches the natural world as a similar source of raw material for the production of consumer goods that have value while the natural world has value only as a resource, not in itself, sport might be reconceptualized along some of the lines that the global economy is currently being reconceptualized. As so many ecologists, sociologists, and even economists have argued, current patterns of consumption are unsustainable, and we can no longer afford to ignore the biological/ecological dimensions, as these are linked to current environmental crises such as diminishing oil and water supplies, global warming, the destruction of ecosystems, and the extinction of species. As I will argue, bodybuilding defined and practiced differently from the competitive model of sport, can, like other physical practices, serve as a mediatory experience between humans and "nature" that can increase our ecological awareness and investment in that ecology – an investment that, in a globalized culture characterized by the ethic of self-fulfillment, is not easy to foster. As Phil Macnagten argues, however, 'in an individualized society environmental concerns are likely to be felt most acutely when they impinge on the body, typically in relation to questions of food and health' (2003: 68). Physical practices such as bodybuilding – because they can so powerfully connect (as well as disassociate) us to our own materiality – might be one way of fostering, in environmental historian Peter Hay's words, a 'pre-rational impulse' that for most people 'establishes identification with the green movement . . . a deep consternation at the scale of destruction wrought, in the second half of the twentieth century, in the name of transcendent human progression' (Hay 2002: 2–3). This is a role for bodybuilding that is counter-intuitive and has been little discussed, and its logic can be most clearly seen in those dimensions of sport that are defined not solely as competition, but also as an "immersive practice."

Despite an emphasis on competitive models of sport perpetuated by the dominant sport institutions and media, a different understanding of sport is possible even within sport constructed in these terms. The biological dimensions of sport experience, as many athletes have found, can themselves be experienced quite differently from the usual regime of measurement and statistics. Rather than an enemy that needs to be transcended or its limitations conquered, looked at differently, the biological becomes something to be embraced. This is another, more positive potentiality that emerges from physical training. This potentiality was there from the beginning but was backgrounded, since, as Mary Mellor discusses, in the cultural logic of transcendence the biological is erased – 'the social relations underpinning current patterns of unsustainability are those that place value on the transcendent/technological at the expense of the immanent/biological' (Mellor 2005: 215). While athletes experience that erasure when they construct their daily practice as a competition between each other leading to the "higher" goal of competing more effectively, something else can be seen as happening simultaneously alongside the reckless quest for "perfection" in these terms.

That "something else" is an alternative experiential modality. This is an experience variously represented as "being in the zone," "flow," being outside of the usual sense of time (the sped-up, hyperreal of technologized time), or being connected to something larger. This kind of effortless physical state of extraordinary achievement marks a different kind of experience than that measured by the scales, measuring tapes, and record books of technologized time. This sense of immanence, a reconnection to biological time as experienced through physical activity, has been termed by sociologist Nigel Thrift, as an "immersive practice."

"Immersive practices" are those that 'constitute a "background" within which nature is encountered as a means of gathering stillness, both inside and outside the body. A central component lies in the temporality of the practice' (Thrift quoted in Macnaghten 2003: 75). That "temporality" is the kind of flow state that physical practices so readily foster. Sports which take place out of doors more easily engender this state of flow, but even if not practiced outside, as most weightlifting isn't, one can still experience this physical practice in this modality if the state of mind is right.

Flow. "In the zone," "athletic high," "creation space," "optimal experience," call it what you will, it's a silent enclave, a soft bed of pine needles hunkered down between the protective branches of enormous trees. Neurologists will tell us it is electrical impulse, neurons igniting in the brain. Mihaly Csikszentmihalyi, who coined the term, will tell us it is focused attention, the space where we impose order on the chaos and entropy of life (Csikszentmihalyi 1990). It is beauty and meaning, it is quiet and calm, it is everything that gathers in us channeled forward to some end, the goal that is paradoxically the moments themselves, sped up, slowed down, outside time, suspended like a spider spinning and dancing its way across its web. And catch flies I might, but as Joseph Conrad's plaintive narrator Marlow says, 'it is like a running blaze across a plain, like a flash of lightning in the clouds. We live in the flicker – may it last as long as the old earth keeps rolling! But darkness was here yesterday' (Conrad 1988: 9). Flow is flicker, flicker flow, channels of energy gathered and released, where self-consciousness disappears, chemical signals conjoined into a steady-state where you and it are one.

So what, concretely, is flow? 'Play, art, pageantry, ritual, and sports are some examples' (1990: 72), Csikszentmihalyi says, and divides flow's conditions of possibility into steps:

> 1) set an overall goal, and as many subgoals as are realistically feasible; 2) find ways of measuring progress in terms of the goals chosen; 3) keep concentrating on what one is doing, making finer and finer distinctions in the challenges involved with the activities; 4) develop the skills necessary to interact with the opportunities available; and, 5) keep raising the stakes if the activity becomes boring.
>
> (ibid.: 97)

Csikszentmihalyi's formulations are based on years of research, and have been applied widely from athletics to artistic practices. The "autotelic" experience is particularly important for Csikszentmihalyi, encompassing as it does many of the other sub-concepts of flow. 'The key element,' he writes, 'of an optimal experience is that it is an end in itself . . . the term "autotelic" derives from two Greek words, *auto* meaning self and *telos* meaning goal. It refers to a self-contained activity, one that is done not with the expectation of some future benefit, but simply because the doing itself is the reward' (p. 58). This seems a contradiction: goal-directedness is so important that it is the very definition of the self, 'the self being the sum and organization of the goals' (p. 178). Can a goal not have an end? However, he mentions a 'benefit' almost immediately after: 'one of the most frequently mentioned dimensions of the flow experience is that, while it lasts, one is able to forget all the unpleasant aspects of life' (p. 58). Immersed in a flow activity, we are left with 'as little room as possible for noticing the entropy of normal life' (p. 226).

Flow is unlikely to be experienced in the competitive mode of measurement and clocks, pounds and standards. If 'the doing itself is the reward,' the mindset where one is lifting to achieve the right definition in one's biceps and hamstrings to appeal to the capricious judges at a bodybuilding show is not likely to produce flow. While the competitive model of sport involves an internal focus while training, concentration on one's breathing, heart rate, poundage lifted etc., based around improving one's performance, what I'm calling "immersive sport" has links to the idea of sport as a form of spiritual practice. In this model, sport is approached as a vehicle through which, as Professor Shirl James Hoffman puts it in the foreword to *Sport and Spirituality*, we 'shape our spirits and create alternative realities and states of consciousness' (Hoffman in Parry et al. 2007: xi). Sport experienced as an immersive practice can involve competition – training hard to perform your best – but it can also involve the joy of sheer participation, an appreciation of the body in movement, a way to step out of the ordinary frenzy of our daily lives filled with the barrage of things to get done and instead experience pure absorption into the activity itself, and a suspension of all other distractions.

Sport formulated as an "immersive practice" takes a practitioner out of tech time and into biological time. The immersive is an alternative to the competitive model of sport and its relentless focus on comparison, on the bottom line of winning to the exclusion of the bodybuilder's health, which in turn embodies the global economy and its relentless focus on economic growth to the exclusion of other factors such as public health and human welfare. If one shifts the lens away from the zero-sum game of winning, a different experiential model based around the idea of immersive practices begins to emerge within sport that reconnects us with biological time (this is why "being in the zone" is also experienced as being "out of time").

The immersive modality is only possible separated from the competitive, comparative world of bodybuilding where your lifting (and other) practices have the end goal of making you bigger, better proportioned, and with a lower bodyfat percentage as opposed to anyone else involved in the same activity. It would involve lifting that foregrounds how you feel and backgrounds how you look, and that sees other lifters not as competitors in reaching a particular physical ideal but rather as people who appreciate a similar kind of physical practice – more like yogis, whose focus in their practice is internal, and rooms that they practice in usually don't have mirrors in order to reinforce this focus. All the health benefits of lifting – stronger muscles, bones, and joints, mood elevation, heightened metabolism, and everyday, functional strength – accrue without competition. A form of bodybuilding that is sustainable might be reformulated and practiced differently in such a way that the focus is no longer on growth but on functionality and health, a different kind of building, a form that, indeed, many bodybuilders would not recognize *as* bodybuilding but rather some lesser, ordinary practice.[6]

Nonetheless, the power one feels when lifting, the links between the movement and the breath, the sense of complete focus one can experience as an end in itself would be an immersive bodybuilding, a bodybuilding practiced otherwise that is more congruent with the present historical moment where everything, including bodies, are being downsized. Maybe it's as simple as calling it "weight training" rather than "bodybuilding." Still, it is "weight training" done and experienced in a particular way. Like Americans struggling with the legacy of outsized American exceptionalism and confronting their actual, less prominent place in the globablized world – part of a much larger network, not "special" or different – in order for their practices to be sustainable, bodybuilders might see themselves less in terms such as 'more than anything else in the world, whatever it takes, I don't want to be like you. I don't want to look like you, I don't want to talk like you, I don't want to *be* you' (Fussell 1991: 137) and more in terms such as 'my physical practice tangibly reminds me of my materiality as part of a much larger, increasingly vulnerable ecosystem, and we need to find a way out of this together.' De-emphasizing preoccupations with measurement and size, bodybuilding as an immersive practice can participate in a re-conceptualized 'flow' modality that brings the individual and his/her bodily processes and practices into alignment with the world around them, the beginning of a physical practice that might lead to a different conceptualization of and relation to the larger world that is sustainable: one that understands the relationship between one's practices and those of everyone else, one that experiences immersion in physicality in order to conceptualize oneself not as a machine but as a flesh and blood materiality irrevocably connected to the bodies of others, and those bodies to the larger ecosystems that are the precondition of each of our existences.

Notes

1 See Leslie Heywood, *Bodymakers: A Cultural Anatomy of Women's Bodybuilding*, especially Chapter Four 'Hard Times: The Pornographic and

Pathetic in Women's Bodybuilding Photography' (91–130); 'Ghettos of Obscurity: Individual Sovereignty and the Struggle for Recognition in Female Bodybuilding', in Frueh, Fierstein, and Stein, (eds.) *Picturing the Modern Amazon* (72–85).

2 Linguistic theorist and philosopher Jacques Derrida often spoke of what he termed *le reste,* the remainder, that thing that 'escapes the horizon of the unity of meaning,' that which exceeds the parameters of discourse, that for which discourse cannot fully account (Derrida 1991 quoted in Peggy Kamuf 1991: 99). The remainder is 'what is left unclaimed' (Kamuf 468), and as this kind of orphan, female bodybuilders can be seen as the literalized figure of *le reste,* the remainder outside speech, the excess flesh for which there is no name. As such, they are subject to ridicule and exclusion, even stigmatization, exiled from any group except their own (and they sit uneasily there) and the sexual fetishists ("schmoes") who largely bankroll their bodybuilding practice. In *Iron Maidens,* Kristin Kaye notes that female bodybuilding has always been a sort of endangered species, writing about extinction as 'the process or fact of disappearing completely from use; the decreasing or dying out of a behavioral response created by conditioning because of lack of reinforcement' (Kaye, 2005: 41–42). If you consider the second definition, then women's bodybuilding has been facing extinction ever since it began. Indeed, since the mid-1990s, Kaye notes, 'sponsorship dollars, prize money, and press coverage for female competitors have dramatically decreased', nudging the sport closer and closer to its demise (Kaye 2005: 42).

3 Kaye's initial awe and sense of female bodybuilders is compromised when she sees who the predominant audience for the show really is, and how most female bodybuilders are forced to make their living: 'An endless sea of slightly balding, slightly paunchy, kind of pasty men surrounded me. Schmoes. I didn't know who they were at the time, but they struck me as remarkably generic. There was certainly a handful of New York artist types mixed in, but these paunchy men were the primary audience for *The Celebration of the Most Awesome Female Muscle in the World.* I felt nauseated realizing that the producer was right. They certainly weren't there for "art"' (Kaye 2005: 201). 'If the competitive arena has failed her, the commercial arena ignored her, and the public arena scorned her, the Physically-Advanced Woman must consider that impulse . . . exotic dancing, private posing, domination, and "muscle worship." It's mixed-wrestling, "lift and carry," and those videos you see advertised back on page 256. It's many of the top names in bodybuilding' (ibid.: 123). A "schmoe" is the name for men who sexually fetishize muscular women, and who are their primary audience: 'A man who pays money to wrestle with a woman who is often more muscular and stronger than he is, for sexual gratification, although no overt sexual activity is performed. "I gotta go. I have a schmoe coming over at 12"' (*Urban Dictionary* http://www. urbandictionary.com/define.php?term=schmoe, accessed June 18, 2010).

4 Paul Solotaroff's account of his bodybuilding blitz in the 1970s depicts a nightmare world of home-brewed steroid stacks and male prostitution, and locates his participation in this world in his naturally slight frame, lack of attaining the hegemonic signifiers of masculinity, and a problematic childhood. It very much struck me reading his memoir next to Sam Fussell's (both, perhaps not coincidentally, had literary fathers) how for male bodybuilders the physiques they build "get them laid," while for female bodybuilders hope to build themselves into something more substantial than a "lay." It is a tragic irony of female bodybuilding that the very practice some use to heal themselves from experiences such as sexual abuse simply reinscribes that 'you-are-your-sex' modality when the bodybuilding industry that hypersexualizes them.

Katie Arnoldi's novel *Chemical Pink* (2001), while not a memoir, explores some of these issues. See also, Richardson (2008).

5 That female bodybuilders competing at the highest levels often have to support their bodybuilding "habits" by performing for "schmoes" who experience them and pay for them to be sexual fetishes is perhaps the ultimate tragedy of the sport in terms of its potential for the "empowerment" of women. See Nicholas Chare, Chapter 10, this volume.

6 I have recently taken up and become certified in CrossFit, an alternative fitness program started in California that has recently gone international. CrossFit bills itself as 'functional fitness' whose 'specialty is not specializing' and that emphasizes 'constantly varied, high intensity, functional movement' that 'prepares one for any physical contingency' (CrossFit Inc n.d.: 3). So while CrossFit's aim is the very functionality I mention here, its psychology couldn't be more different. Advocating a kind of "me against the world" mentality, and, by extension, a "CrossFitters against the world" mentality in CrossFit explicitly defines its program against more dominant conceptualizations of physical training (CrossFitters call bodybuilders/standard gym practitioners members of the "Globo Gym" who've got it all wrong). The 'preparation for any physical contingency' may also share some ideological links with the recent resurgence of survivalism (not that I don't have thoughts of this myself when contemplating the possibility of grid crash). What I find most fascinating is the way physical practices become so much an expression of the material/ ideological conditions of their times. I would argue that CrossFit is in the process of replacing bodybuilding as just this sort of historical expression, but that's another paper.

Since it specifically stimulates your anaerobic pathways, CrossFit is very addictive, very aggro, and a great deal of fun. I love it, but it is nonetheless only directed toward one piece of what I am talking about here – functionality – and remains a physical practice devoted to an in-group/out-group mentality and strength as personal dominance.

Part 2
Representations

Figure II.1 Rene L. Campbell. Courtesy of Rebecca Andrews.

Introduction to Part 2
Bodybuilding *as* Representation

Niall Richardson

As the main introduction has already argued, bodybuilding would probably never have achieved its success had it not been for photography. Without the process to capture images of bodybuilders and, most importantly, disseminate them, the activity of bodybuilding would never have attained any degree of recognition other than by a tiny minority of practitioners or fans. Indeed, one of the key points in this respect is that many people believe they "know" what a bodybuilder looks like but will have probably *only ever* seen this body in representation. In this sense, bodybuilding for many people exists *as* representation.

This is particularly relevant in our contemporary media-saturated society – especially given the rise in popularity of the internet and sites such as YouTube.com and mymusclevideo.com. Although bodybuilding videos/DVDs have existed for quite a while, these products were (relatively) expensive and often hard to obtain other than through mail-order sites or specialist sports and exercise shops. The rise of the internet has allowed an unprecedented ease of access to representations of bodybuilding. When I heard that Jay Cutler had won the Olympia, I had only to do a search for an online video to watch the entire competition. Not so long ago, I would have had to wait for an official bodybuilding publication to publish the photographs and then for a video/DVD to be made and sold. In this respect, we are more aware than ever of the bodybuilder's body – but only in representation.

However, this media saturation of bodybuilding imagery has certainly had an effect on general perceptions of the built physique. To use a personal example, when I first started training all those years ago (I was 14 – I lied about my age so I could sneak into a local "spit and sawdust" gym), I remember going to watch my first bodybuilding competition after a few months of training. I was in *awe* of the bodies on the stage at that regional competition. I had never *ever* in my life seen anything like those amazing physiques flexing on that little stage. Sadly, the same wide-eyed amazement *cannot* be the case nowadays. I recently brought a young, aspiring bodybuilder to a regional competition, hoping that he would share my excitement for the physiques on display. Much to my disappointment, he remarked that all the physiques looked 'small' and 'unimpressive.' Of course, before he left for the competition he had been watching Mr. Olympia online.[1] (In the last section, Leslie Heywood detailed a similar sense of disappointment in encountering regional level competitive bodybuilding.) In other words, the general "fan's" idea of bodybuilding has now been shaped by media representations to such an extent that, for many people, bodybuilding exists in the hyperreal sense. In many ways, bodybuilding can be seen to exemplify Baudrillard's thesis (1983) in that representation *is* the dominant reality.

Yet, this hyperreal idea of bodybuilding can be taken one stage further given our rise in new media technologies. For many bodybuilders, our *own* bodies often exist for us *as* representations. For example, a friend of mine was preparing for a local show and, during a workout, I was chatting to him and enquiring how his contest preparation was going. He remarked that he was very pleased with the striations in his deltoids and how his traps were really "popping" when he did a most muscular pose. He then said that he would show me but instead of doing a crab or bulldog pose, he whipped out his mobile phone and, beaming with pride, showed me photographs he had taken of himself while posing the night before. What struck me as remarkable about this situation was that even though this bodybuilder was wearing a revelatory training tank-top, which revealed his granite deltoids and Dennis James-proportioned traps, he didn't flex to demonstrate his striations but preferred to show a recorded image. Of course, this photograph was taken in "ideal" conditions in that he had positioned himself under a harsh, overhead light to illuminate how "cut" his physique was. The gym, flooded as it was with sunlight at that moment, would have washed out his ripped-ness and not facilitated such an impressive pose as the one recorded last night. My friend's obsession with only allowing his physique to be appraised while it was in re-presentation, continued until the competition as he, in a fashion not dissimilar to Blanche Dubois, developed paranoia about being gazed upon in the "wrong" lighting. When asked to demonstrate a pose, he nearly always refused to do it and instead always extended his mobile phone which contained an image of the specific mandatory pose. In this respect, while the mirror was always deemed an essential prop for the bodybuilder (see Klein 1993: 209–21), I should argue that it has now been succeeded by the recorded image of new technologies, especially mobile phone cameras (see Goggin (2006) for more consideration of mobile phone photography).

Of course, on a technical level, the photograph allows the bodybuilder to see poses, such as the rear lat spread, which he/she could not see without the benefit of a mirrored posing room. Yet I think there is also an element of somehow making the physique appear even more real to the self when it is captured in representation. Arguably, this is what underpins the desires of many of the bodybuilders who perform webcam flexing and place the clips on YouTube. Although this, of course, also relates to the "industry" of muscle worship (see Richardson 2008; Chare, Chapter 10, this volume), in many cases the bodybuilder is not hoping to make any money from this activity but is simply trying to reify the physique to him or herself. While this can simply be dismissed as narcissism, I should argue that it's a way of making the physique seem "more" real to the bodybuilder him/herself when it is seen in re-presentation. Representation is more real than reality.

The other important issue relating to bodybuilding and photographic representations is the relationship bodybuilding holds to art. It is probably fair to say that, more than any other sport (with the possible exception of gymnastics), bodybuilding's origins lie in art. Indeed, many people would classify a bodybuilding competition has having more in common with the spectacle of performance art or dance than with a sporting contest. One of the main explanations offered by bodybuilders (most famously by Schwarzenegger in *Pumping Iron*) as to why they engage in bodybuilding is that the bodybuilder is realizing the artist's vision of the "perfectible" body. What could only have been achieved in marble or clay was now being forged from human tissue. In this respect, bodybuilding exalts the flexed pose where, in that moment of static tension, the bodybuilder *is* a human statue. As the introduction has pointed out, the bodybuilder could only hold this pose for a few seconds. A photograph, however, allowed it to be held forever.

The other important aspect here is the question of realism. Early photography (most notably the work of Alfred Stieglitz and Edward Steichen) aimed for a style known as pictorialism, in that it tried to ape the paradigms of fine art (see Daum 2006). The more a photograph could look like a painting, then the better it was deemed to be. However, as the introduction has outlined, this may have worked with landscape photography but photographers encountered problems when representing the human form in this way. The problem was that the models' bodies often fell short of the classical ideal and presented limbs that were too short, flesh that was too loose or skin that was too blemished. Trying to cloak the image in a veneer of neo-classicism, such as including columns and velvet curtains, often only attained the very opposite effect and made the image appear, at best, kitsch if not merely ridiculous. Therefore, with the rise of the photographic nude came the awareness that the body fell *very* short of the classical ideal. Bodybuilding, of course, was testament to the success of the individual who had sculpted the body into an approximation of the classical ideal and it's hardly surprising, therefore, that bodybuilders should want this success recorded in the photograph, given that early photography was responsible for identifying the shortcomings of the human form. In other words, the photograph, which previously had only succeeded in capturing the limitations of the human form, could now celebrate its "perfection" attained through bodybuilding.

Yet, with the advent of photographic realism and celluloid representations of the human body, entered another dynamic: the pornographic. This is not to suggest that fine art has not been erotic (think of Titian, Caravaggio, Rubens). However, fine art was expensive and so erotic art was, and arguably still is, the preserve of people who can afford to own it. The cheap photograph, by contrast, was widely available to anyone who had a little spare cash. The other important factor is that while the perfected body – the human form in classical sculpture or art – may be beautiful, it is not necessarily erotic. Indeed, gazing upon classical beauty may only inspire a sense of 'erotic numbness' as Kenneth Dutton describes (Chapter 7, this volume) – although, of course, there is no accounting for personal erotic taste. Yet often it is the sense of realism which gives the representation of the human form its erotic potential. It is, for example, the slight imperfections of the skin which make the body in some way tangible and suggestive of sexual interaction.

Obviously, the issue of eroticism is something that representations of bodybuilding have had to fight against since their very origins. If the body is the source of sexual desire (both the focus of sexual desire and the instrument of sexual pleasure), then a representation of the nude or nearly nude body cannot escape the dynamics of eroticism. If bodybuilding representations were not to be labeled as mere pornography, then very distinctive strategies of representation had to evolve.

Kenneth R. Dutton starts this part with a consideration of these very codes employed in the representations of bodybuilding. In 'The Self Contained Body: The Heroic and Aesthetic/Erotic Modes of Representing the Muscular Body,' Dutton asks why people pay good money to look at the representation of muscular humans if not for reasons of sexual voyeurism. Have humans always done this kind of thing, or is it a peculiarly modern phenomenon, a sign of decadence or a culture in decline? Dutton's chapter examines the heroic and aesthetic/erotic modes of representing the muscular body. Whereas the latter classification is exemplified by art photography or pornography, the heroic mode is exemplified by "official" bodybuilding publications/representations. Here it is not the beauty of Jay Cutler's body but its awesomeness of development, not the sensuousness of Schwarzenegger's physique but its perfection of balance and proportion, which is the message intended and, for most people, the message received. Looking at the bodybuilder in such a way suggests an 'erotic numbness' (a term coined by Rudofsky); in other words, there is a curiously asexual quality discernible in the representation of the advanced muscularity of the bodybuilder's physique, and it could be argued that this is the central element in the symbolic language of the developed body.

Adam Locks develops Dutton's argument and in 'Flayed Animals in an Abattoir: The Bodybuilder as Body-Garde' examines the aesthetic implications of the representations of extreme (i.e. competitive) bodybuilders.

The contemporary bodybuilding aesthetic focuses on the body as an incongruent set of muscles, a fragmentary physique which is now so defined that during various poses, the muscle fibers are clearly visible beneath the skin. With their broad shoulders and narrow hips and enormous muscles of the torso, together with bodies so defined that substructures of muscles reveal further substructures, these bodies exemplify the most desired hypertrophic look of the contemporary bodybuilder: a "shredded mass." For this reason many people who are not used to seeing such bodies view these representations of professional bodybuilders as taking ideals of bodily perfection to such an extreme that these very attributes begin to invert themselves. The mesomorphic body shape which became so prized in the visual discourse has become (for those not in competitive bodybuilding) a "freakish image" of shock value. Locks discusses whether such bodies, which are often viewed as straining at the limits of a classically based aesthetics, could be usefully examined in the context of avant-garde art which returns bodybuilding to a more fringe, subcultural status. Professional bodybuilding has transgressed ideals of physical perfection and, conversely, embraces ugliness and extremity.

Niall Richardson follows Locks' argument about how the post-classic physique is represented as extreme or "freakish" by considering 'Strategies of Enfreakment: Representations of Contemporary Bodybuilding.' Richardson's argument is that "freak" is always a construct: the body itself may be strange or different but it is the strategy of representation which renders the unusual body a "freak." As such, "freak" only exists in the mechanism of representation. From the late 1980s onwards, bodybuilding publications have marketed the athletes as "freaks"; as bodies which do not inspire the erotic pleasures of the gaze but stimulate the shivering thrill of the stare. This chapter considers the representation of some contemporary professional bodybuilders, most notably German bodybuilder Markus Ruhl, whose nickname is "das Freak," and speculates on the politics of these bodybuilding representations and why they have emulated the paradigms of enfreakment. Richardson suggests that this is not only bodybuilding's attempt to extricate itself from the stigma of (homo)erotic spectacle but also considers "bigorexia" and how these images fuel masculine fantasies of a homosocial rejection of the tyranny of attractiveness.

The chapters of Dutton, Locks and Richardson all consider the ways in which official bodybuilding representations aim for a strategy of 'erotic numbness'; these representations are emphatic that they should not be "read" as pornography. However, what about the potential eroticism of bodybuilding representations? Most recently, there has been a new form of pornography identified: muscle worship porn. The dynamics of these representations are taken up by Nicholas Chare in 'Getting Hard: Female Bodybuilders and Muscle Worship.' Although muscle worship representational strategies are also employed for male bodybuilders, Chare focuses on the female bodybuilder. Obviously, this is a particularly sensitive debate given that, for so many years, female bodybuilding was praised as feminist resistance, given that these women's physiques were read as a challenge to hegemonic feminine iconography. However, how much challenge is offered when these bodies are so readily represented within the arena of pornography? Chare examines the erotic spectacle known as muscle worship in which the built physique provides erotic gratification. Chare argues that beauty resides not solely in the look of the body but also in its fleshly substance and physical strength. While "official" bodybuilding representations aim for a sense of distance, muscle worship aims for spectatorial engagement. Chare, therefore, considers how beauty resides within actions of the body and how this vigorous aesthetic manifests itself in the representation of muscle worship sessions. Most importantly, the chapter stresses the importance of representation in that a body in "official" bodybuilding representation may attain the goal of erotic numbness while this very same body in a muscle worship representation can achieve the very opposite.

While Chare's chapter addresses the eroticism of muscle worship in a critical fashion, Joanna Frueh's chapter makes a definite investment in the representation of the erotics of muscle. Frueh, is a rare breed of academic in that she is both a critic and a performance artist who actually manages to combine artistic performance with cultural criticism in the same piece (see, for example, Frueh 2003). In 'Aphrodisia and Erotogenesis,' Frueh, in her inimitable erotic prose, addresses bodybuilding as a model of pleasure that extends the types of beauty and sexuality available to mid-life women – matron, crone, and ingenue-sexpot. Frueh discusses the mid-life body as an artistic medium whose creator can be the subject of erotogenesis, which is the creation of a vibrant, radiant energy, the life energy that is Eros and that contemporary Western culture generally denies to older women. As Frueh argues for the erotic agency of "extreme," "excessive," and "difficult" beauty of the mid-life female bodybuilder, she asserts that an older woman *can* be an aphrodisiac body, sensually gratifying to herself and others, sexually and aesthetically arresting. This chapter is an interesting, meta-critical conclusion to the debates raised in the representations part, as it very deliberately blurs the boundaries between representation and reality, critical distance, and erotic investment.

As I've stressed already, one of the issues that representation studies raises, is how the images are "read." For example, the *intended* message of a nurse's uniform is to identify a hospital official who administers medicine and medical attention but yet, as we all know, many people *read* an erotic element in that semiotic. Short of doing an enormous ethnographic study, it is impossible to discern how people consume the plethora of bodybuilding images now available via new media. What is intended as an image of "erotic numbness" may well be consumed by a spectator who has a box of tissues to hand.

My own response to this current availability of muscle in representation has always been ambivalent. As something which increases the visibility of the practice of bodybuilding, then I believe it is a worthwhile development. Yet given that most representations are comparable to *Big Brother* realism (a camera which is pretending that it isn't lying when, in fact, it is), I become a little worried as to how representations have eclipsed bodybuilding practice. What happens to regional level bodybuilders' identifications if Jay Cutler's body becomes canonized *as* bodybuilding? What happens to recreational lifters' investment in the health enhancement properties of bodybuilding (see Bailey and Gillett, Chapter 4, this volume), or bodybuilding as immersive practice (see Heywood, Chapter 6), if professional bodybuilders are marketed more and more as chemically induced "freaks"? What happens to the amateur level female bodybuilder, struggling to find a gym space in which she can be free from macho hassle while she trains (see Bunsell and Shilling, Chapter 2), and negotiating a space in a regional competition, if female muscle is represented in online sites as erotic display rather than an athletic activity?

Most importantly, if cult followings, composed of fans who have never engaged in training themselves, develop around this "spectacle" (and the number of naïve comments available on YouTube suggest that many spectators have never set foot in a gym in their life), what does it do to the very *concept* of bodybuilding as a practice as opposed to an exhibition? As technology allows people to watch bodybuilding as a "media spectacle," bodybuilding seems to have arrived at a curious pose-down between the actual and the virtual. Do we take the cynical view and say 'it's only a representation' or do we suspect that bodybuilding may well have entered a new evolution in its life? As many fans stare at the muscle-bulked-ripped-to-shreds figures on their screens, both the ease of access and the unremitting acceleration of technology (that offers increasing levels of interfacing, for example 3D) might suggest that the future of bodybuilding may have already been decided.

Note

1 There is a counter-argument to this. Recently there has been a rise in popularity of posting "unflattering" images of bodybuilders on various online discussion websites/boards. These are often images of professional bodybuilders taken when they are extremely off season and "bulked." Another trend started by some fans (whom I believe have simply too much time on their hands) has been the posting of images of bodybuilders who have forgotten to keep their "roidguts" crunched in and so the image is a most unflattering representation of an off-season bodybuilder with a distended abdomen. Therefore, there is an argument to be made that the rise in internet media has not, in fact, reified the competition-ready physique as "the" image of bodybuilding but allowed the naïve fan to appreciate that bodybuilders only look competition ready for a short period of the year.

Figure 7.1 James Llewellin. Courtesy of Rebecca Andrews.

7 The Self Contained Body

The Heroic and Aesthetic/Erotic Modes of Representing the Muscular Body

Kenneth R. Dutton

BODIES BOLD AND BEAUTIFUL

Human beings are more than bodies, and a preoccupation with the world of physicality or outward appearance to the exclusion of deeper and ultimately more meaningful concerns can turn the pursuit of the developed body from an engrossing imaginative exercise into a futile obsession with the shallow surface of existence or a narcissistic cult of the self. More dangerously still, the distortion of physical development from a subjective means of personal expression into an ideological program is to pervert its creativeness and reduce it to the crudest form of physical suprematism and social intolerance. The bigotry of the body can take possession of an individual, a group, a society or a regime. Only when the quest for physical perfectibility is held in balance with a desire for the general good of our fellow man and woman can it ever be a fully, and admirably, human aspiration.

Yet to those who have learned to read the language of the developed body, it can open up a world rich in imaginative associations. At the purely representational level, freed from the accretions of higher or lower purpose, the heavily codified display of the bodybuilder is a unique expressive exercise, all the more inexhaustible in its allusive suggestions because of that absence of utilitarian aims which is the mark of pure play as it is of art. It gives concrete form to one of the limits of our potentiality as physical beings, and explores the symbolic and expressive capacity with which the developed body has been endowed by the inventive imagination of Western civilization. The bodybuilding display is, in a peculiarly twentieth-century form, the inheritor of what we have called the "heroic" tradition in Western art. Its inception coincided almost exactly with the final abandonment of the heroic style of representation of the body as a leading theme of high art, and the conventions of one medium of expression passed with little modification into another. Since the time of the early bodybuilders and their mock-classical poses and accoutrements, the convention has undergone further evolution in conformity with the changing tastes of successive generations, but its basis in the metaphorical language of its beginnings remains clearly in evidence.

The heroic figure in Western art is often referred to as 'self-contained,'[1] that is, it is seen as an end in itself and not as reaching out to us to seek, or produce, gratification. We admire it because of the fascination that a human physical structure can hold on account of its perfection of purpose and function – a perfection found in harmony and proportion, in the muscle and sinew which indicate the discipline of control and mastery, in the classical attitudes which convey an inner energy and a striving toward ideal form. As Rudofsky puts it:

> The erotic numbness that emanates from a perfectly proportioned body assured generations of city fathers that all the mythological statuary that clings to public fountains or dots a town's parks, and the caryatids and atlases carrying sham loads of palace porticos, are incapable of arousing sensuous pleasure.
>
> (1971: 52)

This is not to deny the presence, even the importance, of the erotic element in high art. It is to distinguish a particular tradition in the depiction of the body, in which the self-containment of the representation restrains any overt sexual response.

The heroic tradition can be distinguished in principle from what might be called the "aesthetic" tradition in the rendering of the muscular male body. Both conventions use muscularity as an important element of the visual message, though in the aesthetic convention the muscularity tends to be subordinated to the overall impression of physical beauty – whether of the body itself, the facial features, or the graceful elegance of the pose. The aesthetic tradition has always co-existed alongside the heroic: the commanding statues of Greek gods stand alongside the vase paintings of lithe young athletes; the Herculean giants of Michelangelo alongside the coltish *David* of Donatello; the chiseled muscularity of Sandow alongside the burnished grace of Sansone; the imperturbable body-landscape of George Butler's photographs of Schwarzenegger alongside the lingering curiosity of Robert Mapplethorpe's photographs of muscular nudes.

The distinction being proposed here is one of principle. In practice, an individual representation or display of the developed body may contain elements of both traditions; one or the other may predominate, or both may be present in more or less equal measure. While in general the aesthetic tradition has favored a more lithesome, less massive muscularity than the heroic tradition (bodybuilders are generally not sought as male models, even for beachwear or in advertisements requiring a sexually attractive male physique), only the context can determine which if any of the two traditions is dominant in a particular instance. The aesthetic tradition can never be divorced from a hint of mild eroticism, and while the overtly erotic (or pornographic) representation of the body may appear to eliminate any traces of "aesthetic" appeal, it is best seen as an extreme or (in some cases) perverted instance of the aesthetic as opposed to the heroic mode of depiction.

A telling illustration of the distance which separates the heroic and aesthetic/erotic modes of representing the muscular body can be found in a comparison between the bodybuilding magazine photograph and the "art" photograph. As examples of the latter medium we can take the studies of muscular black nudes made by one of the most original and gifted of late twentieth-century photographers, Robert Mapplethorpe (1946–1989). The very ambiguity of Mapplethorpe's portrayals of these lithe and well-developed bodies – enigmatically caught at mid-point between what Hollinghurst calls the 'intensely sexy silkiness' of their skin texture and the 'aestheticizing into sculpture' of their body outline (1983: 8) – serves to bring more clearly into focus the extent to which the world of bodybuilding as sport has established its distance from the world of eroticism. It is true, for example, that in Mapplethorpe's photographs we are in a sense looking at bodybuilders, but what is significant about them is precisely what makes them different from the conventional bodybuilding photographs which fill the pages of the popular monthly bodybuilding magazines. It is not simply a matter of the nudity of Mapplethorpe's figures (actually a very chaste nudity by his standards), though this clearly marks an important difference in convention and overtones. It is rather the hesitancy between detached and formal appreciation on the one hand, and on the other, the lingering attention to sensuous detail in the curve of a buttock or the glint of light on a nipple, which not only characterize Mapplethorpe's work but also give it an unforgettable beauty. His attempt in these photographs to prevail over the sexual seductiveness of the physique by the sheer sculptural beauty of line and texture has divided critical opinion – some believing that formal elements dominate emotional involvement while others consider that the two are inextricably intertwined – but what is clear is that they never leave the world of aesthetic for that of purely heroic depiction.

If the equally meticulously photographed physiques in the quality muscle magazines seem totally uninspired by comparison, it is precisely because they are lacking in mystery and desire, directing our attention immediately and unambiguously to the formal quality of the body and the technical criteria of the judging panel. In the case of these Mr. Olympia aspirants, it is not the beauty of the body but its awesomeness of development, not the sensuousness of the physique but its perfection of balance and proportion, that is the message intended and, for most people, the message received. The role of the camera here is purely to record, to reproduce in minute detail the physical presence of the body itself. It is not the photographer who has taken over the role of artist as author of the "heroic" message: it is the subject of the technically flawless but neutral photograph – the bodybuilder as author of his own muscularity, as sculptor of his own body. He speaks to us without the intermediary of art, even of photographic art: the only transcendence involved is that of the body's capacity for self-transcendence.

THE ALL-INCLUSIVE BODY

The term 'erotic numbness' used by Rudofsky to characterize our response to heroic art applies equally well (but for different reasons) to the effect produced by the bodybuilding display. In both cases, this observation must obviously be confined to "typical" responses, since, as we have already noted, the possible range of human reactions to the sight of the body, whether in art or in real life, is determined by the psychological disposition of the individual at the viewing end of the transaction. Though the *Laocoön*, the Farnese *Hercules* or Michelangelo's *David* can in no meaningful sense of the term be considered erotic art, it is at least conceivable – and probably factually the case – that some people would find these statues irresistibly exciting in sexual terms. So too with the bodybuilding display: the phenomenon known as "muscle fetishism" is well known to psychologists dealing in the area of psycho-sexual fantasy, and such a disposition makes the very sight of muscularity a powerful source of sexual arousal (see Chare, Chapter 10, and Richardson, Chapter 9, this volume). Hence the associated activity referred to as "muscle worship." In this area, any general proposition that one may advance will apply only within the bounds of what can be considered typical or "normal" human reaction.

With this caveat, it is possible to suggest that there is a curiously asexual quality discernible in the advanced muscularity of the body-builder's physique, and it could be argued that this is a central element in the symbolic language of the developed body. It is not so much that the body is here devoid of sexual connotations, as that it combines in a unique fashion elements of both male and female sexuality, or that by simultaneously affirming and denying male and female sexual messages it manages to escape or even transcend the male–female duality and attain a symbolic completeness which comprehends them both. Implausible though such a theory may at first seem, it not only accounts for some of the particular conventions of bodybuilding display which defy explanation on other grounds, but also corresponds to a deep-seated aspiration toward sexual unification which has found expression in various forms since antiquity.

It should be noted that this is a somewhat different concept from that of unisexuality or the elimination of visible differences between the sexes, a tendency which has been found in certain idealistic movements from the apocryphal writings of the first century AD, through medieval and Renaissance mysticism to modern incarnations as disparate as the rock musical *Hair* and Maoist China.[2] It differs also, at least in mode of presentation, from the androgynous or sexually ambivalent characteristics and mannerisms adopted by a number of male pop performers from David Bowie in the 1970s to Prince and Michael Jackson in the 1980s and 1990s. What is suggested by the bodybuilder's physique is not a diminution or denial of masculine qualities, so much as their explicit affirmation in a context which simultaneously suggests complementary messages associated with opposite qualities. There is a basic principle of selective perception involved here, one long recognized by traditional scholastic philosophy which neatly encapsulated it in the maxim *expressio unius rei est exclusio alterius*: the presence of a characteristic or quality implies the absence of an opposite quality (hardness implies the absence of softness and vice versa) and thus suggests incompleteness of being. Conversely, the reconciliation of opposing characteristics can lead to our apprehension of a sense of completeness or self-sufficiency. Kenneth Clark, for instance, has observed that 'the disposition of areas in the torso is related to our most vivid experiences, so that abstract shapes, the square and the circle, seem to us male and female' (1960: 25); in this context, 'the old endeavor of magical mathematics to square the circle' is related to the ancient cosmology which saw the union of opposites as a restoration of primordial harmony and perfection.

The combination of male and female characteristics has been noted by a number of observers of the bodybuilding display. George Butler has vividly described one of his photographs of Arnold Schwarzenegger as follows:

> He seems to float, suspending himself palms down on the rails of two back-to-back chairs . . . His upper body – trapezius flexed, deltoids rolled forward, abdomen vacuumed into a small shadow – is an accumulation of striking details. The pectoral muscles beneath are large and sweeping. They glisten so shockingly in the air of the shabby room that the figure who bears them seems neither man nor woman.
> (1990: 13)

Equally, Lisa Lyon has characterized the image projected by the female bodybuilder as 'neither masculine nor feminine but feline' (Chatwin and Mapplethorpe 1983: 12). Margaret Walters has commented that 'for all his super-masculinity the bodybuilder's exaggerated breast development, as well as his dedicated self-absorption, can make him look unexpectedly, surreally feminine' (1978: 295). Whilst the latter comment is part of Walters' dismissal of bodybuilding which she sees as 'the most purely narcissistic and, in that sense, most feminine, of pastimes,' it is nonetheless possible to endorse her perceptive identification of the crucially suggestive elements of the bodybuilder's physique without sharing her distaste for this form of bodily manifestation.

The three elements identified here are the basic shape or outline of the body ('super-masculinity'), the modeling of the body's surface ('unexpectedly . . . feminine'), and an overall air of self-absorption (characterized as 'narcissistic'). With regard to the last-named characteristic, it is no doubt possible to draw different conclusions as to the extent to which it is a universal trait of bodybuilding performance. For one thing, there are considerable individual differences between bodybuilders in the degree to which they seek to interact with their audience, and in any case the extent to which such interaction is possible differs in the "compulsory" and "free" posing of which competition is made up. The extreme concentration required by any high-level competitive sport is here directed toward the body itself, in maintaining the "pump" and flexion of the muscles; in this sense, the self-absorption of the bodybuilder may not differ greatly from that of the diver standing on the platform and mentally rehearsing the movement of his or her body in a high dive.

If the term "self-absorption" accurately conveys the self-directed concentration of the posing display, a more revealing indication of its distinctive and perhaps unique character as a form of spectacle is the alternative term "self-containment." The pose does not look beyond itself; it is meaningful only in terms of the body's ability to suggest, by its inherent expressivity of mass and gesture, the exaltation of physical existence.

In this sense, the bodybuilding display can be compared to ballet, not to those scenes in which the performers advance the action by way of a superior and aesthetic mime related to the events of the plot, but to those in which the action is halted and a dancer performs a bravura solo in which the body expresses nothing beyond an inner mood. Even here the analogy falters, however, because what the bodybuilder seeks to express has about it nothing cerebral, no reflection of an interior life, but the evocative power of the body itself, the ability of visible form to conjure up in the minds of those who understand its language deep-seated images and fantasies of perfection and completeness. There is little difference in principle between such a form of contemplation and the delight of the mathematician confronted by a "perfect" theoretical equation, the rapt wonderment of a musicologist studying a Bach fugue, or the intent admiration of an art-lover standing before an abstract sculpture by Brancusi. In each case, the intimation of formal perfection is real, though it can be appreciated only by those who have learned the language of the medium by which it is conveyed. In each case, as in the so-called classical ideal of art, form takes precedence over content; in one sense, indeed, the form *is* the content.

The posing display suggests self-containment because it is not "about" anything other than itself. The so-called "archer" pose, for example, mimics the bodily attitude of a person drawing a long-bow in a lunging position; its reference, however, is not in any sense to the sport of archery but purely to the muscular configuration and line of the body which can be displayed in that particular position. The 'three-quarters twisting back pose' is precisely that of the antique *Torso Belvedere* and one of the *ignudi* (sometimes known as "The Athlete") from Michelangelo's Sistine Chapel ceiling. Once again, there is no sense in which the pose "refers" to these artistic works, of which the bodybuilder – and no doubt most of his audience – are very likely unaware given their cultural background; it is rather that the bodybuilder, like the artist, has chosen that pose because it expresses a potentiality of the body. Handed down to the contemporary poser by his predecessors (the art-studio models), it reveals in Clark's words 'a compelling rhythmic force [which] drives every inflection of the human body before it' (1960: 199). Like its artistic forerunners, the pose indicates nothing beyond the power of human anatomy to transform itself into an instrument of expression.

Pursuing the terms of Margaret Walters' analysis, we can discuss in closer detail her reference to the co-existence of 'super-masculine' and 'surreally feminine' characteristics in the bodybuilder's physique. In its fundamental shape and outline, the latter is unmistakably, even aggressively, masculine, emitting precisely those super-normal stimuli of masculinity to which we have already referred. The ideal bodybuilding physique, says Robert Kennedy,

> should have wide shoulders, trim hips, a small waist, arms with balanced development from the wrist to the shoulders, legs that flow aesthetically from the hips to the knees, and then into a full calf development. The lats should be wide, but not too much at the lower lats. The neck should be developed equally on all sides. Pectoral muscles should be built up in all aspects, especially the upper and outer chest region. The glutes should be rounded but not overly heavy in appearance. The overall muscle separation and definition should be clearly visible when contracted or flexed.
>
> (1985: 98–99)

The broad shoulders, trim hips, wide latissimus dorsi, small buttocks, and relatively thick neck are all super-normal masculine stimuli. All of them, it will be noted, are characteristics of body shape and are visible features of the body when seen in silhouette. The development of the pectoral muscles, on the other hand – what Walters refers to as the 'exaggerated breast development' of the male bodybuilder – seems somehow to be of a different order, having more to do with the modeling of the skin surface and the tactile quality of body-texture than with the outline of the body. It is here that we enter into a world of body-imagery strangely different from that of masculine stimuli.

The tactile quality of the body's surface is clearly an important component of the messages emitted by the bodybuilder's physique. The skin, as psychologists have recognized, has a vital role in erotogenic stimulation, related as it is to the considerable suggestive power of the sense of touch.

Physical love-making is intensely reliant on touching, and certain parts of the body (the so-called "erogenous zones") are especially sensitive to erotic messages conveyed by stroking, kissing, fondling or other forms of skin-to-skin contact. The powerful imaginative force of tactile messages is so great that the mere sight of bare skin can act as an erotic stimulus, without the need for actual touching to take place (Rudofsky 1971: 212). (The same applies, it should be noted, to tactile experiences involving non-human objects: fur, leather, silk and velvet, as well as garments associated with another person, can all act as erotic agents and take on the patho-logical dimensions of fetishism.) The erotic role of the skin itself is inti-mately associated with the polarized attitudes toward the display of nakedness which have long been characteristic of Western society.

While skin is not of itself a purely female characteristic, as a mode of conveying bodily messages it belongs to a different order from that of super-masculine stimuli. The latter are all related to the outline of the body, and are observable even when the body is clothed; indeed, some male clothing (from padded shoulders to tight-fitting jeans) is designed to accentuate the super-masculine body shape. Bare skin, however – endowed with all the erotic overtones mentioned above – is suggestive of the body-as-object rather than the body-as-agent, of the "sex that is looked at" rather than the "sex that looks." To present the skin surface as an "object of the gaze" is not a traditional male dominance signal, but on the contrary a sign of submissiveness or seductiveness. Not for nothing did the erotic tradition in art, from the seventeenth to the nineteenth century, typically depict a clothed male in the presence of a nude female – never the other way round.

That a man should bare his body for presentation to the objectifying or fantasizing gaze of others – whether women or (even more) other men – is so signal a departure from Western sexual convention that it would almost be unthinkable as a public spectacle but for the simultane-ous display of super-masculine stimuli which obliterate or even deny any suggestion of female role play and provide a sexual "neutral ground." The legitimizing context of the posing display leaves the spectator's mind, if not "erotically numb," at any rate erotically uncertain. Not so much transcending sexuality as rendering it illegible, the bodybuilder's perform-ance aims at a kind of sexual self-containment which sublimates desire.

THE TRANSFIGURED BODY

Over the years of its evolution, bodybuilding has adopted a set of conven-tions related to the grooming and attiring of the body for competition and public display. Designed to enhance the visible muscularity of the physique, these measures have an obvious cosmetic purpose and can readily be understood in terms which apply also to other types of public spectacle: the bodybuilder, like other performers, must appear "in character." Like stage make-up and costume, these are part of the accepted practice of theatrical presentation and are aimed at the improvement of the performer's appearance. At a deeper level, however, the conventions of presentation can be related to the implicit metaphorical language of the developed body, and can be read in symbolic terms as significant (if subliminal) elements of the message it transmits. Some of these practices have subsequently been transposed from the specific context of competitive bodybuilding into other, more general spheres (such as film and advertising) which make use of the expressive character of muscular development.

The shaving of body hair is a case in point. Since the super-normal stimuli of masculinity are to be found in those characteristics by which male and female bodies are most sharply differentiated, one would expect that the presence of male body hair would be an important component of the messages of the muscular body. Yet the opposite is the case. Competition bodybuilders shave all exposed parts of the body, including the chest (where necessary), legs, and armpits. The common and most obvious explanation of this practice is that body hair tends to conceal muscular shape, so that the definition and striation of muscles are not visible. In this and a number of other aspects of body presentation, however, the obvious practical explanation, while entirely valid so far as it goes, is only a part of the total picture. If its practical purpose were accepted as the complete explanation of the practice of body shaving, there would be no reason why the underarm should be shaved, since it is not the site of a muscle group. The practice of body shaving, in both men and women, clearly has an additional set of connotations connected with the heightened messages conveyed by hairless skin.

In this respect as in several others, the conventions of bodybuilding have merely articulated in somewhat exaggerated form a set of widely held, if latent, cultural attitudes toward the body. Given the significance of facial and bodily hair as biological markers of masculinity, the male ideal might logically be the figure of a hirsute, bearded he-man; yet in fact the masculine images portrayed in Western media as ideal models are those of lithe, smooth-bodied youths. Only by reference to the symbolic language by which the body has been interpreted in the Western cultural tradition can we understand the conventions underlying this shift.

The shaving of the whole or parts of the body has been practiced in human societies since primitive times, sharpened stones having originally been used as a form of neolithic razor. The practice has possessed various kinds of significance – religious, political, social or sexual – from one culture to another. In ancient Egypt, both men and women commonly shaved their heads and bodies, possibly as a matter of hygiene (Gunn 1973: 31); in ancient Greece, the athletes who appeared naked in the gymnasium or arena were known to go so far as to shave (or pluck out) their pubic hair (Rudofsky 1971: 94). In contemporary Western society, certain parts of the body only (the face for men, the legs and underarm for women) are commonly shaved. The wearing of a beard is more frequent amongst certain male groups – academics and students, for instance – just as unshaven legs among women may be a social sign of feminism. The shaving of the head has often been required by authorities as a mark of submission: prisoners of war have had their heads shaved to humiliate them, and men and women who join religious orders have traditionally received the tonsure as a sign of humility and devotion (Polhemus 1973: 141).

Although the various messages involved in shaving are complex and disparate, it is possible to hazard some suggestions as to those connected with the modern bodybuilding display. The anthropologist Robert Brain has suggested that the shaving of body hair is associated with man's desire to make "cultural" human qualities prevail over "natural" beastly attributes, to distinguish us as humans from brute creation around us. As he states: 'A hairy body is an animal body. Wild men, like Esau the hunter, are hairy. Body hair is beastly and has to go in the interests of humanity' (1979: 146–147). This distinction appears to have prevailed in fifth-century Greece, where the civilized, "Apollonian" bodies of gods and athletes were hairless while those of more elemental, "Dionysiac" figures were often misshapen and hairy. Other ancient cultures used a somewhat different symbolism: R.D. Guthrie notes, for instance, that in earlier and more authoritarian Western societies 'full beards, woolly chests, and rancid odours reinforced the lines of authority by giving a rather awesome or even fearsome visage.' As he writes:

> Hairiness is associated with most of the more important components of status – sex, age and size. It is easy to see why, in the locker room, a hairy body is nothing to be ashamed of. In a society that must emphasise co-operation and de-emphasise direct serious competition, excess hair may be too gross for most tastes, because it is a symbol for rough masculinity. If the best key to physical prowess among humans is the amount of body hair, the corollary is the more body hair, the greater the intimidation.
>
> (1976: 67)

In relation to facial hair, Guthrie's observation certainly accords with a number of social practices, from that of the heavily bearded kings of Persia and the Pharaohs of Egypt (who wore false beards on ceremonial occasions to emphasize their power and authority) to that of the biker gangs of today who often cultivate beards as part of the image of fearsomeness.

In the case of the bodybuilder's shaven body, it is doubtful that the message has directly to do with co-operation as the opposite of intimidation. On the other hand, it could have a good deal to do with a slightly different antithesis proposed by Guthrie: that between the older male and the baby or new-born, baby skin being 'our standard of inoffensive child-like beauty (p. 67). He suggests a variant form of the behavior known as *neoteny* – the reversion to an earlier state of evolution or life-cycle – which he calls 'social neoteny' (p. 159): this is a particular means of reducing the messages of intimidation by reverting to a more childlike appearance. Nakedness, a hairless body and smooth skin texture are all forms of social neoteny, signaling a childlike non-threatening quality and thus denying messages of aggression. In the light of such suggestive (if not conclusive) evidence, it could be argued that the point of shaving the body is to contradict, and thus neutralize, the aggressive or intimidating message of the super-normal adult male body shape: to demonstrate, in other words, that this is not a body to be feared on account of its dominance, but rather to be looked at or touched – a body that places itself in the submissive role of "object."

It is clear, in any case, that the hairless body conveys a particular message or set of messages, possibly related to the attenuation of hyper-masculinity by the enhancing of those submissive tactile qualities associated with the skin of the infant. So pervasive has the association become that body waxing and electrolysis for men is becoming increasingly common in some Western societies. The proprietor of a firm specializing in men's skin care has reported a marked trend towards hair-free torsos and limbs:

> . . .the increase in hair removal for men [she says] reflected a reversal of roles. While women had undergone treatment for years, men were following suit. Women's aesthetic expectations of men were such that many gave their husbands or boyfriends gift cards for treatment. A lot of the women tend to send the guys to have it done.
>
> (Mostyn 1991)

It would appear that the influence of bodybuilding on the presentation of the male body has extended, possibly by way of the film and television screen, into the wider world of social fashion, and that it has been affected at least to some extent by the increasing acceptance of the male body as an object of aesthetic or erotic contemplation.

In a number of its manifestations – from heroic art to the erotic pin-up – the history of muscular body display has been that of the nude male body. On the other hand, the one part of the bodybuilder's physique that is always kept covered is the genital region. Again, the most obvious explanation – social mores, the need for decency and a respectable sporting image, the avoidance of erotic overtones – is entirely correct but not entirely complete. It is well known, for instance, that penile display is an important part of the intimidation behavior of primates other than man, and it would follow that it, like hairiness, must be reduced to the minimum if the messages of sexual (or other) aggression are to be neutralized. We may note here the unusually small size of the penis in many nude sculptures of the Classical period, and more than one commentator has pointed to the apparent discrepancy between the bulging muscles of the bodybuilder and the apparent tininess of the male organ hidden beneath the posing trunks (Guthrie 1976: 84). Those who have seen professional bodybuilders naked will attest, not only to the unfoundedness of this assumption, but also to the remarkable adaptability of the male sexual organs and the compressive powers of Lycra. According to the interpretation proposed here, this is precisely the point of the exercise: once again, it is to neutralize the aggressive sexual message of the male body, in this case by giving the genital region the inoffensive and undeveloped appearance of the baby or pre-pubertal youth. In contemporary bodybuilding practice, posing trunks are worn as brief as possible, as if to reinforce the neutralizing message.

In the ancient world, the diminutive and almost childlike penises of Greek vase paintings (and, to a lesser extent the often disproportionately small sexual organs of heroic statuary) contrasted markedly with the exaggerated phalluses seen on satyrs, in pornographic figures and in Dionysiac celebration. The latter tradition is still reflected in homosexual toilet graffiti, of which Delph writes: 'If one compares the proportions of the penis and testes to the rest of the torso in these drawings, they assume enormous size . . . the larger the penis, the more virile the individual is thought to be, enhancing the amount of attention he receives' (1978: 71).

At a more generally acceptable level of eroticism, it is a fact well attested by those "in the business" – though seldom publicly admitted – that the G-strings and posing trunks worn by male strippers are commonly padded so as to give the genital region an appearance of greater size. As distinct from the bodybuilder's miniaturizing trunks, the "posing pouch" favored in the sexually provocative physique magazines of the 1960s tends to draw attention to the genital area, often revealing a few tufts of pubic hair. The subsequent banning of this form of dress in competition bodybuilding may have had less to do with what it actually revealed (modern posing trunks are practically just as abbreviated, and any visible pubic hair is shaved) than with the extent to which it accentuated the bulge of the genitals.

Over the last ten years or so, male posing trunks have tended to be cut higher at the rear, exposing at least the lower half of the buttocks. This practice has become more common since a number of leading bodybuilders, beginning with Richard Gaspari, have made a feature of their impressive gluteal striation (the visible separation of muscle-bands in the gluteus maximus or large muscle of the buttocks). As in previous instances, however, there are perhaps more latent suggestions underlying this development in fashion. Unlike the male sexual organs, the buttocks are seen as non-intimidating, a symbol of passivity associated with infancy or childhood: a baby's bottom can be patted, pinched or even admired for its "dimples." Women's bodybuilding costume (like some women's beachwear) is often cut so as to leave some, if not all, of the buttocks exposed; the recent adoption of this fashion for men, as in the G-strings or "thongs" which are now worn on some beaches, can here be seen as a further shift in gender roles which has rendered the male body an acceptable object of aesthetic or erotic curiosity.

The skin which the bodybuilder exposes to our gaze is hardly ever the "natural" skin, but rather a skin surface which has been subjected to processes designed to enhance the message of muscular development. In Sandow's generation, the practice was to cover the already pale skin with a coating of white powder, in order to stress its resemblance to marble statuary. By the 1930s, however, social customs had undergone considerable change as the leisured classes had both the time and the means to take summer holidays, usually in a sunny climate.[3] This meant a complete reversal in fashion as compared with earlier generations in which tanned skin was the mark of the peasant or the outdoor laborer: the tan now became the badge of the upper classes, as the French Riviera and the beaches of Rio became the favorite resorts of the wealthy. Pale skin was the sign of the lowly office or factory worker, whose long working day was spent entirely indoors. The association with leisure and exercise gave rise to the notion of the "healthy tan," which soon took over from the earlier pale skin as the new bodybuilding convention. By the time of the leading American bodybuilder of the 1940s, John Grimek, it had established itself completely and has since become almost mandatory.

Even in the present age, where the dangers of exposure to ultra-violet light are well publicized and the medical profession issues frequent warnings of the risk of melanoma or skin cancer, there is no sign of a change in the convention of bodybuilding, and the tanned body is the universal norm. This being the case, it is probably fortunate from the medical point of view that those who do not tan easily have access to a wide range of chemical body dyes, tanning lotions, vegetable-based "body-stains," canthaxanthin (or Vitamin A) tablets and a host of other artificial means of producing the desired color. That the tan is fake is unimportant: it is essentially a form of stage make-up. The skin need not *be* tanned, but it must *look* tanned.

The metaphorical meaning of the convention is not far to seek, and is even clearer when seen in conjunction with the other chief mode of skin preparation: the oiling of the body. Though much disputed as late as the 1960s, the coating of the skin with a light layer of oil is now standard practice. If inexperienced bodybuilders tend to overdo the effect and present the glistening spectacle of a body which appears to be wrapped in cellophane, more seasoned competitors seek the effect of a low sheen rather than a high gloss.

The tanned and oiled body replaces the symbolic associations of marble with those of polished bronze: the glint of light on the rounded muscle surface contrasts with the deep color of the depressions, so that the musculature stands out in dramatic and highly tactile contrast, a dark and polished surface which emphasizes the rises and hollows of the muscles more vividly than can be achieved by the pale, matt texture of marble. The association is even more obvious in French, where the terms *bronzé* and *bronzage* are used to refer to tanned skin. The rise to eminence of a number of black bodybuilders in recent years, though mainly attributable to their genetic endowment and often formidable muscularity, has no doubt been assisted by the fact that their deeply colored and naturally polished skin allows them to achieve the sought-after effect without resorting to artificial means.

The visual effect in question is often described by bodybuilders themselves as "looking hard," an optical impression which suggests the tactile firmness of the flexed muscle. At the level of metaphorical suggestion, however, the aim is not simply to resemble the appearance of burnished bronze, but to convey what the bronze statue and the bronze-like body alike suggest to us. No art-form, not even sculpture, is more purely concerned than the bronze with the visible *surface* of things: it is in its surface, says Jennifer Montagu, that the supreme quality of bronze resides, its particular effect being chiefly dependent on 'the interplay of its shapes and the movement of light and shade on its modelling' (1963: 9, 16). The frequently made bronze copies of marble statues seem to speak a different language from that of their originals, the translation of light-absorbing stone into light-reflecting metal concentrating all attention on the outward play of highlights and shadows. Its dark, gleaming surface is suggestive of impenetrability or even invulnerability, as Jean-Paul Sartre recognized when he made the bronze statue in his play *Huis Clos* ('In Camera') the symbol of the inanimate world of fixed being as distinct from the human world of shifting inner consciousness.

Yet the body we see on the stage is not a statue, an attitude captured at a moment of time. We are in fact conscious of opposing and neutralizing messages: this medium of representation is not impenetrable metal, but living and resilient flesh. The body moves, it breathes; it is part of our human world of mutability and transience. The muscles flex and unflex, limbs are extended and retracted, the abdominals turn suddenly from a cavernous vacuum into a glistening washboard, the pectoral muscles are bounced up and down. The performer's face is at one moment serene and smiling, at the next contorted with effort; the body is now a road map of vascularity, an anatomical drawing, now a series of soft and rounded planes, as sweeping as though drawn with a compass. At once aloof and intensely present, the body we see before us belongs to both the world of inanimate objects and the world of subjectivity and feeling, to the world of fixed being and the world of becoming.

It is obvious that this sophisticated array of self-canceling messages of affirmation and denial could never have been designed or introduced as a pre-planned system. Despite its relatively recent origin, bodybuilding (like most sports) has evolved over the years more by experimentation and the processes of trial and error than by deliberate design. As innovations were introduced, they would either be adopted because they seemed somehow "right" or would be abandoned. As with any internally consistent but outwardly hermetic code, the elements can be developed and elaborated only by those who speak and understand the symbolic language by which it operates. Had anyone set out in advance to devise a means whereby the human body could suggest, purely by its own visible configuration and presentation, a totality of physical being which by subsuming and reconciling opposing qualities both completes and somehow transcends them, one may well doubt that such an enterprise could ever have been successfully achieved. Only the accumulated and refined perceptions wrought by centuries of cultural tradition could have endowed the developed body with such imaginative potential.

Notes

1 See, for example, Edward Lucie-Smith (1972: 50).
2 See John Passmore, *The Perfectibility of Man* (1970: 313–314) and Desmond Morris, *The Human Zoo* (1971: 188).
3 See Guthrie (1976: 164–165) and Stephen Bayley (1991: 151–153).

8   Flayed Animals in an Abattoir
The Bodybuilder as Body-Garde[1]

Adam Locks

This chapter examines the aesthetic implications of extreme (i.e. competitive) bodybuilders. Elsewhere I refer to such bodies as "Post Classic" (see Introduction, this volume). By this I refer to a body that remains rooted in the classical style – but a style which has been applied very selectively, creating what I consider to be a new ideal, a hyper-muscular, but essentially fragmented body, in which the sculpting of individual body parts and the display of body poses have come to supplant the whole body. I want to debate whether such an aesthetic can be recuperable, particularly as bodybuilding is palpably transgressive and adheres to certain features of the avant-garde.

MUSCLE AESTHETICS

Aesthetic images of the muscular male have been evident throughout history; more specifically, in ancient Greece, the Renaissance, the late nineteenth century and throughout the twentieth century, the muscular male body has been celebrated in sculpture, painting, drawing and latterly photography. The contemporary is marked by the ubiquity of images of such bodies in magazines, television, cinema, adverts and other forms of media and so to possess such a look is to be considered to live up to what is known as the "mesomorphic" ideal, a term signifying a man who is lean with high levels of muscular definition – assumed to be the result of healthy exercise. However, as many commentators have noted, men desire to be mesomorphic not for reasons of health and fitness, but for the symbolism this muscularity has latterly come to signify: sexual attractiveness, self-discipline, and personal success. There is nothing new in seeing the body being linked to socially and culturally motivated ends as evinced by Nazi Germany's idolization of the muscular male. The Renaissance was also a key period where various depictions of the muscular male were established. The art historian Margaret Walters comments how Florence 'put a new premium on aggressive individualism, mobility and competitiveness' and, she continues, 'those qualities are seen as defining a man' (1978: 11).

Thus commentators have suggested that the 1980s also reflected a similar period where such "individualism" was significant. For instance, John Rutherford suggested that one 'of the nastier fall-out effects of the Thatcher (and Reagan) revolution [was the] glorification of strength and masculinity which comes as a side effect of the culture of success' (1992: 175). This did seem especially evident in the Hollywood action films during the 1980s and early 1990s, many of which featured bodybuilders in the leading role. In ascending order of size, Jean Claude Van Damme, Sylvester Stallone, Dolph Lundgren, and Arnold Schwarzenegger all possessed bodies whose hyper-muscularity was critically considered to reflect the politics of America at the time. As Yvonne Tasker observed of the *Rambo* series of movies: 'The pumped-up figure of Stallone seemed to offer more than just a metaphor, functioning for various cultural commentators as the literal embodiment of American interventionism [in Vietnam]' (1994: 92). Commentators have also noted that this muscular representation was also palpable when looking at toys sold to young boys (see Richardson, Chapter 9, this volume). According to a study by Harrison Pope, Kate Phillips, and Roberto Olivardia, bulked-up action figures in the toy market – exemplified by the G.I. Joe doll and *Star Wars* action figures – have 'acquired the physiques of bodybuilders, with bulging "pecs" (chest muscles) and "delts" (shoulders)' (2000: 43).

At the same time, since the late 1980s there has been much discussion over a so-called "crisis in masculinity" and there has been much debate about what the rise of the mesomorph means. Considered as a crisis, by 2000, Anthony Clare could identify the male predicament as follows:

> Serious commentators declare that men are redundant, that women do not need them and children would be better off without them. At the beginning of the twenty-first century it is difficult to avoid the conclusion that men are in serious trouble.
>
> (2000: 3)

For Clare and other cultural commentators such as Robert Bly and Roger Horrocks, this crisis has come because men have lost their dominance in the home and in the workplace. The reasons for this loss are varied, yet the main factors can be related to increasing levels of consumerism, feminism, and a pervasive abhorrence for traditional versions of masculinity (Whitehead and Barrett 2001: 6). As a result of these changes in gender roles and, also, the value placed upon the body itself, body ideals have become increasingly exaggerated (Dutton 1995: 346). It is often noted that this is marked by an application to the male body of the types of advertising images which were once reserved for women. Certainly, from the mid-1980s onward, advertising has become notable for featuring muscular men, for instance in Calvin Klein's advertising campaigns. Although there are other different images of masculinity on offer – for example, androgynous males and muscular males – the meso-morphic figure is the more ubiquitous in media imagery and so allegedly the more desirable (for men and women). Indeed, an ideal of men that are muscular and women that are slim has become noticeably more pronounced, especially since the 1980s. Again, thinking in terms of "crisis," the psychologist Marc Mishkind discusses these changes via his "polarization" model where such ideals 'may be a reaction against sexual equality, an expression of a wish to preserve some semblance of traditional male-female differences' (quoted in Persaud 2001: 537). Female bodybuilding provides an example of the complex relationship which men and women have gained toward the modifiable body.

These issues surrounding the body have necessarily been tied to issues of identity. Discussing consumption and identity in 1991, Mike Featherstone claimed that individuals today were increasingly being encouraged to follow practices of 'body maintenance' (1991: 182). As Featherstone defines it, 'body maintenance' refers to a process whereby men (and women) are encouraged to adhere to 'idealised images prolifer-ated in the media' which, in turn, increases the body's own 'exchange-value' (ibid.: 177). The key characteristic of 'body maintenance' has been the hard muscular body – the antithesis of which is fatness, often projected in the media as signaling personal failure and apathy (Ewen 1985: 189). The hard and muscular body has become an indicator of social and cultural worth in film and advertising where idealized images of the meso-morph have been most commonly represented. However, in the same year (1991) Anthony Giddens argued for a concept of the body which posi-tioned it not as a victim, but as a territory to be reclaimed. Giddens claimed that since these changes in social roles were a product of late modernity (rather than postmodernity) they offered a 'reflexive project of the self.' This means, as Giddens wrote, that: 'the body is less and less an intrinsic 'given', functioning outside the internally referential systems of modernity, but becomes itself reflexively mobilised' (ibid.: 7). This theme of the reflexive project of the self has been expanded upon considerably by many critics since (see Richardson, Chapter 9, this volume). For instance, Susan Bordo defines the contemporary body as 'cultural plastic,' in reference to the various ways in which bodies can be modified and manipulated through exercise, diet and also surgery (1999: 246). As such the body becomes the contemporary site of what is quite literally to be considered as *self-expression* (even to the extent that obesity has been argued to be a justifiable state). Most recently, the role of modifications of the body which are transgressive has gained considerable critical atten-tion and practices such as piercing, tattooing, and branding have likewise been considered to be part of a self-reflexive attitude to the body.

Yet in women's professional bodybuilding, this transgressiveness has been curbed. Since 2000, the IFBB has placed a cap on the degree of size and "rippedness" permitted in women's bodybuilding, with the emphasis placed on smaller and more "feminine" competitors illustrated by the Dutch bodybuilding champion Juliette Bergmann (see Bolin, Chapter 1, this volume). Upon winning the 2000 Ms. Olympia title, Bergmann announced: 'The future of this sport is to promote women who are sexy and beautiful – that's the example I will set as the reigning Ms. Olympia' (Rosenthal 2002: 114).

For male bodybuilders no such compromise has emerged – indeed as I have argued elsewhere (Locks 2003), these developments in female bodybuilding themselves acted as a concession to the men, and so have not slowed down the male quest for even greater mass and ultra-shredded muscularity in the least. At the 2002 Mr. Olympia, Ronnie Coleman faced a competitor who threatened to usurp his Mr. Olympia crown: Jay Cutler. Cutler was a bodybuilder who showed a size and level of conditioning that seriously contested Coleman's position. Journalist Ron Harris observes: 'How could anyone even come close to beating Ronnie Coleman, a genetic mutant who trains with heavier weights and more intensity than any other bodybuilder alive today (or in the past, to be sure)? Jay Cutler was actually ahead of the now four-time Mr. Olympia after prejudging ended for the 2001 contest' (2002: 110). Cutler, who has since won the Olympia title three times, is viewed by many as heralding an even greater phase of extremity in the sport.

Thus, as I asked at the beginning of this chapter: does this reveal that even if it is the result of near perverse social practices, the aesthetic *image* of the contemporary male bodybuilder can be considered recuperable? Bodybuilding, like the body modification subcultures from which it is often excluded, blatantly rebels against definitions of the "normal" and conventional. Look no further than the comment of the psychologist quoted by Kenneth Dutton who described competition level bodybuild-ers as 'straining, fleshless monsters with ugly knotted and veined torsos, suggesting nothing so much as flayed animals in an abattoir' (Dutton 1995: 278). Bodybuilding has not only always been open to such criti-cism, it has already successfully challenged these boundaries with the example of Arnold Schwarzenegger in the 1970s. In doing so, it trans-gressed ideals of physical perfection and, conversely, ugliness and extremity. As such, perhaps questions of art ought to intervene.

Relevant here is Lisa Lyon. Lyon was the first female bodybuilder to gain critical attention from the major magazines. As bodybuilding jour-nalist and photographer Bill Dobbins once gushed: 'She combined body-building poses with a series of graceful, aesthetic, and athletic transitions in a style that became the model for presentation still used by women today' (1994: 26). Lyon perhaps became one of the better-known female bodybuilders because of her work during the early 1980s with the photographer Robert Mapplethorpe. Of their initial encounter, Mapplethorpe recalled: 'I had never seen a woman like that before . . . It was like looking at someone from another planet' (Morrisroe 1995:

231). A woman 'like that' had also never been seen working out at Gold's Gym and although the owner – bodybuilder Ken Sprague – was most keen to rid the gym of its gay image, he was less willing to encourage the opposite sex to take up membership and Lyon remained exceptional (231–232). Highly unconventional in her training at Gold's Gym – for example, she would regularly use LSD rather than steroids to help her weight train – Lyon attracted a significant amount of media attention (232). She also became the first female bodybuilder to be given a color photo feature for Joe Weider in the 1979 July edition of the magazine *Muscle Builder*. Lisa Lyon aimed to surpass gender and Judith Stein notes that Lyon perceived herself as first a 'Performance Artist' and second a bodybuilder (Stein 1999: 21). For Lyon, her body *was* art. Stein places this in a wider artistic context when she explains:

> During the 1960s and 1970s, many avant-garde art works prominently featured performing bodies. Performance Artists, who were not necessarily trained as actors or dancers, used their bodies as their medium, gleefully scrambling distinctions between art and life, subject and object, and artist and model. One of the earliest examples was the British artistic team Gilbert and George, who in 1969 began exhibiting themselves as Living Sculpture.
>
> (ibid.: 24)

Although postmodern artists such as Gilbert and George have gained recognition and notoriety for proclaiming to be the first examples of "living sculpture" since the late 1960s, in fact they belong to a considerable artistic tradition which bodybuilding popularized (Farson 2000: 49). For example, popular interest in the muscular male body was such that in the early 1880s famous boxers such as John L. Sullivan and William Muldoon acted as examples of "living statuary" in which they were paid to be viewed by audiences standing in "artistic" poses considered to be evocative of ancient Greece (Budd 1997: 36).

Art critic James Hall comments how it was during the latter part of the nineteenth century that many public "heroic" statues were erected in a period of, what he terms, 'statuemania' (1999: 230). Hall remarks statuemania became usurped after the Second World War due to 'an increase in abstract monuments' typified by the prolific Henry Moore (ibid.: 243–244). A return to the representational art might therefore be found displaced into the flesh sculpture of bodybuilding – as the term "body sculpting" which has been used in American and British gyms instead of bodybuilding suggests (see Heywood, Chapter 6, this volume). (It should also be pointed out that numerous bodybuilders have compared the process of bodybuilding to a sculptor at work, most notably Schwarzenegger in *Pumping Iron*.) However, bodybuilder Frank Zane's comparison of his body with sculpture was ridiculed by an art academic who replied: 'If you are a work of art, you had a bad teacher because, to me, your poses are the personification of nineteenth-century camp' (Stein 1999: 24). However, it is only in artistic referents such as camp or performance art that a potential recuperation of the image of the contemporary bodybuilder might lie.

In this respect – and here we come to the crux of the chapter – bodybuilding shares a selection of traits with the avant-garde which similarly aimed to disturb and disrupt. In his *Dictionary of the Avant-Gardes,* Richard Kostelanetz defines the term thus:

> Used precisely, avant-garde should refer, first, to rare work that on its first appearance satisfies three discriminatory criteria: It transcends current aesthetic conventions in crucial respects, establishing discernible distance between itself and the mass of recent practices; it will necessarily take considerable time to find its maximum audience; and it will probably inspire future, comparably advanced endeavours.
>
> (2001: xix)

Professional bodybuilding generally adheres to these criteria. First, considering the history of bodybuilding, those viewed as the top bodybuilders in the sport have always transcended the more moderate aesthetic conventions of the mesomorphic body; most notably, Eugene Sandow during the Physical Culture movement in the nineteenth century. The admiration accorded Sandow's physique was such that his body was examined, detailed, and recorded by scientific authorities. In 1893 the Director of Gymnastics at Harvard University, Doctor Sargent, took measurements from Sandow for his research, while, shortly after Professor Ray Lankester made a plaster cast of his whole body for exhibition in the Natural History Museum in London (Webster 1982: 32–33).

More recently, there has been the example of Greg Kovacs who competed for just over ten years from 1995. Canadian Greg Kovacs allegedly weighed 350 lbs in competition and managed to be ripped (if not yet shredded). His popularity in hard-core bodybuilding magazines such as *Flex, Ironman* and *MuscleMag* came from his embodiment of two key features of bodybuilding: one related to the competition arena and the other to the training gym. Bodybuilding has always been concerned with increasing muscle mass and, thus, Kovacs' size apparently made him symbolize the future of the sport. However, in another way, admiration for him functioned more anachronistically. All top bodybuilders lift tremendous weights, yet Kovacs' ability to lift was legendary within bodybuilding: barbell rows of 545 lbs, flat dumbbell presses of 250 lbs, squats of 855 lbs, and leg presses using up to 40 plates are typical (Schmidt 1997: 149, 151). The focus in the magazines on his exceptional ability is reminiscent of the early physique contests in which strength was seen as a vital demonstration of successful bodily development. Thus Kovacs, even though he was not a consistent winner of major titles, and indeed never won a Mr. Olympia, nevertheless remained – and still remains – a source of fascination for bodybuilding fans.

A further factor to realize is that body weights refer to bodybuilders who have dieted down for competition. During the off-season (when a bodybuilder is not competing) most bodybuilders are many pounds heavier. Kovacs, who weighed in at over 400 lbs in the off-season, was 100 lbs heavier than any other professional bodybuilder out of competition (Hesse 2001: 179). Bodybuilders in the past were often exceptionally heavy in the off-season, typified by Bruce Randall in the 1950s who weighed up to 410 lbs (and stated that he could have reached 500 lbs if he so wished) (Webster 1982: 100–101) and although off-season is traditionally a period when a bodybuilder could, ironically, sometimes be considered fat, continual advances in training, nutrition, cosmetic alteration, drugs, and perhaps relatively soon, gene manipulation may make a 400 lb ripped competitive bodybuilder a reality. Until then the apparent genetic advantage possessed by bodybuilders such as Kovacs will suffice. It is noticeable that Kovac's genetic inheritance was lauded in the following fantastic description of his birth given in the August 1997 edition of *Flex* magazine: 'In the silent, brittle, predawn cold of December 16, 1968, on a tranquil farm muffled with snow outside Ontario, Canada, the great northern tundra cracked, a caldera gaped, a fissure hissed, magma spewed to the heavens and Greg Kovacs was born' (Schmidt 1997: 146). With such blatant (though probably unconscious) vaginal imagery, Kovacs' emergence is given all the resonance of Greek myth, with his propensity toward size given all the wonderment and unfeigned splendour of the birth of a god; he was quite simply represented as another "authentic" wonder of the world (and this has strong echoes of the constructed nature of the "freak" as discussed by Richardson, Chaptper 9, this volume). Such divinity apparently comes from the fact that Kovacs was "naturally" big and muscular. As the reader was told in a 1997 issue of *Flex*, this 'plinian eruption of muscle' already weighed 240 lbs at the age of seventeen before even starting weight training (Schmidt 1997: 146). At his largest, Schwarzenegger's chest measured 57 inches, his biceps 22 inches, and his quadriceps 28.5 inches (http://www.bodybuilders.com/arnold.htm, accessed August 18, 2010); this compares with Kovacs' chest that was measured at 70 inches, biceps 26 inches, and thighs around 35 inches (http://www.bodybuildingpro.com/gregkovacs.html, last accessed August 16, 2010). Bruce Randall's off-season weight was 400 lbs and at this he looked obese, and yet at this same off-season weight Kovacs remained muscular (Schmidt 1997: 148). What is evident here is how Greg Kovacs' hypermorphic size reveals changes in the sport which have rendered past academic research and enquiry often outdated. Alan M. Klein wrote in 1993 that:

> Comic-book depictions of masculinity are so obviously exaggerated that they represent fiction twice over, as genre and as gender representation. But for bodybuilders these characters serve as role models.
>
> (1993: 267)

Klein's comment is verified by the nicknames bodybuilders are given once they reach a certain level of fame. Hence, Dorian Yates becomes the Shadow, Schwzarzenegger the Oak, Lee Priest the Blond Myth, Branch Warren the Quadrasaurus, and Dexter Jackson The Blade. However, given the size of Kovacs and other professional bodybuilders, these roles have reversed. Australian bodybuilder Lee Priest's physique was used as the model for the computer-animated version of *The Hulk* (dir. Ang Lee, 2003), a superhero with gargantuan physical development (http:// www.elitefitness.com/forum/entertainment-movies-tv/lee-priest-works-computer-double-new-hulk-movie-164450.html, accessed August 8, 10). Certain comic strips during the late 1980s, particularly those of *Image Comics*, began to exaggerate the size and shape of their male heroes to such a degree that as Scott Bukatman remarks in his analysis of masculinity and this medium: 'the superhero body becomes auto-referential and can only be compared to other superheroes bodies, rather than the common world of flesh, blood, muscle, and sinew' (1994: 106). Kovacs again proves this verdict premature. It is not comics but professional bodybuilding that has become auto-referential, since the hypermorphism on display is now beyond the archetype drawn upon by the comic book.

Second, although the popularity of professional bodybuilding remains subcultural, muscularity in general has become a desired commodity exemplified in various media discourses that can be seen as directly influenced by bodybuilding. This is also true athletically; athletes in other sports have also significantly increased in mass in recent years (palpably in American Football and rugby, especially since the latter's professionalization in the late 1990s). However, bodybuilding is atypical in that its competitors prize size for its own sake, and can still dramatically surpass previous achievements and records.

Thus, third, and to paraphrase Karl Frederick Robert writing on modernism, bodybuilding, like the avant-garde, is always 'point[ing] toward the future' and the further transgression of aesthetic standards, thus confirming its avant-garde status (1988: 15). Additionally, T.S. Eliot claimed that the roots of the avant-garde lay in a turn toward art as a means to combat the 'immense panorama of futility and anarchy which is contemporary history' (Pegrum 2000: 24); likewise bodybuilding magazines continually turn to the body to regulate the chaos of the world outside. For example, in response to the terrorist strike on the World Trade Center on September 11, 2001, a number of bodybuilding magazines (most notably *MuscleMag* and *Flex*) discussed bodybuilding in image and practice as a means for combating the terrorism. The editor-in-chief of *MuscleMag* responded to 9/11 thus:

> At times like these there is much for our elected leaders to do. Each of us, on the other hand, must renew our own resolve to become as strong in mind and body as we can . . . Try to be courageous in the presence of danger, and keep a cool head – but above all, keep up those visits to the gym! The best way to survive the destruction of what surrounds us is to not self-destruct. What every successful man thrives on is self-confidence against all odds – and superior muscle power takes you more than half way there.
>
> (Fitness 2002: 14)

Bodybuilding is often presented in magazines such as *Muscle and Fitness* as using the aestheticism of the body for personal and public salvation. This echoes Nietzsche's notion of the "Overman" (or Ubermensch), a difficult and often confusing term, but one loosely referring to what Dave Robinson calls those who are 'artistic creators of themselves that strive to go beyond human nature' (1999: 30). Daniel O'Brien reads the contemporary overman as concerned with the 'enhancement of the human species [using] technology, the modern Ariel, to aid him' (2000: 39). The most frequently imagined development is the cyborg, which is a human who has been technologically modified. The body-builder might be understood as a proto-cyborg: a body aesthetically redesigned through chemical and cosmetic surgery – and so in body-building magazines, the sport is often presented as in the vanguard of social change in its receptivity to the bio-technology which promises to transcend the human form.

However, notions of the avant-garde are themselves suspect. Steve Best and Douglas Kellner define the avant-garde as: 'a military metaphor that implies that artists are in the "front line" in bringing change . . . [in] existing culture and society in the project of creating new forms of art and life' (1997: 190). Such a definition is profoundly modernist in ambition and suggests why the avant-garde is often seen as no longer possible in postmodernism in a period where artifacts from the past are suggested to be constantly recycled. However, art critic Matthew Collings offers another possibility when he comments that the objective of postmodern art has become increasingly to shock its audience. In art, states Collings, 'the grim stream has become the mainstream'[2] an observation that I think applicable to the enormous, ripped, diced, sliced, and shredded appearance of bodybuilders. Although it may seem facile to compare bodybuilding and the work of the contemporary postmodern artists who for Collings exemplify this move toward the provocative and sometimes unpalatable – Damian Hurst, Jake Chapman, Dinos Chapman, and Paul McCarthy – there does appear a shared interest in an aesthetic of shock and a focus on the visceral. Whereas the avant-garde attempted to break the boundaries of representational art (for example, with Cubism, Vorticism, Futurism, Dadaism, Surrealism, and so forth), postmodern art has often attempted push at the boundaries of taste. We read something very similar in this description of the Post Classic professional bodybuilder. Greg Zulak writes:

> These guys are trying to become monsters and freaks. Their goal is to shock the audience with their level of size, development, and ripped-to-shreds muscularity. If this means the waist is blocky, or the abdominals are thick and bloated and hang out if not consciously held in, or the thighs are so big that they touch when a bodybuilder walks, but the guy's traps [trapezius] are up to his ears, or his upper arms are bigger than his head and out of proportion to his forearms, or the pecs bloated with bitch tits . . . so be it.
>
> (1997: 59)

There are some fascinating relationships to performance art here, ones which differentiate bodybuilding from body modification. Paul Sweetman notes that certain body modification practices – namely tattooing and piercing – represent an attempt to 'fix, or anchor one's sense of self through the (relative) permanence of the modification acquired' at a time where postmodern notions of identity suggest a play of surfaces and shifting signs (in Featherstone 2000: 71). But such permanence is precisely the identity which the professional bodybuilder cannot achieve. This is never more apparent than at the moment of contest when a bodybuilder is seen at his most dramatic, most ripped and shredded, most muscular, most vascular, and most fleeting. Several professional bodybuilders now compete for just the Mr. Olympia contest; Dorian Yates was well known for this. This meant that Yates' grueling exercise and diet regime over a year was all for a competition held on one day. The day of competition represents a climax so acute that bodybuilders appear noticeably more shredded and cut in the morning than the evening or vice versa. During his brief period as a competitive bodybuilder Sam Fussell noted: 'Even standing was excruciatingly painful. The soles of my feet, without their padding of fat, couldn't take my body weight' (1991: 22). Caught on camera, the photograph captures the transitory moment of 'peaking' where the bodybuilder is huge, sharp (or cut) and dry (dehydrated enough to reveal muscle separation). The photograph alone provides the bodybuilder with what he cannot have: lasting vitality.

As such does professional bodybuilding become an example of a naïve performance art? Andrew Graham-Dixon once described Francis Bacon's paintings as 'something like the manic celebration of someone who knows he does not have long to live but has decided (what the hell) to enjoy being alive while he can' (1996: 225). The bodybuilding aesthetic is certainly composed of the manic: manic eating, manic dieting, manic working out, and manic drug taking. All this is done for the singular moment of competition. Therefore, bodybuilding has, especially since the late 1970s, pushed against its own "classical" limits. Hence the irony that bodybuilding's continued move toward a kind of anti-aestheticism – a primary characteristic of the avant-garde – has made it derided and scorned (inside and outside the sport) as unacceptably transgressive, but equally not accepted by the art avant-garde.

NO LIMITS?

One final issue remains: how far can bodybuilding go? Andrew Blake has remarked: 'the performance curve is beginning to flatten. The strength and malleability of the body must have finite limits, whatever the resources of equipment, training, sports psychology and drugs: in the case of the male body in particular it may be close to those limits' (1996: 154). Is there a similar cul-de-sac in professional bodybuilding? When is big enough big enough?

In 1995 (former) magazine editor Bill Philips predicted the Mr. Olympia 2005 with a body weight of 335 lbs and 2 percent bodyfat at a height of 5'10" (1995: 11) while five years later, bodybuilding journalist Greg Merrit foresaw a future Mr. Olympia of 2010 who would stand 6'3" tall, weigh 405 lbs and have next to no bodyfat (2000: 91). Such predictions construct bodybuilding as a sport with muscular definition aplenty for many years to come, making bodybuilding noticeably different from other sports. Blake continues: 'it is beginning to appear that an end is in sight to the constant and astonishing rollback of record times and weights which have so far characterized the century of modern competitive sport. The pace of change in most men's records has slowed dramatically: new records are set in tenths of a second in many events' (1996: 154). But what is being dealt with here has two parameters: the limits of the *literal* and the limits of *judging*. In a 100-meter race, the literal limit does seem to have almost been reached and so it is extremely difficult to imagine an 8 second race ever being run. Bodybuilding may also have reached such a literal limit, however, its continued drug abuse and now other interventions such as Synthol have allowed increases in size to continue – in effect, if the International Olympic Committee were as lenient about the use of drugs as the IFBB, then times would be pushed back and records would be broken. However, it could be argued that in another way professional bodybuilding has reached a limit. The quadriceps of Branch Warren, the shoulder width of Markus Ruhl, the overall size of Jay Cutler, and the biceps of Lee Priest are already so big that fans are running out of superlatives and judges out of criteria. Hence, the second limit lies in judging, and an instructive comparison can be made to other aesthetically based sports, for instance ice-skating, a sport with similarities to bodybuilding since both are performed to music in front of a crowd, each is closely linked to show business, and both have judging criteria that rely on aesthetics. Until 2004, ice-skating marks ranged from 0.0 to 6.0, but recent debates provoked by the increasing award of perfect scores begged the question: how much better than a perfect 6.0 can a performance become? However, in bodybuilding this problem has existed for years and judging has been far from trans-historical. Scores sometimes stand still, but the aesthetic being assessed has not. Thus Schwarzenegger's perfect score of 20 in 1975, Lee Haney's score of 20 in 1990, and Ronnie Coleman's score of 20 in 1999, all gained the same marks, but they are clearly not the same bodies.[3] In other words, the problems for bodybuilding are compound: the invalid limits of the judging criteria would only be exposed if the limit of the literal were valid, but that would only happen if judges genuinely enforced the rules about substances, or at least did not reward their manifestation.

Somewhat ironically, the catalyst for the Post Classical trajectory – Arnold Schwarzenegger – has suggested that the only way forward is to curb the use of drugs by altering the IFBB's rules so as to penalize size. He recommends:

> The fastest way to get rid of performance enhancing drugs in bodybuilding is to change the rules to pay less attention to size. You can't simply say, "We're going to test you all". That hasn't worked with any sport, from the Tour de France to the Olympic Games. Not only should the judging criteria change for judging physiques, but also performances should become a large part of the equation. If a guy hits 30 perfect poses, including splits and handstands, to great music, he gets a perfect 10. Anything short of that is a 9, or an 8, and so on. If a guy lumbers out with a distended stomach and hits three or four perfunctory poses before falling apart, he gets a zero! He can be the biggest guy in the world, but he doesn't get a point in that round. Posing would become critical, and training would head off in a much different direction, placing more emphasis on cardiovascular fitness to sustain extended, more elaborate posing routines.
>
> (O'Connell 2000: 50)

What other options exist to control or halt bodybuilding's ever onward moving dynamic aesthetic? One preference might be to radically amend the judging criteria in a similar fashion to that of women's bodybuilding in 2000; such a sea-change did dramatically stop the forward direction of the female aesthetic (admittedly with negative implications for the cultural critic). However, it is far more difficult to see this applied to the male. Perhaps the only means might be a rebellion by bodybuilders against the IFBB. This has happened once before in 1993 when many of the Weider's top athletes temporarily defected to the WBF for financial reasons. If enough bodybuilders expressed concerns over health issues and refused to get larger or more ripped and shredded, then changes would occur. Both these remain (so far) unlikely options, given that the sport is what John Romano calls a: 'sports entertainment, not a sport' (2003: 242). This option would require not just a new aesthetic for professional bodybuilding, but a new professional organization to support, administer and judge it. Bodybuilders do not belong to a union. What is on offer, beyond bigger is better? Schwarzenegger suggested a different emphasis on extended posing and penalties for excess. Another answer might be "Retro" bodybuilding; in other words, an aesthetic in bodybuilding which looked backward to the American Classic ideal of Steve Reeves, and where lesser size and less radical definition would combine with symmetry and proportion. The problem here is that in many ways this ideal is already apparent in "natural" bodybuilding and, although there are numerous organizations and several well-known "drug-free" bodybuilders, fan interest is limited. Also, bodies of the mesomorphic male is visible in advertising and other discourses outside competitive bodybuilding. For the aficionado of the Mr. (and Ms.) Olympia, what is there to compete for? Thus at present it seems unlikely that any of these changes will be implemented.

CONCLUSION

In his book on the world of professional bodybuilding, journalist Jon Hotten discusses 'tigers' and 'lambs' as labels for those who watch and those who compete at bodybuilding contests (2004: 259). Initially, he sees professional bodybuilders as the lambs, a term clearly not complimentary when taken into consideration with the bodybuilder's unhealthy condition during competition, the physiological side-effects and appearance induced by pharmaceuticals, and the control wielded by the IFBB; all suggest a set of personal restrictions within the context of a competitive professional sport. Such a derogatory labeling also seems apt as some professional bodybuilders have expressed their unease about having to become ever larger and more defined each year in order to win any competitions, fearing the dangers this poses to their health, but their doubts give way given the circumstances of bodybuilding's economic and ideological imperatives. But then Hotten changes his mind remarking how the audience who watched these men 'with five per cent body fat standing between them and disaster . . . were the lambs, living . . . soft lives and staring up at all that muscle' (ibid.: 260). The word 'soft' suggests not only a non-bodybuilder, but more importantly, one who doesn't take risks.

The professional bodybuilder has always been a body pioneer, pushing at the limits of physical development. Perhaps bodybuilding should be thought of as analogous to the participants in "extreme sports" in which the activity is undertaken with awareness of considerable risk of injury or even death. In their discussion upon extreme sports, Robert Rineheart and Synthia Sydnor remark how extreme sports 'connect the athlete and audience with ineffable meanings with life and the universe' (2003: 12).

By the 1980s and the emergence of the Post Classical body, professional bodybuilding can be viewed as supporting the ultimate transgressive – and hence avant-garde – act of all: suicide. The fact is that bodybuilders are now recorded as often taking enormous dosages of substances, the consequence of which cannot easily be known. This exemplifies one of bodybuilding's most "freakish" characteristics: its drive toward self-destruction, a subject often recounted in bodybuilding texts. Steve Michalik, a professional bodybuilder who also appeared in the film *Pumping Iron*, illustrates one typical example in a newspaper article from 1998 (Solotaroff 1998). Hit by a tractor in 1975, Michalik was told that he would never walk again and could no longer compete as a professional bodybuilder (p. 9). But following the notion oft-discussed in bodybuilding magazines that one needs to fight on (often against the wishes of the medical establishment), he secretly injected himself with testosterone while lying in traction in an effort to hasten his recovery (p. 9). Out of hospital, his legs regained some sensation, which allowed Michalik to begin a relentless exercise and dietary regime. Several months later Michalik entered one of his last competitions. An account described it as follows:

> Steve Michalik only wanted two things. He wanted to walk on stage at the Beacon Theatre on 15 November, 1986, professional body-building's Night of the Champions, and just turn the joint out with his 260 pounds of ripped, stripped, and shrink-wrapped muscle. And then, God help him, he wanted to die . . . and leave a spectacular corpse behind.
>
> (p. 8)

Michalik did not die on stage, and today is an active campaigner against steroid use. However, there have been numerous deaths attributed to excess drug use. Andreas Munzer died when, according to Jon Hotten, his liver 'dissolved almost completely' from the drug Erythropoetin (2004: 16); Michael Hall likewise died of liver disease, and Don Ross and Mike Mentzer allegedly both died as a result of prolonged use of anabolic steroids. And Mohammed Benaziza managed to fulfill Steve Michalik's ideal by expiring from the over use of diuretics within hours of winning the Night of the Champions in Holland in 1983; he achieved the ultimate transgression – dying for your "art."

Notes

1 'Flayed animals in abatoir' is coined by psychologist Ronald Conway, cited in Dutton (1995: 278).
2 Quote is taken from Matthew Colling's documentary, *This Is Modern Art* (1999), Channel Four.
3 All statistics are taken from http://www.getbig.com/results/e-mroly.htm (last accessed October 15, 2008).

9 Strategies of Enfreakment

Representations of Contemporary Bodybuilding

Niall Richardson

The definition of the true freak in many ways also describes the contemporary bodybuilder.

(Cecile Lindsay, 1996: 356)

In an article in *Flex* magazine, published in 1992, IFBB professional bodybuilder Mike Matarazzo wrote that, 'Consensus has it that I'm a freak. To the general public, I'm an object of ridicule . . .' but, 'I *love* being a grotesque horrifying freak. I just love it! To me, this is bodybuilding' (1992: 42). Describing *himself* in terms such as 'gross' and 'nauseating' (p. 44), Matarazzo explained how bodybuilding fans delighted in his "freaky" dimensions which he described as 'huge gobs of twisted, sickening muscle hanging off my body' (p. 47). Matarazzo detailed how his unclassical, grotesque body was a source of great pride rather than shame as 'what's especially great is having freaky bodyparts. It makes me feel unique, as though out of the entire world, I have something very special to offer, even if it is a quality as weird as mutant muscularity' (p. 42). Another example from around the same time was the lesser-known professional bodybuilder Troy Zuccolotto who, writing in 1988, expressed his lifelong ambition as being, 'I want to be big. I mean, so huge, it'll make you puke! I want to be gross!' (Zuccolotto, quoted in Newton 1988: 42). Similarly, in a 1989 edition of *Flex*, Franco Santoriello, another young professional bodybuilder, is described as 'a fissiparous freak of frightening size, a perpetual shock wave of emotional tumescence that threatens to annihilate all life forms that wander within the range of his fallout' (Schmidt 1989: 59). Adam Locks lists the type of descriptions which bodybuilding publicity material would employ in representing its stars: 'Freak-enstein, Meat Monster, White Buffalo, Freaky Guns, Monster Mass, Jurassic Thighs, Thunder Thighs, Humungous Hams, Cantaloupe-Size Delts, Titanic Thighs, Monstrous Delts, Bulldozer Quads, Canons (for biceps), and Barn Door Shoulders' (Locks 2003). What we find expressed here is the celebration of abject freakishness: a representational tactic which would become the norm for the world of contemporary competitive bodybuilding. Welcome to the strategies of enfreakment used to market contemporary professional bodybuilding.

As this book's introduction has detailed, there was a move in professional level competitive bodybuilding from the ideal of the classical physique to the disproportionate or "grotesque" physique. While the classical ideal celebrated symmetry, proportions, and overall aesthetic harmony of the body, the "post-classical body" (see ibid.) is an inharmonious shape in which certain parts have been distended so that they are too large and therefore overpower the rest of the physique. Arguably, the first example of bodybuilding's celebration of this body type was Tom Platz, whose extreme quadriceps development overshadowed the rest of his body and managed to make even his hugely muscled torso appear small. (Arguably Larry Scott, the "Master of Biceps" was the first to anticipate this move given the size of arms (see ibid.: 68) but it was Platz who became the first main example of the post-classical physique.) After Platz, bodybuilding publications would start *marketing* other bodybuilders as having "freaky" and grotesque muscle groups, including Eddie Robinson (famous for his "guns" – arms), Dorian Yates (famous for his enormous lats – back) and, Platz's successor Paul 'Quadzilla' DeMayo. In other words, what was being sold to the "fan" or "consumer" of bodybuilding representations was no longer the pleasure of gazing upon a 'perfectible body' (Dutton 1995), but the thrill of staring at a grotesque body. Indeed, terms which would enter into bodybuilding currency would include 'monster,' 'grotesque,' 'gross,' and, most importantly, 'freak.' From the late 1980s onwards, professional bodybuilding was "sold" to the consumer through the representational strategy of enfreakment.

WHAT IS A "FREAK"?

In my last monograph, *Transgressive Bodies: Representations in Film and Popular Culture* (2010), I suggested that the archaic entertainment spectacle of the freak show has been creeping back into contemporary popular culture – if, indeed, it ever left. The most influential writers on freakshows have been Leslie Fiedler (1978), Robert Bogdan (1988), Rosemarie Garland Thomson (1996), Rachel Adams (2001) and, most recently, Nadja Durbach (2009). One of the main critical points to remember when considering freak shows is that the "freak" is *always* a construct (Bogdan 1988: 10, 95, 267). The body may be different – for example, it might be extremely tall – but it is the mechanism of the freak show – the strategy of representation – which *renders* this body a "giant." As Bogdan explains, '"freak" is a way of thinking, of presenting, a set of practices, an institution – not a characteristic of an individual' (ibid.: 10). For example, in most freak shows there was usually an exhibit titled "the giant." This was a man who was undoubtedly very tall, yet his tallness was re-presented to the public as "giantism" and so the presenters would usually have the "giant" wearing shoelifts to give him another few inches and a hat to add to the impression of extreme height, while the *mise en scène* of the stage would also conspire to increase the illusion of even greater height through the use of under-sized furniture. Likewise the "world's fattest lady" always gained quite a few pounds in the programme blurb and through padding under the clothes. As Bogdan explains, in the freak show, 'every person exhibited was *misrepresented* to the public' (ibid.: 10, my emphasis). The critic David Hervey aptly describes this process of stylizing and, most importantly, marketing the non-normative body as 'enfreakment' (1992: 53).

Of course, the above debates raise the question of *why* spectators are still interested (perhaps even more than they ever have been) in staring at "freaks." Leslie Fiedler, adopts a totalizing psychoanalytical approach and makes the valid argument that freak shows bring to life our darkest, most secret fears. For example, we stare[1] at the dwarf because this body touches our darkest fears about never growing up and remaining a child forever. Yet this nightmare is made safe as it is removed from us, contained within the representation (the freak show stage – or the contemporary film/media text) and establishes a "them and us" boundary. Nevertheless, as we stare at the "freak" we shiver with anxiety as we are reminded that this "difference" may not be as firm or clear-cut as we like to imagine it is (1978: 24). Although Fiedler makes a valid argument, psychoanalysis makes little allowance for cultural variation (some cultures, given the specificities of its cultural history, may have a greater fear of the image of, say, "the fat lady" than others) and also this does not suggest why "freaks" seem more popular now than they ever have been. More recently, critics such as Margrit Shildrick (2002), Rosemarie Garland Thomson (1996, 1997) and Rachel Adams (2001) have developed Fiedler's argument by pointing out that the concept of the freak is a fluid one which continually evolves in relation to cultural norms. In other words, the "freak" of the dwarf may signify differently in relation to contemporary spectators than the way it did for spectators of the Victorian freak show. As Adams points out 'the meaning of freaks is always in excess of the body itself' (2001: 54). There is no fixed meaning to the body of the freak because there actually is no essential body which exists prior to the discourse which "creates" it. The freak's body is the product of the institution or discourse known as the freak show. As Thomson explains, the freak show exhibits become 'magnets for the anxieties and ambitions of their times' (1997: 70). These 'magnets' can function as abject sponges, absorbing all the fears and worries of the particular period. As such, the signification of the "freaks" and ways in which they have been exhibited have evolved over the years.

However, why "freaks" may have returned in popularity in recent years *may* be due to a growing realization on the part of the general public of the key theory in body studies: that there is no fixed, inherent or essential body. Arguably, the media's fascination with the "freak" body – the 500 lb teenager; the woman with the most augmented breasts in the world; the self-*elective* eunuch; the most beautiful transsexual in the world – is that these images remind us (perhaps subliminally rather than explicitly) that the body is not an essential attribute but instead is shaped by culture. A key difference, of course, is that in recent years we have seen a growth in the minor category of "freaks" which Bogdan identified as the 'self-made freak' (1988: 234). At the heyday of the freak show, these were "freaks" such as the excessively tattooed person, the person with innumerable piercings or the sword swallower or the fire eater; in other words, bodies which had no physiological difference but who enhanced/modified their bodies or forced their bodies to perform extreme actions. Given advances in science, surgery, medicine, technology and – most importantly for this chapter – exercise and nutrition, one of the things we are witnessing is a growth in the category of the self-made freak. (Examples, of two famous self-made freaks have been the late Lolo Ferrari (see Jones 2008, discussed in more detail below) and the late Michael Jackson (see Yuan 1996)). Therefore, what a documentary focusing on a woman with the most surgically augmented breasts in the world suggests is not the terror of a freak of nature but the horror of the overwhelming power of contemporary regimes of culture in shaping the body. This documentary reminds us that the body is formed through specific discourses and, in the case of a woman such as Lolo Ferrari, shows us how frighteningly powerful these discourses can be. If these discourses are the way the woman identifies – Lolo Ferrari, for example, identified *only* in terms of her augmented mammary glands and was 'the woman *with* the world's largest breasts' – then the body will be formed in accordance with the cultural demands. Ferrari had to have more surgery to accede to the ranks of having the most augmented breasts in the world. What Ferrari demonstrated, in a nightmarish fashion, was how the human body was shaped by specific cultural discourses; performatively constituted by the discourse of surgically enhanced breasts.

Arguably, the same thrill is the case when we stare at the bodybuilding "freaks" in the Mr. Olympia line-up. We marvel at the demands of contemporary bodybuilding culture which has forced these bodies to develop to such extreme proportions. While Schwarzenegger had competed in the Mr. Olympia at about 230 lbs and at a height of 6'3", the 2010 Mr. Olympia – Jay Cutler – weighs-in at about 270 lbs and a height of 5'9". More than any other contemporary activity, professional level bodybuilding testifies to the overwhelming power of culture in shaping and coercing the human body to the dictates of specific regimes.

However, given that bodybuilding representations are hardly mainstream (a bodybuilding training DVD will never make Amazon's top seller list), it is fair to say the fans of these representations have considerably more investment and, in most cases, identification in these "freak" bodies than a spectator who, surfing through the television channels, stumbles across a documentary about a woman with the most surgically enhanced breasts in the world. It is this investment/identification which the bodybuilding fan has with the "freak" body of the bodybuilder which makes this particular strategy of enfreakment markedly different from other contemporary representations.

ENFREAKMENT: MARKUS RÜHL

As I have emphasized already, "freak" is a re-presentation (a misrepresentation) of an unusual or non-normative body in which this body's difference is coded as "freakish." Undeniably, the professional bodybuilder quoted at the start – Mike Matarazzo – is an exceptionally (unusually) muscled man who has body parts which are disproportionately bigger than the rest of his physique. However, it is only the representational discourse which renders this unusual body a "freak." In other words, "freaks" only "exist" as re-presentations.

This has particular relevance for bodybuilding given that (as outlined already in the introduction to this part) the world of extreme, competitive bodybuilding only exists for the majority of people *as* representations. These competition-ready bodies, so stripped of fat and dehydrated that their veins looks like snakes slithering underneath paper-thin skin, only look this way for a short period of the year and so the majority of people only "know" this body because of representations. Most competitive-level bodybuilders do not walk around in public, flaunting their extreme muscularity in tank-tops and training vests but tend to cover their vast bulk with loose clothes, known in bodybuilding circles as "baggies." As Adam Locks points out (2003: 211), the bodybuilder, dressed in baggies, looks to the general public as someone who is merely bulky or fat and, as we all know, in our contemporary culture of fast-food plenty, bodies which are bulky or "overweight" are hardly unusual, let alone warranting the status of "freak."

Bodybuilding representations, however, have strained to represent the extremely muscular body as a "freak." One contemporary star of the professional bodybuilding circuit, who has been subject to bodybuilding culture's strategies of enfreakment, has been the German bodybuilder Markus Rühl, an athlete (in)famous for the sheer enormity of his physique. Although never having been crowned Mr. Olympia, Rühl continues to attract a legion of fans enthralled by the huge dimensions of his body. Jon Hotten employs enfreakment discourse to describe Rühl as having 'no real neck to speak of, although there must have been one somewhere. His lats were so big his arms had nowhere to go but outwards.

His thighs moved past one another like two men in a narrow corridor' (2004: 160). Indeed, it is hardly surprising that Rühl's nickname is 'Das Freak.' In a description of the free-posing round of the Mr. Olympia, one journalist describes Rühl as: 'Das Freak! One of the more popular body-builders to grace the posing dais in recent years. Rühl was his usual beastly self. Freakish, hard and separated, Markus is finally getting his props and deserved his placing' (http://www.animalpak.com/html/article_print.cfm?ID=201, accessed July 26, 2010). Indeed, this element of Rühl's freakishness is the way bodybuilding publicity material always "markets" his body, especially in his lifestyle DVDs.

Lifestyle DVDs are publicity material for professional bodybuilders. These documentaries are, unsurprisingly, composed of sequences of the bodybuilder training in the gym, and talking about his exercise regime and diet, but it will also feature sections which represent the athlete in his recreational leisure time. In Rühl's first publicity DVD, *Markus Rühl: Made in Germany*, the documentary features all the usual sections of gym training, nutrition, and competition preparation but also includes a rather entertaining segment entitled 'Rühl goes Shopping,' which repre-sents Rühl and his wife, Simone, shopping for their groceries in the local supermarket.[2] The humour of this sequence is observing the stares which Rühl receives from all the other shoppers. As the sequence begins, Rühl, dressed in training tank-top and workout pants, lumbers along the aisle pushing his shopping trolley.

Figure 9.1 Markus Rühl.

Diegetic "musak" plays, suggesting the everyday banality of the situation. It is also intended to suggest the "virtual-realism" of the sequence and to downplay that this is an "enfreakment" marketing scenario, used to sell the image of Rühl to bodybuilding consumers. As Rühl swaggers around the supermarket, filling the trolley with huge quantities of groceries, he manages to turn every head in the place as people stare in astonishment, unable to fathom what this body actually is. Some people giggle, some simply stare and a few more arrogant individuals feel it is their right to make jokes about the man's extreme proportions. The sequence culminates in Rühl queuing at the check-out while a woman standing at the next queue is visibly nauseated by the sight of Rühl's body. The woman makes the classic "stifling vomit" face and clasps her hand to her mouth as if to stop herself from puking. It is interesting that this particular moment was deemed so important to the whole documentary that it was used in the trailer and, should the spectator fail to notice that a woman was nauseated at the sight of Rühl's "monstrous" body, this was even highlighted on the screen by an arrow superimposed onto the image.

Of course, one way of interpreting the shopper's stares is to read their astonishment due to a masculine invasion of a gendered space. Some could argue that Rühl's shopping is a hyper-masculine invasion of a feminine space and therefore this produces horror, if not even nausea, by the female occupants. Since the iconic ending of *The Stepford Wives*, in which a troupe of gorgeous, pre-feminist women (or are they androids? – we never really know) navigate their way around Stepford supermarket,

Figure 9.2 Markus Rühl.

in a sequence of such beauty that it almost looks like a finely choreographed ballet, the supermarket *may* be read as an exclusively feminine space. In this respect, the 'shopping sequence' is almost akin to a masculine invasion of the feminine. This (arguably) hyper-masculine body invades a space which is normally a safely feminine haven and intimidates, if not even terrorizes, the female shoppers.

However, reducing the supermarket to an exclusively feminine space is, in contemporary culture, not accurate. It hardly requires a quantitative investigation to discern that supermarkets are now frequented by men as well as women although, certainly in some areas, the majority of shoppers will undoubtedly be female. Instead of viewing the supermarket as indicative of femininity, it is probably more appropriate to consider it in terms of the banal, the everyday or, more importantly for these debates, the normative.[3]

Therefore, I read the 'Rühl Goes Shopping' sequence in Rühl's DVD as a celebration of how this body no longer "fits" (quite literally in his case) into the regimes of the normative. Through his intense program of training and supplementation Rühl is represented as having built a body which has transcended the everyday and therefore upsets the normative bodies of the supermarket who find his body impossible to read. In this respect, extreme bodybuilding is represented as attempting a form of deconstruction, offering a challenge to accepted ideas of beauty.[4]

Arguably, extreme bodybuilding could be related to other body modification practices such as tattooing and body piercing. Like bodybuilding, tattooing and body piercing can be interpreted a form of resistance, critiquing (often through caricature) culture's notions of normative beauty. In one respect, what the extreme body-piercing practitioner does is to take something which is deemed attractive or ornamental by contemporary culture (pierced ears are usually regarded as attractive ornamentation) and then caricature this through excessive piercing. Pierced ears are deemed "sexy" by normative Western culture but what about if nose, lips, cheeks, and eyebrows have piercings in them as well? Similarly, tattooing can have a comparable trajectory. If contemporary Western society deems one subtle tattoo to be a risqué, quirky ornamentation, what about when the body becomes covered with these "ornaments"?

Arguably, a comparison could be drawn between the politics represented by the hyperbolic body of the extreme bodybuilder and another embodiment of cartoonish dimensions: the late Lolo Ferrari. Ferrari was a Belgium porn star who attained a relative degree of notoriety for having (while she was alive – I believe she has been succeeded now) the most surgically enhanced breasts in the world. She sprang to media recognition largely because of her regular appearances on the British television show *Eurotrash* where she did very little else other than flaunt her enormous breasts for the spectator's attention. Ferrari's slot on

Eurotrash was entitled "Look at Lolo" and every week spectators would marvel at how such an extreme body could manage to do a basic chore such as polish the silver or wash a car.[5] Ferrari's breasts were indeed "freakish." After a huge number of operations (18–25 – reports vary), Ferrari had indeed attained the dimensions of a living Barbie doll. Reports (but, again these may simply be 'enfreakment' marketing ploys) suggest that she suffered intense back pain, from supporting the weight of the breasts, and had trouble sleeping at night (Jones 2008: 90). Ferrari died of a drugs overdose – or so the reports suggest, but this is open to debate and many believe that her husband was implicated in her untimely suicide (ibid.). While most critics would simply dismiss Ferrari as a woman suffering from serious mental health issues, most obviously body dysmorphia, Meredith Jones makes some very interesting points about the politics of Ferrari's cartoon dimension breasts by suggesting that Ferrari's surgically enhanced body can be read as transgressive. By having attained the dimensions normally associated with a Barbie doll, or a masculine fantasy cartoon, Ferrari is actually making an ironic comment on the "perfect" woman's body. If society deems the extreme dimensions of tiny waists and enormous breasts as the feminine ideal, the representations of Ferrari ask *how* attractive it is when these dimensions are exaggerated to cartoon proportions. As Jones points out, 'Ferrari was quite aware of the borders she was transgressing' (p. 93) as something deemed ideal in feminine beauty can become very unattractive, if not even ugly, when it reaches excessive dimensions. In this respect, Ferrari was enacting a form of femininity that was 'overly subversive' (p. 93). Like the extreme bodybuilder, Ferrari can be read as a 'freak of conformity' (see introduction) in that she takes something which is deemed ideal in contemporary culture but twists or even carnivalizes it.

Arguably, the extreme bodybuilder can be read in a similar fashion. This celebration of the "freakish" body, a body which has pushed idealized proportions to a ridiculous extreme, can be read as making a subversive comment on idealized masculinity. Most importantly, as the 'Rühl Goes Shopping' sequence demonstrates, male bodybuilding is represented as a celebrating a rejection of traditional ideas of attractiveness.

Of course, a comparison with Lolo Ferrari obviously ignores the issue of gender. When a man challenges regimes of masculine attractiveness/ beauty it is not the same cultural taboo as when a woman does it.[6] While women have always been considered simply *as* their bodies (Spelman 1982), and their appearances have always been policed by patriarchal culture, men by contrast have had the liberty (until recently) of not having to be overly concerned about their appearance. The male body is a tool for getting the job done but never something that should be the cause for concern about whether or not it is beautiful (Bordo 1999: 197). Yet this links to one of the tensions within bodybuilding in that the *appearance* of the body is the ultimate *goal* of the bodybuilder.

Unlike powerlifting, which is concerned with the ultimate heavy lift, irrespective of how this alters the body's appearance, bodybuilding is not concerned with the amount of weight lifted as long as it effects changes in the physique. Therefore extreme bodybuilding stands as a curious activity given that its concern is purely appearance – the bodybuilder works out to create a specific body shape and not to achieve maximum strength – but that this "appearance" is excessive and *unattractive* by contemporary culture.

It is important to remember that the sight of Rühl's body is represented as managing to evoke nausea in a woman queuing at the checkout but yet this abject spectacle is represented to the bodybuilding fan (who, arguably, wants to copy Rühl's training and nutrition so that he *too* can look like that) as something desirable. Therefore, is it not rather odd that this sequence proclaims to the bodybuilding fan that looking like Rühl will only lead to public shame and ridicule? If you look like this, everyone will stare rather than gaze. To reference Matarazzo once again, you will be an 'object of ridicule' and a 'grotesque, horrifying freak.' It is here that I wish to consider how these enfreakment representation strategies fuel fantasies of bigorexia in the bodybuilding fan.

BIGOREXIA

The term 'bigorexia' is derived from the established medical term known as anorexia nervosa. While the anorexic believes that the body is too fat,[7] the bigorexic believes that the body is too skinny and seeks to increase overall (muscle) bulk. Obviously, there are very different political and psychological agendas between anorexia and bigorexia which I consider in more detail later.

However, there is still some debate about the term bigorexia itself given that some critics use it as a synonym for "The Adonis Complex" while others, myself included, draw a distinction here. The Adonis Complex was a term made famous by the trans-academic text of the same name which argued that more and more men are now feeling victim of the beauty myth of contemporary culture (Pope et al. 2002). Besieged by images of perfected bodies and six-pack abs in every advertising image, men are starting to feel the tyranny of impossible standards of beauty in a way previously experienced only by women. One of the most interesting examples cited in the Adonis Complex has been the recent transformation in the physiques of boys' toy dolls – especially action figures. The original GI Joe and *Star Wars* figures (Luke Skywalker and Hans Solo) had body types which could be deemed "average." By contrast, contemporary models of these toys now display pumped biceps and washboard stomachs. This fetishization of chiseled muscularity in popular culture has, arguably, exerted an influence on male body image and induced an obsession with the appearance of the body in a fashion similar to those which women have labored under for years.

Yet I should draw a distinction between the Adonis Complex and bigorexia. While the Adonis Complex aspires to a body type which is deemed *beautiful* by the standards of contemporary culture, bigorexia fetishes "extreme" muscular mass, often to the point of excess, which moves the body *beyond* the spectrum of traditional attractiveness. The bigorexic reveres Markus Rühl or the other "mass-monsters" of the professional bodybuilding circuit while someone consumed by the Adonis Complex aspires to the "beautiful" dimensions of a Calvin Klein model. In this way bigorexia can be read as relating, in some respects, to anorexia although there are definite political differences.

On an obvious level both bigorexia and anorexia are about the subject gaining control of the unruly, wayward body. Many people who suffer from anorexia often feel that their lives are out of control and the only thing that they actually *can* control and discipline is the living tissue of their bodies. Bodybuilding obviously holds a similar trajectory which explains its popularity in prisons, and other establishments where civil liberties are denied, and also areas of socio-economic deprivation. As Susan Bordo explains, like anorexics, 'body-builders put the same emphasis on control: on feeling their life to be fundamentally out of control, and on the feeling of accomplishment derived from total mastery of the body' (1993: 152). Yet there is another area deserving attention in the similarity between the two – the correspondence these activities have to sexual attractiveness and the awareness the subject has of this. Although, on one level, anorexia can be read as women simply trying to adhere to the standards of beauty found on the contemporary catwalks (where womanly curves have been replaced with reed thin, if not skeletal-thin, models), it is also possible to see anorexia as a form of resistance. Many anorexic women talk about *hating* the sexual characteristics of their body. Bordo quotes an interview with one anorexic woman who describes how, at puberty, she hated the development of her womanly curves and other sexual attributes such as full breasts (1993: 155–156). Indeed, many anorexics express a desire to be removed from the constrictions of sexuality altogether and of remaining in a time (childhood) where sexuality was not an issue (ibid.).

Arguably, this idea of being removed from the dictates of sexuality is also at work in the agenda of the extreme bodybuilder or bigorexic. While the anorexic wishes to subdue her womanly curves so that she is not recognized as a sexual subject, and not driven by uncontrolled sexuality herself, the bigorexic wishes to step outside the regimes of sexual attractiveness too but obviously in a much more confrontational, aggressive fashion. The anorexic wants to become small and unnoticed; the bigorexic wants to become so "gross" that he is unfathomable within the dictates of sexuality. This is why bodybuilders such as Troy Zuccolotto (quoted at the start) express a desire to disgust people, to the point of puking, by his enormous, grotesquely muscled physique. Certainly a distinctly different agenda from that expressed by someone held in the thrall of the Adonis Complex, idolizing the beautifully sculpted musculature of an *Abercrombie and Fitch* model.

One of the most outspoken ambassadors of bigorexia is bodybuilder Greg Valentino.[8] Known for having the biggest arms in the world, Valentino is famous for a *very* disproportionate physique (the arms are far too big to be in proportion to the rest of the body) and, most recently, for the trauma his arms suffered when they literally *exploded*. In the documentary, *The Man Whose Arms Exploded*, Valentino explained how he wanted to have the biggest arms in the world so much that he not only performed site injections of steroids (injecting testosterone directly into the bicep muscle) but also used an oil known as synthol which he pumped into the muscle in order to inflate it to even more enormous proportions. Unable to cope with the sheer amount of synthol, Valentino's arms, quite literally, exploded when his immune system decided that it could no longer tolerate this foreign oil being pumped into the body. His biceps developed internal abscesses which eventually burst and oozed out. This rather disgusting image – indeed it would not be out of place in a gross-out horror movie – has delighted and intrigued many fans, most notably teenage boys. Valentino has appeared regularly in teenage, gross-out lad magazines such as *Nuts* and *Zoo* which often delight in the horror of exploding bodies, pus and gore, and also the scatological delights of piss and shit. These abject substances are, of course, notoriously the fascination of pre-pubescent boys who often delight in all things disgusting and gross, especially when they are the cause of the disgust themselves. In the documentary about steroid use in American sports, *Bigger, Stronger, Faster*, Valentino explains that he was not interested in bodybuilding to make himself more attractive to women. Indeed, with a grin of satisfaction, Valentino proclaimed that his arms are disgusting and put women off. His face breaks into a beaming smirk when he describes how women look at his arms and think 'Gross.'[9]

This rejection of sexual attractiveness, of building a body which is outside the regime of sexual allure, obviously accords with the anorexic's trajectory of preventing the body from being sexual. Of course, the anorexic tries to prevent the development of sexual features while the bigorexic seeks to exaggerate features which are deemed sexy, such as gym sculpted biceps, and caricature them to an unattractive extreme. It could be suggested (although without ethnographic research this is speculative) that bodybuilding representations therefore support homosocial fantasies in which men create their bodies to impress other men and disgust women. In this respect, it is hardly surprising that the most avid fans of bodybuilding are pubescent boys who, being at extremely difficult points of their lives – the onset of hormones, lust and the "threat" of girls – may find some solace in the fantasy representations of bodybuilding as "removed" from the dictates of conventional sexual attractiveness. Arguably what can interpreted from the representations – or rather enfreakment fantasies – of bodybuilding imagery is the dream of a petulant rebellion against societal norms. The bigorexic is saying he will not conform to this tyranny of making his body conform to dictates of masculine attractiveness – will actively reject the tyranny of the Adonis Complex – but will make his stand of resistance through the very mechanism which the Adonis complex says men should do; namely, gym training and bodybuilding.

WHY THE MOVE TO THE BIGOREXIC "FREAK" IN CONTEMPORARY BODYBUILDING?

The question this "look" raises is why the change in iconography of bodybuilding representations? From representations which had revered the proportions of classical beauty they have become images which glorify the "grotesque" and the "freaky." The reason for the change might be attributed to various developments in the sport and fitness industry and cultural politics.

First, a factor which has undoubtedly influenced the extreme hypertrophy of contemporary male bodybuilding physiques is the development outlined in this book's introduction: the growth in popularity of women's bodybuilding and, most importantly, the change in female bodybuilding physiques. Indeed, while the developments in nutrition, pharmaceutical enhancements, and training techniques promoted changes in the physiques of male bodybuilders, it also permitted extreme advancements in female physiques. As female bodybuilding started to change, with female bodybuilders attaining a degree of muscularity which previously was considered only possible for a male body, male bodybuilding had to progress alongside it.

Second, the late 1980s saw the growth of a new strand of male body type springing into public view. This was a more lithely muscled, toned and, most importantly, *eroticised* body which came to grace the cover of other alternative health and fitness magazines and started the cultural trend already described as 'The Adonis Complex.' As Susan Bordo summarizes, by the late 1980s, 'beauty (re)discovers the male body' (1999: 168–225). Eventually this body type would be canonized as the *Men's Health* magazine physique – a body which is distinguished by its sculpted abs, low body fat and most importantly *moderate* muscular development. The rise in popularity of this body type was connected to the growth of the gym and fitness industry. While gyms had previously been filthy, underground bunkers (often tagged onto a boxing club), in the 1980s they became luxurious health clubs and gym membership became a standard work bonus for white-collar professionals. Now, having a lithely muscled physique became the goal of the average professional who would often train after his day at the office.

The rise in popularity in the *Men's Health*-type physique meant that bodybuilding – as a competitive sport – had to assert itself as something different or more extreme from this body type. With advancements in training, nutrition, and pharmaceutical drugs (where once steroids where the only chemical recourse, growth hormone and insulin use started to prevail), competition level bodies started to become more extreme and pushed the envelope out in relation to muscular development.

However, the key factor which is certainly implied in the above discussion of the *Men's Health* physique and the Adonis Complex is the question of who is doing the gazing and whether or not this is underpinned by eroticism. As I have argued already, the investment in the "freakishness" of extreme bodybuilding fuels fantasies of being released from the pressures of the conventional Adonis Complex and of sexuality altogether. The subject fantasizes about challenging these pressures in deconstructive, confrontational fashion rather than simply ignoring them and being accused of "letting himself go." Similarly though, one of the reasons why contemporary bodybuilding has embraced the idea of "freakishness" may well be its paranoid attempt to extricate itself from the connotation of homoeroticism.

Bodybuilding has *always* held an uncomfortable relationship with gay culture. One of the most famous early "muscle" publications was Bob Mizer's *male*-order *Physique Pictorial*. This magazine was soft porn masquerading as an exercise magazine, and featured young toughs as its models (usually straight out of prison) whose physiques ranged from "some" muscular development to none at all. One of the reasons why gay soft porn stopped disguising itself as a bodybuilding publication was simply the question that the pornography legislation changed in the 1970s and porn could now legally exist. No longer did porn fans have to buy publications which claimed to be dedicated to "sun bathing enthusiasts" but could buy actual pornography. Indeed, one of the Weiders' biggest struggles – and their bodybuilding ambassador, Arnold Schwarzenegger was very important here – was to free bodybuilding from the taint of homosexuality. Schwarzenegger's indisputable heterosexuality and charisma greatly helped in erasing the stigma of bodybuilders as closet gays.

However, the rise in the 1980s of gay pornography, which became a multi-million dollar enterprise, reified the representation of the classical bodybuilder's physique as ultimate object of homoerotic desire (see Mercer 2003). While images of bodybuilders engaging in homosexual activities had previously been the stuff of fantasy drawings, such as those produced by Tom of Finland, now these could be watched on the home videotape. Of the gay pornography studios, Falcon became synonymous with the bodybuilder look and often featured impoverished, amateur bodybuilders having sex with other bodybuilders. Of course, these bodybuilders had more in common with the type of physique predating Schwarzenegger than with the "mass monster" or "freak" of the 1980s competition world. (This, of course, was *why* they were impoverished as their physiques had not attained the "freakish" proportions necessary to gain entry to the professional ranks.) Therefore, while the classical physique was being crowned as the ultimate in homoeroticism, with gay men (especially those based in metropolitan settings) taking up bodybuilding as a serious hobby (see Benzie 2000), professional bodybuilding needed to distinguish itself from that look and so espoused the excessive, grotesque body.

Another factor in this debate may well have been the lasting impact of early 1980s professional bodybuilder Bob Paris. Paris was (and still is) the *only* professional bodybuilder to have taken the very brave step of announcing his homosexuality to the bodybuilding world. A noted writer and critic (1991, 1997; Paris and Jackson 1994), Paris has written a considerable amount about his experiences of professional bodybuilding and has always maintained that "coming out" was damaging for his career (Paris and Jackson 1994: 120–127; 1997). As the only openly gay professional bodybuilder, Paris has attained iconic status within gay culture. For example, London's most famous gay gym is *The Paris Gym*, although, sadly, many of the gym-bunnies training in it nowadays are unlikely to be aware of the significance of the gym's name. Yet Paris is not only famous for being openly gay identified but for arguing that the classical physique *should remain* the goal of professional bodybuilding. Writing about the shift in professional bodybuilding toward freaky, grotesque proportions, Paris argued:

> By the time I had stopped competing, I hated bodybuilding and the direction it was headed in. And, in fact, I still disagree with the direction the sport was and is taking. I saw bodybuilding as a road toward the 'perfect' physical specimen. The dominant culture of the sport for the last ten years has been grotesque freakiness for the sake of freakiness.
>
> (1994: 149)[10]

What this did, of course, was help cement the link between the classical body and homosexuality. If Paris, an openly gay man, exalted the "beauty" of the classical physique, then most people interpreted that this was a look which appealed to gay men. If bodybuilding was not to be a homoerotic beauty pageant, then it needed to transform the look of the bodies on the stage. Indeed, this emphasis on how a bodybuilding competition should *not* be read as a beauty contest, and these men were not hunk pin-ups, was exemplified by one of the most popular "mass-monsters" of the late 1980s/early 1990s – Nasser el Sonbaty. The journalist Jon Hotten described Sonbaty as having 'the head of a professor . . . and the body of a genuine freak' (2004: 64). Sonbaty did indeed have the stereotypical head of the professor given that he was balding – yet did not simply shave the head but emulated a style which was not far from being labeled a "comb-over" – and always wore a pair of big, thick specs – even on the competition stage. Sonbaty's specs were not fashion glasses but heavy, unglamorous spectacles. Yet beneath this professorial-looking head was a physique which, at a height of 5'11", often weighed an astonishing 300 lbs plus. Sonbaty's appearance certainly made the point: professional competitive level bodybuilding is not a beauty contest and the contestants on stage are not hunk pin-ups.

CONCLUSION

This chapter has argued that in order for professional-level bodybuilding to survive it had to change its strategy of publicity representations and market itself as a postmodern freak show. Given the rise in female body-building, the cultural trend of the Adonis Complex, and the growing articulation of a metropolitan gay bodybuilding culture, contemporary professional bodybuilding had to repackage itself as something different from the canonization of male beauty. Enfreakment discourse became

Figure 9.3 Nasser el Sonbaty.

the accepted way of marketing professional bodybuilders to the fans. I have suggested that these representations *may* fuel homosocial, bigorexic fantasies for the bodybuilding fan; the idea of challenging regimes of normative attractiveness and creating a body which moves outside the dynamics of sexuality altogether.

However, it should be remembered that, historically, 'the freakshow was a place where human deviance was *valuable*, and in that sense valued' (Bogdan 1988: 268; see also Stephens 2006 and Durbach 2009). Joshua Gamson points out that this "value" is the way in which the "freak" can challenge received dictates of normativity (1998). Indeed, Gamson argues that one contemporary evolution of the freak show – the daytime chat show – is not simply a vehicle for permitting normative people to stare at the freaks but can also be read as spectacles which 'mess with the "normal," giving hours of play and often considerable sympathy to stigmatized populations, behaviours, and identities, and at least partly muddying the waters of normality' (Gamson 1998: 18). It is this idea of 'muddying the waters of normality' which, arguably, intrigues most critics interested in enfreakment.

Perhaps the final word should be with Greg Valentino who in his own charming style states that the fans of bodybuilding demand the disquieting pleasure of watching "freaks":

> In bodybuilding, nobody gives a shit about Milos Sarcev up there all symmetrical with a beautiful body. You ask the crowd who they like to see. They like to see the freaks, Markus Rühl or Paul Dillet, even though he can't pose to save his life. People love to see mass. They like to see freaks. It's what gets them into this sport.

And what the fans want – the fans shall get.

Notes

1 I use the term "stare" here suggesting the dynamics of staring analyzed by Rosemarie Garland Thomson (2009). The "stare" is different from the "look" and the "gaze." The look is simply the biological action of the eye. The gaze, by contrast, is an act of discipline which oppresses and subordinates its victim (see above). This term was revised in relation to Film Studies by Laura Mulvey in her famous 'Visual Pleasure and Narrative Cinema' article (1975) which, drawing upon John Berger's famous paradigm 'Men act, women appear' (1972: 47) argued that the spectacle of the woman's body in the cinema, engineered through the mechanism of the cinematic apparatus, connoted "to-be-looked-at-ness." Underpinning the male gaze is the question of eroticism. (Mulvey's article has inspired a small library of feminist film criticism including, Kaplan 1997; Rodowick 1982; Silverman 1992; Mayne 2000; and most recently Merck 2007.) The stare, however, is different from the gaze in that it is not always driven by the erotic and, most importantly, is not an engineered activity, manufactured by the process of spectatorship. Instead, the stare is an

involuntary, biological response or, as Garland Thomson describes it, 'an urgent eye jerk of intense interest' (2009: 3). Yet it is also constrained by culture given that, from childhood, we have been instructed that it is rude to stare. As such, staring connotes a dangerous taboo; it is something which the body feels it wants to do but yet is constrained from doing it by culture. Obviously, the thrill of the freak show was the "stare."

2 This sequence is available online: http://www.youtube.com/watch?v= mAOuIqXJwb0 (last accessed July 26, 2010).

3 The image of the 'supermarket' as suggestive of the hyper-normative can be discerned by thinking about how it has entered into common discourse. 'It's hardly the sort of thing you'd wear in the supermarket' is a phrase used to describe a non-normative or non-everyday item of clothing. If it is not something you would wear in the supermarket it must, in some way, be distinguishing itself from being everyday apparel. Similarly, the non-gender specificity of the supermarket has been suggested in various advertising campaigns, most notably the Sainsbury's campaign which represented Jamie Oliver – a celebrity chef famous for his new-laddist performances of masculinity – shopping in Sainsbury's.

4 Arguably, there is also a comment being made on consumer society. Rühl's enormous is body is fueled by the vast quantities of food available in the supermarket. By representing this huge body in the process of shopping it can be read as a visual testament to the excess of contemporary consumption – something which society would like to disavow. However, because Rühl is not simply fat – but instead "built" through a sustained process of exercise – the shoppers cannot merely dismiss this body as a passive victim of overindulgence.

5 Ferrari can be seen in action online:http://www.youtube.com/watch?v= ICUBcdhNuLM (accessed July 26, 2010).

6 In this respect, it is interesting to note that Rühl's wife, Simone – also a professional bodybuilder – is shopping with him and undoubtedly would receive the same amount of stares as he does. However, the sequence is carefully edited so as to remove these stares, presumably because the idea of a woman violating regimes of beauty is not as light-hearted and comical as when a man does it.

7 I am not suggesting that men cannot also be anorexic and indeed the condition is becoming increasingly common for men.

8 For an interview with Greg Valentino see: http://www.tmuscle.com/free_ online_article/sports_body_training_performance_interviews/the_most_ hated_man_in_bodybuilding;jsessionid=81872F052DC3912AEB0E4A6CC7 71D929-hf.hydra (accessed July 26, 2010).

9 Of course, there is no accounting for personal taste. There may, indeed, be many spectators who are gazing upon images of Valentino with a box of tissues to hand.

10 Paris's civil partner, Rod Jackson, was also a bodybuilder but maintained a more moderate, "beautiful" physique. Jackson worked as a model and was famous for having been a *Playgirl* centrefold. His disgust for extreme bodybuilding is even more vehement than Paris': 'I hated the whole freaky culture of bodybuilding. I thought it was a silly sport full of a bunch of goons supported by a lot of freaky people. [. . .] Other sports don't have this underground, low-life quality that bodybuilding does, especially the 400-pound gorillas who think everybody wants to look like them. Ugh! Golf and tennis aren't freak shows' (Paris and Jackson 1994: 148).

10 Getting Hard
Female Bodybuilders and Muscle Worship

Nicholas Chare

WARM UP

A clip, titled simply *Catherine Boshuizen*, plays on YouTube.[1] It lasts for approximately one minute and shows a hard-bodied woman facing the camera, repeatedly flexing her biceps. Boshuizen, who looks in her late twenties, is of medium height, with black shoulder-length hair. She is wearing a light grey open-shouldered top with sequinned trim which fastens at the front just below her cleavage. The top leaves much of her upper body exposed displaying a highly toned but not hyper-muscular physique. The clip has attracted 23,032 views and has drawn several comments. One of these, a post, by 1crazysupertrucker, exclaims: 'Those nice huge muscles of hers were popping, twisting, twitching and throbbing just about the same manner my main muscle has been twitching, throbbing, and hungry!!!'

The choice of adjectives used to describe this sensual posing is noteworthy. Muscle, the focus of attention in the comment, is here 'nice,' a commendable attribute. The reference to niceness is coupled with a remark on mass. It seems size matters in this context. By implication, small muscles are not nice or as nice. Muscles that 1crazy feels are unusually big elicit compliments. These muscles are also, as the list of verbs emphasize, doing things. In the clip, Boshuizen does not actually "pop" her muscles, taking them from totally unflexed to flexed, but she does make her right bicep, shown in close-up at one point, bulge and ripple by repeatedly twisting her wrist and forearm slightly (Figure 10.1). This creates continuous motion in the muscles of her arm.

1crazy's 'main muscle,' presumably a penis, responds to this display (1crazy's gender is not actually stated). The penis is, of course, strictly speaking not a muscle although it possesses musculature. The twitching and throbbing 1crazy experiences is the product of the action of, amongst other muscles, the bulbospongiosus (which contributes to erection and ejaculation) and the ischiocavernosus (which stabilizes the erect penis). 1crazy becomes erect, gets hard, at the sight of Boshuizen's hard body, specifically at the poses she has been striking with her 'nice

Figure 10.1 Catherine Boshuizen Flexing.

huge' biceps. There is therefore a physical connection forged between these two people by way of distinct muscle groups: the sight of the actions of Boshuizen's biceps stimulates the genitals of 1crazy.

The pair of bodies, in their interconnectedness, brought together by way of the internet, mirrors the behavior of muscles. Female bodybuilders such as Boshuizen and the men, such as 1crazy, who find their built bodies sexually arousing, rely upon each other in a way comparable to the workings of muscle. No muscle can stretch itself, rather it must be stretched by its antagonist: when Boshuizen's biceps contract, for example, her triceps are stretched. Pairs of muscles are mutually dependent as are women such as Boshuizen who need income and men such as 1crazy who require each other to fulfill their lifestyles. The prize money offered for bodybuilding, figure, and fitness competitions is seldom substantial. In 2006, the winner of the Ms. Olympia bodybuilding competition was awarded $30,000, the winner of Fitness Olympia, $23,000, and the winner of Figure Olympia, $20,000. Those in sixth place were awarded only $2,000 in these categories.[2] Some women therefore supplement their income by selling photographs and videos, posing via webcam on subscription-only websites, or engaging in muscle worship sessions in locations such as hotel rooms.

Muscle worship has, so far, received little scholarly attention. Niall Richardson's pioneering work on the subject provides a notable exception (Richardson 2008). Richardson describes muscle worship as a form of sexual fetishism which, like all forms of fetishism, 'is about the adoration of the fetish object itself rather than copulation' (p. 290). Muscle worshippers gain sexual gratification from actions such as 'oiling up and massaging muscles' and 'watching a bodybuilder flexing (especially seeing the muscle bulge and swell) and displaying feats of strength' (p. 290).

1crazy's enjoyment of the size and throb of Boshuizen's muscle identifies him as an exponent of the emergent phenomenon of muscle worship. He is sexually aroused by muscle per se. It is integral to his sexual fantasy life.

This chapter will examine muscle worship both as an internet phenomenon and as a real-world sexual practice which usually occurs in apartments or hotel rooms. I have explored the potential for muscle worship to expose the labile meanings of body parts and to resist the penis–vagina coital model of sexual gratification elsewhere (Chare 2008). Here I want to focus instead more precisely on what is found erotic in muscle worship and on the reasons behind why this erotic has emerged recently. The chapter concludes with a consideration of what muscle worship reveals about the nature of all identity.

DEFINITION

Muscle worship sessions usually involve clients, popularly known as "schmoes," paying women bodybuilders for the privilege of worshipping their muscles. Schmoes are usually, but not exclusively, non-bodybuilders. The term "schmoe" is frequently perceived as derogatory (Kaye 2005: 109). Outside of muscle worship, it usually refers to someone who is thought to be a dullard. Within muscle worship, it carries the additional connotation of sleaziness.

This is evinced by Bryan E. Denham's description of schmoes as individuals who 'sit in dimly lit auditoriums watching the bodybuilders pose and then approach them after contests, often seeking to wrestle' (2008: 239). By drawing attention to the shadiness of the auditorium, Denham implies that something sordid is being practiced there, the propositioning of the bodybuilders, but also, perhaps, their actual posing. Additionally, the wrestler Bill Wick has described schmoes as 'little nerdy guys who weigh a hundred thirty pounds, wear glasses, and have nineteen pens in one pocket' for whom wrestling with a female bodybuilder is a 'sweaty-palms, exciting, heavy-breathing kind of event' (Kaye 2005: 110–111). The stereotype of the weedy schmoe is, however, sometimes at odds with the reality of the men who engage in sessions. A British bodybuilder, Antoinetta, has stated that although 'geeks' attend sessions, there are also 'strong, muscular guys who are into weights' (Plummer 2001: 79–80).

Muscle worship, the practice of adoring another's muscularity and/or feeling their physical strength, is not solely restricted to men worshipping muscular females. Some women, for example, find the muscular male body desirable. Leslie Heywood, for instance, has described the erotic beauty she discovered in Linford Christie's muscle definition and how some male pole vaulters she saw at the Olympics 'had abs and biceps worth hours of watching' (1998: 108). Other women fantasize about female muscle.

The lesbian activist Sandra Kirby has waxed lyrical about Martina Navratilova possessing 'this amazing vein that runs the length of her bicep' (Robinson 2002: 76). The vein is appreciated here in the same way as a deep cleavage or a well-turned ankle might be. Muscle definition is registered as a marker of sexual appeal. Lesbians do, in fact, sometimes express interest in booking worship sessions with female bodybuilders (who may, or may not, identify as lesbian themselves).[3] Muscle is also widely recognized as desirable by gay men (Alvarez 2008; Campbell 2004). In his study of competitive bodybuilders, Alan M. Klein explores the phenomenon of hustling: 'the selling of sex or sexuality by bodybuilders to gay men' (1993: 155). This activity, in which posing forms a precursor to fellatio (usually performed on the bodybuilder), appears closely related to muscle worship (ibid.: 278).

In the case of men who worship muscular women, there is significant variety in the kinds of bodies that are found desirable. Muscle fantasies operate along a continuum. The woman bodybuilder represents the apex of muscular development but other female athletes such as rowers, sprinters, swimmers, and tennis players also possess powerful physiques and can become the "material" from out of which such fantasies are woven. This is illustrated by the photographic images of female climbers, rowers, rugby players, and track and field athletes, amongst other kinds of sportswomen, which are available to view on the website of Diana the Valkyrie (a site which advertises itself as the premier portal for people with an interest in women's bodybuilding). The income of a professional sportswoman, however, is often sufficient for her not to need to supplement her earnings in order to practice her sport.

Muscle fantasists also show variations in their desire for female bodybuilders with some, for instance, preferring women of a particular ethnicity. The links available via Diana the Valkyrie includes ones to sites specifically dedicated to Asian muscle, ebony muscle, and Scandinavian muscle. Some fantasists also exhibit a preference for "mature muscle," for middle–aged female bodybuilders.[4] There are clips on YouTube, for instance, titled *Mature muscle – pumping up* and *Grandma48 Old Lady Flexing* (Figure 10.2).

This last clip has generated the observations 'whoa, getting big and strong, nice' from luvsbuffgirls and 'My G-d [sic], you look fantastic. I love the way you can make your forearms ripple as well as your biceps. Your trapezius muscles are beyond words' from avilachs.[5] If these clips did not highlight the age of the women they represented, then the responses they have generated could be interpreted as evidence to support Al Thomas' claim that muscle can be erotic irrespective of getting older (Frueh 2001: 66). The possibility that muscle fantasies may transcend conventional ideas about age and desirability will be considered in greater detail later.[6]

Figure 10.2 Grandma48 Flexing.

THE BURDEN OF REPRESENTATION

The clip of *Grandma48* mentioned earlier, like many other videos of its kind, features footage of a flexed bicep being touched. This gesture, pressing a finger into the flesh, sliding it the length of the muscle, is carried out by the woman herself. It appears designed to assert the solidity of the flesh. This is because hardness is highly erotic for muscle worshippers, as illustrated particularly well by another video on YouTube titled *Rock Hard Biceps Grooowing*.[7] The clip, which lasts for approximately two and a half minutes, is of a woman called Crystal Rivers (Figure 10.3). Her build is athletic, highly toned rather than massively muscular. Whilst Rivers seeks to appeal to muscle fantasists, she evidently does not possess the physique of a bodybuilder. The clip, however, is worth discussing here because of how knowing it is about the limits of video as a format. It seeks to compensate for this deficiency and engage senses other than the visual in spite of the restrictions imposed by the medium. The clip also includes many characteristics generally found in muscle worship videos.

The video starts with a shot of Rivers, who wears a Lycra singlet (an item of clothing closely associated with physical fitness), measuring her right bicep. As she carries out this task she is audibly breathy as if she has just been working out or is, perhaps, aroused. The camera is centered on her flexed arm and face as she fixes the tape measure in place to show her bicep is just over 14¼ inches in circumference before stating: 'Thought maybe we should do a measure today and see if I've made any progress.' The importance of the process of expansion, of building muscle, for fantasy is also encapsulated in the clip's title, the elongation of the word 'grooowing.' A desire to see transformation in action,

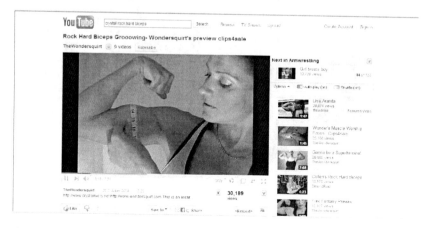

Figure 10.3 Crystal Rivers Flexing and Measuring.

albeit of a more rapid kind, is also reflected within actual muscle worship sessions where flexing assumes great importance. The flex makes relaxed muscle bulge with the skin becoming taut. Flexing is carried out repeatedly in sessions. There therefore appears to be an erotic revolving around transformation present here. It is a performance centered upon change: soft to hard and back to soft and then to hard again repeated over and over. The significance of this play of contrasts will be returned to later.

In the video, these states, the firm and the solid, the delicate and the fragile, assume considerable importance. Rivers' hard body, for example, is contrasted with her soft voice. Her impressive muscles, traditional signifiers of masculinity, combine with her carefully managed feminine appearance. She is meticulously made-up. Rivers wears eye shadow, mascara and lip gloss, sports a slender, silver chain, and is prudently coiffed, her long black hair worn in a ponytail. This last action perhaps also functional: it prevents her hair from falling across her shoulders and obscuring the camera's view of her bicep. Her sports top is predominantly pastel pink, a color traditionally associated with femininity. There is therefore an echo of what Maria Lowe has described as the feminine apologetic. The most applicable feminine apologetic in women's bodybuilding is 'the exaggerated use of feminine accoutrements such as makeup, jewellery [and] breast implants' (Lowe 1998: 115). Rivers' appearance combines visual markers of both masculinity and femininity.[8] This is common to many videos of female bodybuilders.

The shot of Rivers measuring her bicep is followed by one in which she is shown further away from the camera, her upper torso visible as she oils her right bicep whilst saying 'I love to flex for you.' Rivers continues, 'I want to know how bad do you want me to flex for you in person,' and then looking straight at the camera, 'what would that be like for you?' Rivers maintains an impassive expression whilst she speaks.

She is restrained, emotionless. Her demeanor contrasts with the excitement, the loss of control, she is seeking to elicit in the viewer. There are aspects of the professional dominatrix evident here. Muscle worship has, in fact, been identified as a form of BDSM activity (Connolly 2006: 91; Richardson 2008: 295–297).[9] Rivers is visibly cool and controlled, whereas the spectator is summoned to surrender to their fantasies.

In Rivers' commanding address there is both the recognition of technological mediation and an invitation to the viewer of the clip to imaginatively overcome it. This directive to the spectator to think their way into the situation on the PC or laptop screen requires them to draw upon memories of senses other than the acoustic and the visual in order to *feel* what is being seen. Pornography regularly strives to trigger multi-sensory associations and identifications. Joanna Frueh, for example, has remarked that seeing a close-up of female genitals in a *Playboy* video caused her to see and feel her own genitalia, 'the particularities of folds and plumpness, the pleasures embedded there' (2001: 94). The visual and the acoustic both hold the potential to stimulate tactile, olfactory, and gustatory responses for someone. Muscle erotica is no exception in this regard.

Rivers appears to be calling on the viewer to sense the solidity of her body, to grasp it as rock hard. The muscle erotica available on the internet strives, through careful use of sound and image, to overcome its inbuilt deficiency, its ethereality. It is composed of mere code, combinations of zeros and ones, impalpable and elusive, the product of software even if it achieves a tangible hardening in its consumers. Much of the careful staging that accompanies videos designed to appeal to muscle worshippers is informed by the wish to overcome the inherent intangibility of the onscreen image. Depth and mass must be brought to the screen. Heaviness must be carried to it.

The accoutrements of the gym, which often form part of the backdrop to muscle fantasy imagery, therefore have a key role to play here. Weights are akin to lingerie in muscle erotica, they are sexy accessories that add to the allure of the woman bodybuilder, yet, depending on the context, they can also function, when they are being lifted, to emphasize the reality of her strength. They are burdened with being guarantors for the reality of the muscle that is being seen. This is captured well by the cover of the documentary *The Bicep Bombshell* (Simon Hicks 1991) in which Tonya Knight is depicted side on with her head turned toward the spectator. The pose allows the photographer to capture her firm gluteus muscles and her flexed right bicep. Her right hand clasps a 10 lb free weight.

PERIOD MUSCULATURE

Knight is lifting the dumb-bell. Her strength can be seen in action. For someone who is familiar with weights, lifts them or perhaps eroticizes them, it can also be felt. This phenomenon, the weighing of the image by the beholder, can best be grasped by turning to the work of Michael Baxandall. In *Painting and Experience in Fifteenth-Century Italy*, Baxandall famously demonstrates how social factors at a given moment in history inform the visual habits and skills, the cognitive style of seeing, of individuals (1988). He terms the particular form viewing takes at a specific time the 'period eye.' In Italy in the Quattrocento, Baxandall suggests that a merchant (the class of person who often commissioned artworks at the time) would be particularly adept at gauging the volume of containers such as barrels and sacks because it was necessary for their business (ibid.: 86). This meant an artist could invoke a response to a work that was centered upon gauging if he included forms familiar to a merchant from his education in geometry, such as columns and towers, in it. If these were present, the merchant could appraise the skill with which the artist has represented them. Baxandall has been criticized because he does not acknowledge the fact that visual skills are not uniform in a given society but differ between groups (Rubin 2007: 93–133). There are always period eyes.

Baxandall also does not consider the way in which perceptions gained through hearing, touch, taste, and smell are similarly informed by the particular forms of knowledge that exist in a given period of history. Cognitive style is not restricted to sight but extends to all the senses. This would include kinesthesia: the sense of the body's muscular effort. The advent of modernity, for example, impacted on the way in which muscles were used, when, as Walter Benjamin has explained, the changing nature of everyday experience that accompanied modernity 'subjected the human sensorium to a complex kind of training' (1997: 132). This training included the ability to avoid potential shocks and collisions in the crowd. In the modernized body of the city dweller, muscles are used to twist and angle, to dash and dodge. The ability of a spectator to appreciate skill in modern sports such as rugby and football stems, in part, from this period kinesthesia. The corporeal knowledge of motion in the city informs the supporter's judgments of sporting events.

The muscle worshipper looking at an image of a woman bodybuilder lifting weights does not draw on the same kinesthetic education (although in all likelihood they possess it) to make sense of what they are seeing, or feeling. They derive their response to the representation from muscular knowledge gained in another modern phenomenon, the gym. The person who has lifted a 10 lb weight and looks at the dumb-bell in Knight's hand can potentially feel that weight, the exertion required to hold and raise it, in and through their own arm. The schmoe who looks at muscle erotica is a connoisseur of such exertions. Not all schmoes will have lifted weights but given the popularity of the gym in contemporary culture many probably will have. Those who have not will still take an acute interest in the practice of weightlifting and its accompanying paraphernalia. Schmoes who have attended actual worship sessions will also have gained a tactile education. They will be able to feel the hard bicep and firm gluteus muscles in the image of Knight, or the video of Rivers. Their period hand is familiar with the sensation of touching a hard body.

The images of muscle erotica that incorporate aspects of weightlifting technology in their *mise en scène* permit kinesthetic learning to be brought into play. They make representations heavy. The beholder lifts with the bodybuilder or, perhaps, baulks at lifting, feels failure, is unable to mentally match the feat of strength they are seeing, knows their musculature is incapable of such exertion. The weedier schmoes may, in fact, deliberately cultivate flabbiness or lankiness, perfecting a feeble physique incapable of lifting heavy weights, the better to contrast their bodies with images of the powerful figures of female bodybuilders they revere pumping iron. The schmoe eroticizes his weakness as is particularly evident in actual rather than virtual muscle worship sessions (Richardson 2008: 296).

The key point that needs to be focused on here, however, is that muscle fantasies are not primarily scopophilic. Seeing is secondary, merely a means to bring other, more important, senses into play. The schmoe sees with fibers and sinews, looks with and through their fleshly knowledge. This knowledge, as already mentioned, is also frequently tactile. The muscle worshipper who has attended sessions will know the texture of hard muscle. The muscle worshipper who has attended the gym will know the feel of a weight, its density, its smoothness, its temperature upon initial contact. The weight in a picture such as the one on the cover of *The Bicep Bombshell* mirrors, in its solidity, the unyielding flesh of Knight's physique. I would argue that the presence of iron or alloyed steel, of indurate metal, contributes to flex appeal, and is in itself part of that appeal. Muscle worship is reverence for the adamantine, for impregnable hardness.

The sexual desire for solidity, whilst amplified in muscle worship, has increasingly crossed over into mainstream fitness culture. This is evinced, for example, by the cover of the May/June 2010 issue of the mass market health magazine *Muscle and Fitness Hers*. The cover girl, Amanda Latona, a bikini competitor rather than a bodybuilder, is shown gripping two 25 kg weights, one in each hand. These weights, which would usually be attached to a bar, are not being lifted. Latona holds them, instead, by her sides. The magazine markets the benefits of physical activity but the pose of the cover model is a passive one (albeit one which implies action). This passivity, as Shari L. Dworkin and Faye Linda Wachs have suggested in their analysis of fitness magazines, works to reinforce stereotypical sexual differences (2009: 155).

The cover is carefully staged, not simply in terms of this implicit reassertion of patriarchal values, but also on other levels. The wardrobe has been judiciously selected. The bright blue Elisabetta Rogiani bra top and shorts have been chosen to mirror the ultramarine of Latona's eyes and also to echo the faint blue of the veins in her arms. She is, in fact, clothed in the color of muscle: wearing striation. Latona is also slightly bedraggled, or seemingly so, her hair wetted and combed so as to hang limp and close to her shoulders. Perspiration, or its simulation, shows on her upper torso. The image is intended to possess a post-workout look. Yet, as with the breathy audio of the Rivers clip described earlier, there is another interpretation being courted here. Latona's glossy lips are slightly parted. Her expression is not one that signals exertion or exhaustion but rather allure. She is sultry. The image is highly sexualized.

The picture is quite conventional in that it suggests that lifting weights, working out, contributes to sex appeal. The hard body is made desirable through associating it with the elicitation of desire. The spectator, the magazine reader, is encouraged to emulate it. This is made obvious by an arrow that directs the eye to Latona's abdominal muscles and is accompanied by the words 'Get abs like this.' I would argue, however, that the weights Latona carries form an important component of the message here. The weights are not just the means to the end that is this body: the image is creating equivalence between iron and flesh.

Alphonso Lingis has suggested that through pumping iron the bodybuilder 'receives from the metal its properties' (1994: 42). The muscular physique of the built body can be seen to 'acquire for the eye the opaque impenetrability of metal' (ibid.: 42). Like the bodybuilder, Latona is here figured as a woman of steel. She is solid, inscrutable. There has been a hardening of fitness images as the eroticization of muscle, or more precisely of the solidity signaled by enhanced muscularity, of the visible shift from toned to vascular flesh, has become part of the mainstream.

The carefully posed covers of *Muscle and Fitness Hers*, for example, frequently feature images of models with weights, either barbells or dumb-bells. The images of barbells (such as the covers of April/May 2001, July 2003, and September/October 2003) have the knurled crosshatch pattern on parts of the steel bar clearly visible. Two of the covers depict the models clasping this metal hatching. This gesture asserts solidity and texture. The magazines with cover models lifting free weights (such as Spring 2000, October 2004, September/October 2007, May/June 2008, and September/October 2008) usually opt for those that are purely metal rather than plastic coated. This despite the fact, as the pink free weights being lifted by the model on the cover of the Spring 2000 inaugural issue demonstrate, that those that are plastic coated can come in colors that are traditionally coded as feminine. The October 2004 issue is also notable in that the model is lifting 15 lb weights and she is a fitness model. This is a third more poundage than Knight has in her hand and demonstrates how mainstream the strong, built body is becoming.

The cover of this issue bears the tagline 'Now with 50% more muscle': the hard body, and the means to achieve it, is increasingly in demand.

HARD STUFF

Hardness, strength, shifts between states of solidity and motion, the held pose, the fluid rendered static, form part of the erotic appeal of muscle worship as it is encountered on the internet. These attributes also characterize actual muscle worship sessions in which devotion moves beyond seeing to encompass caressing, kissing, and licking muscles, being lifted and carried, and/or being wrestled by the bodybuilder. Touching muscle with the hand or tongue enables its hardness to be savored. Whilst wrestling begins as fluid movement it frequently ends in immobilization: to be pinned is to be kept in place, stilled. It involves complex, carefully choreographed ways of inducing inertia. It is an inaction which, for the muscle worshipper, is felt as exquisite. To tap out, to accept defeat, is to acknowledge one's reduction to immobility. The practice of lifting and carrying also requires stillness, a diminution to simple substance, a becoming dead weight.

For the schmoe, seeing is not believing, he has to feel solidity, rather than experience it vicariously. Sessions are intensely tactile involving touching muscles and massaging oil into them. Holding a muscle involves grasping its shape, understanding it. The reality of the muscle may, of course, differ from previously held fantasies about it. Its contours are not formed of cold, smooth steel. The carefully crafted surface of the bodybuilder, waxed and depilated, tanned, is designed to fetishize the look of skin (Richardson 2004: 56–57). To the touch, however, the bodybuilder's perfected sheen, their uniform surface, is composed of warm, variegated flesh that abounds in wax-induced bumps and ingrown hairs. It is, however, despite its bumps still predominantly solid.

The schmoe's faith in the muscularity of the female bodybuilder is therefore affirmed, in large part, through touch. He does, however, get off on a multi-sensory experience. The speech of the bodybuilder, her trash talk, for example, forms an often key part of the complex ritual that comprises the session.[10] Seeing is, of course, also not without a role. Sessions end half the time, as Christine Fetzer explains in the muscle fantasy documentary *Highway Amazon* (Ronnie Cramer 2008), with the hard worshipper "wacking off" whilst looking at the bodybuilder from a distance. The schmoe's erection is triggered by encounters with solidity and strength.

Michel Serres' "given," which refers to our sensory experience of the world, is described as something hard (2008: 111–113). For Serres, an individual's everyday experience of the world is mediated by language which renders it soft and insubstantial. He wishes to combat this state of affairs asking that 'we remember hardness' (ibid.: 112). For him, his memory of the hard world is held in his ears still ringing from stone-breaking in his youth. It is therefore a sound that has acquired mnemonic substance. This echoes Don Ihde's assertion that things bespeak something of their material nature in their sounding (2007: 190). The clang of an iron weight in a gym, for example, voices its solidity. In a muscle worship session, hardness is audible in the bodybuilder's silence. The gasps and grunts of the men being wrestled in *Highway Amazon*, for instance, contrast markedly with Fetzer's lack of vocalization. Her lack of audible exertion signals inexorable stamina and strength. This silence is palpable and enduring when contrasted with the continual moans and pants of her adversaries. These last sounds, however, can be heard to signal the kind of linguistic breakdown that can occur in a session.

Serres writes 'softness belongs to smaller-scale energies, the energies of signs; hardness sometimes belongs to large-scale energies, the ones that knock you about, unbalance you, tear your bodies to pieces; our bodies live in the world of hardware, whereas the gift of language is composed of software' (2008: 113). Here, hardness is conceived of in terms that relate well to the activities enjoyed by both bodybuilder and muscle worshipper. They combine in a delight in hard activities. For the bodybuilder, the building of muscle literally involves tearing muscle fibers and then allowing them to repair. For the worshipper, wrestling involves being unbalanced by an opponent, thrown, and pinned. The bodybuilder and the worshipper therefore both, in different ways, appear to savor the hard over the soft.

It is the hard given of bodily experience that, I would argue, is becoming increasingly eroticized in contemporary culture. The sexual appeal of this given is given its most obvious expression in the muscle worship session. This desire for the rigid, the stiff, the still, the static, as it manifests itself in muscle fantasies by men about women bodybuilders has, on occasion, been interpreted as an expression of repressed homosexuality (Parker 2003: 70). This reading is rendered possible primarily because muscle is conventionally gendered as a masculine attribute: the man who finds muscle sexually appealing ultimately finds men sexually appealing. The way the clitoris can become hypertrophied in women bodybuilders may, however, also constitute a contributing factor to such interpretations. Either way, woman is positioned as a stand in for man. This explanation, whilst in many ways wide of the mark, is revealing in that it is, as mentioned, based upon the cultural coding of muscle as masculine. I do believe that culture coding, as it is manifested in terms of gender difference, can provide an explanation for the rise in popularity of muscle fantasies.

The Information Age, in which we now live, has been characterized by a reduction in heavy industry and a rise in the importance of information generation and transfer. The best machinery of the Information Age is light and clean, and comprises 'nothing but signals, electromagnetic waves, a section of the spectrum' (Haraway 1991: 153). These machines are materially hard to see. They are elusive, evanescent. The rise of an information society has also led to a shift away from industrial labor and toward a rise in what Michael Hardt and Antonio Negri have called immaterial labor (2005). This type of labor takes one of two forms: it is either intellectual or linguistic or it is affective (p. 108). Most actual jobs involving immaterial labor, however, share characteristics of both. Immaterial labor 'creates immaterial products, such as knowledge, information, communication, a relationship, or an emotional response' (p. 108). The products of this labor, like much of the machinery that sustains it, is intangible.

Information society with its emphasis on codes and languages can, in Serres terms, be characterized as soft. This is also a verb that has been used to typify the form of capitalism that exists at the moment (Thrift 1997). Soft capitalism is exemplified by management discourses which address liquidity, changeability, and acknowledge constantly shifting economic circumstances. The present is therefore a period in which social experience can often be described as soft and fluid in nature. These states have traditionally been allied with femininity by patriarchy. In a phallocentric economy focused upon the hard-on, the hard one, softness and fluidity are fantasized as feminine (Johnston 1996: 333–334; Chare 2010: 23–25). These fantasies maintain their cultural currency in the present despite the real gains achieved in society by feminism.

The rise in muscle fantasy, in the eroticization of practices that venerate hardness and immobility, should be understood as a response to the emergence of an information society that creates individuals who feel emasculated by the nature of their economic circumstances and of the labor they undertake. The schmoe who pays to worship the body of a woman bodybuilder exhibits the same erotic desire for hardness and fixity that prompts a person to view a bodybuilding competition. It has been suggested that erotic desire for muscle can, at times, be distinguished from its aesthetic appreciation (Dutton 1995: 16). As I have argued elsewhere, however, all aesthetic enjoyment is ultimately underpinned by sexual need (Chare 2008: 158). The wish to look at a bodybuilder posing – to see them hard and fast – is of the same tenor as the wish to worship that bodybuilder's body in an apartment of hotel room. It is a wish for the solid and the static. In the phallocentric economy of the present, these terms are privileged.[11] The desire for hardness and fixity, their eroticization, results from anxieties induced by the rise of feminine identified qualities such as softness and fluidity in the fabric of everyday life. Under patriarchy these last attributes are, unfortunately, frequently experienced as negative by both men and women.

In the context of muscle worship the implications of the knowledge that the solid and the still are what are sexually desired is considerable.

In sessions, schmoes often show partiality toward particular muscle groups. Some prefer biceps or pectorals or glutei or quadriceps over all the other groups.[12] I had previously perceived this focus on certain body parts to simply be a variation of the reduction of Woman to 'tits and ass,' with the female bodybuilder compacted instead into 'biceps and ass' or 'biceps and calves' (ibid.: 160). The choice of muscle groups, however, now strikes me as more arbitrary. Underlying the preference is ultimately the desire for firm, unyielding flesh. The woman is, in the end, being admired because she is hard. This is, of course, another kind of objectification and of fetishization.

It must be remembered, however, that men and women essentially possess the same muscles with the exception of the genitalia. The desire for hardness as it is exhibited in a built physique is not tied to a given gender. Bodybuilders, either male or female, share in solidity. They both possess the capacity to look and feel engorged, their anatomies 'pumped like priapic erections' (Lingis 1994: 30). Either sex, young or old, can assume this physical resemblance to the hard on. Schmoes who exclusively seek out female bodybuilders to venerate do so because of the pressures of living under a hetero-normative imperative. Muscle worship does appear to hold the potential to challenge culture's delineation of sexual identity as based upon sexual object choice.

Richardson, drawing on Eve Sedgwick's work, has suggested in relation to muscle worship that 'it would be equally viable to label sexualities in terms of, say, a preference for a specific sensation, type of activity or frequency of sexual acts' (2008: 297). Richardson does not focus specifically on the role played by hardness in sessions but I would argue it is this sensation which is venerated as erotic by schmoes. Their sexuality is, therefore, a hard one. The reassertion of solidity as a privileged state that forms the impetus for muscle worship is therefore accompanied by an undoing of the fixity of sexual pleasure, an expansion of what can engender sexual gratification.

WARM DOWN

Muscle worship is complicit with phallocentrism in that it is engaged in order to compensate for the increasingly soft character of society and reassert the fantasized superiority of the hard and the fixed. The schmoe experiences a sense of substantiality in the session which ruptures his immaterial identity, his soft existence, creating instead a phenomenon similar to what Michel Serres has referred to as 'incarnation' (2008: 133). For Serres, incarnation is an undoing of the alienating effects of language, a working backward toward what he terms the 'given,' our sensory experience of the world. Serres rails against the mediation imposed by language between the individual and the surrounding world. He does this, however, by way of language. Steven Connor has, in fact, suggested 'his is the effort to incarnate, with the very language that he insists is toxic or paralyzing' (2005: 165). Muscle worship similarly uses language, the carefully crafted internet videos, the trash talk of the session, to bring about a situation favorable to this incarnation, this hardening.

It is, perhaps, a sensation not even experienced by the bodybuilder. Fulfilling another's fantasy, being another's fantasy, is not the same as possessing that fantasy. It is possible that the woman bodybuilder has also perfected a hard body for reasons similar to that which motivates the schmoe's fantasy. Often, however, as Leslie Heywood has suggested, the impetus derives from a desire for self-ownership inspired by the violence of patriarchy (1998: 185). Klein's insight that muscle worship is an economic strategy rather than a sexual preference for many male bodybuilders can also be extended to female bodybuilders (1993: 197).

The session will ultimately frustrate the schmoe even as it satisfies. The incarnation, the getting hard, the fixing in place of a solid sense of surroundings and, by extension, of identity, will always be fleeting. The identity of the participants in worship can only be properly understood if being is, as Nikolas Rose suggests, rendered intelligible 'in terms of the localization of routines, habits and techniques within specific domains of action and value' (2000: 321–322). It is in such domains, a hotel room, a website, that 'repertoires of conduct are activated that are not bounded by the enclosure formed by the human skin or carried in a stable form in the interior of an individual' (ibid.: 322). The behavioral repertoires which are galvanized into being, the beings which become in muscle worship sessions, are twofold. In the session, either online or in person, two discrete subjects are activated: the worshipper and worshipped – one of whom is erotically invested in the activity, the other economically.

The flesh of both is infused with significance by the space which it occupies, the situation given at a particular moment but, more importantly, also by a specific place. Being is repeatedly built out of specific situations. It never, however, hardens. There is no solid being only an endless fluidity: a greater or lesser fluctuation of becoming. Rose states that human beings 'live their lives in a constant movement across different practices that address them in different ways' (ibid.: 319). This is brought out strongly by the example of Fetzer in *Highway Amazon* traveling from venue to venue providing sessions. In the motel rooms she stays in, her identity as a hard body for adoration, or as she might perceive it as a commodity for sale, is activated. It becomes clear, however, in the documentary that at home she is the competitive body-builder, a girlfriend, a friend amongst friends. She practices her life differently on the road and her identity adjusts accordingly. The same can be said for those who visit Fetzer to venerate her body. Once they leave, their identity as worshipper deactivates. The worshipper and the bodybuilder, like two antagonistic muscles, also require the presence of each other, actually or virtually, for their identities to emerge.

The identity of 1crazy, of the online worshipper mentioned at the beginning of this chapter, can be understood as similarly fluid, changeable. He travels a different kind of highway to Fetzer, the information superhighway, surfing it in search of amazons, of hard bodies. In moments such as his viewing of the Boshuizen clip, when he finds a suitably built body and gets hard at the sight of it, his identity as muscle worshipper is turned on. Once, however, 1crazy's bulbospongiosus muscle has done its work and his worship is over, his penis will return to its flaccid state, he will soften, and a different aspect of his identity repertoire will come into the ascendant. The desire to get hard, like all desire, is one that can never, ultimately, be satisfied.

Notes

1 http://www.youtube.com/watch?v=aRo8rQwgxgA (accessed April 12, 2010). Catherine Boshuizen, also known as Catherine Holland, is a figure competitor.

2 See http://blog.bodybuilding.com/OlympiaBlog/2006/09/26/ms-olympia-figure-fitness-prize-money (accessed June 28, 2010).

3 This information was received in response to an email interview conducted with a woman bodybuilder whose muscle worship services were advertised via the links on the Diana the Valkyrie website. The reply was received on December 5, 2009. The respondent, who wished to remain anonymous, stated that whilst lesbians sometimes expressed an interest in booking a session, they seldom followed through on their initial enquiry.

4 This facet of flex appeal also manifests itself in gay gym culture (see Alvarez 2008: 223–245, particularly 238–239).

5 http://www.youtube.com/watch?v=PmW8ETdRFOI (accessed April 27, 2010).

6 The desire for muscle may also transcend gender categories. As yet, there has been no research conducted into whether at least some of the men and women who admire muscle and/or strength no longer strongly require those qualities to be tied to a specific gender. Certain individuals may find musculature erotic in itself irrespective of the biological sex of the body that sports it.

7 http://www.youtube.com/watch?v=xm3RmWuZiz0 (accessed April 12, 2010).

8 The combination of masculine and feminine attributes even extends to her name which combines crystalline solidity and riparian fluidity: two states, the hard and the soft, traditionally coded as masculine and feminine respectively.

9 BDSM is the acronym for Bondage/Domination/Sado-Masochism.

10 In the interview mentioned earlier, the bodybuilder stated that trash talk usually only assumes importance for a schmoe after a few sessions although ultimately it can end up becoming the dominant feature of worship.

11 This has also been the case in phallocentric cultures of the past. See, for example, Timon Screech's discussion of the problem of manhood in relationship to fluidity in eighteenth-century Japan (1999: 79–87).

12 This information was gleaned from the interviewee I have already mentioned. She also stated that some men preferred the upper body to the lower body and vice versa.

11 Aphrodisia and Erotogenesis

Joanna Frueh

'She's an abomination,' said the owner of a fashionable New York gym chain about a bodybuilder in her early forties. 'I could love them all,' wrote semiotician Marshall Blonsky about the twenty-seven bodybuilders in *Evolution F*, a 1995 performance that included three women in their forties and one each in her fifties and sixties.[1] These two statements, both made in 1995, bracket the extremity of response to an aesthetic spectacle, which is not just the female bodybuilder, but also, more complexly, her older incarnation.

A bodybuilder friend of mine in her forties used to train herself and others at this voguish gym and reported the owner's remark to me. She told me she thinks the "abomination" was labeled so because of her stupendous shoulder and biceps development. A risky body, such as hers and my friend's, a risk-taking soul-and-mind-inseparable-from-body, inspires hatred and disgust as well as stimulates erotic and aesthetic pleasure.

The bodybuilder's aesthetic and erotic overarticulation provokes discomfort and lust. Whether the bodybuilder has created a sculpted form that merely exceeds a normative (relatively flaccid) appearance, or that is hyper-muscular, the deliberately built older female body violates categories; it is uncategorizable according to binary laws. Illicit and anomalous, the mid-life bodybuilder speaks the paradox of pleasure that is monster/beauty. In my book *Monster/Beauty*,

> I define *monster/beauty* as an extremely articulated sensuous presence, image, or situation in which the aesthetic and the erotic are inseparable. Monster/beauty is a condition, and it can also describe an individual. Because extremity is immoderation – deviation from convention in behavior, appearance, or representation – and starkly different from standard cultural expectations for particular groups of people, monster/beauty departs radically from normative, ideal representations of beauty.
>
> (Frueh 2001: 11)

The mid-life bodybuilder's immoderate appearance ruins and increases visual pleasure. She is an erotic assault on the prevailing erotophobia regarding older women because she brings into consciousness by literally bringing into being supposed oppositions and dissonances: youth and age, the feminine and the masculine, touchability and dominatrix toughness. She is the sign and embodiment of confusions and dilemmas. A comic body based in hyperbole, she is a joke: on "feminine forever," because she crosses genders, anatomies, and generations; on the archetypal crone, the wise soul in a withered body; on sex-myth, which requires the respectable invisibility and matronly spread-and-shrivel of older women.[2] The mid-life bodybuilder is a cliché that shatters clichés; a nude who is also an actual woman; a purposive exerciser whose "purposeless" muscles expose the workings of eros as an aesthetic discipline.[3] She is the return of the repressed – older women's erotic agency and urgency – and she is proof that an older woman can be an aphrodisiac body, sensually gratifying to herself and others, sexually and aesthetically arresting. She can be the subject of erotogenesis.

THE ANAPHRODISIAC BODY

Myths of so-called graceful aging and acceptance of reality – submission to time and gravity – construct an anaphrodisiac body for the older woman. These myths essentialize her body by relegating her to a no-body. She may gain wisdom by modeling herself after the crone archetype or simply by living as long as she has, but she loses her body, the corporeal and carnal vitality and presence wrongly associated with only younger women.

Freud wrote, 'Dirt is matter in the wrong place' (Freud, quoted in Pacteau 1994: 94). This describes the older female body in its conventional contemporary configuration of de-forming matter or verging-on-formless matter: time has polluted the older female, and dirt manifests itself as sagging flesh and atrophy. A statement by artist Joan Semmel, who is now in her late sixties and who has worked out regularly, serves as counterpoise to Freud: 'the human body is always sensual no matter what age, twenty or fifty.'[4] Semmel's words suggest that age cannot separate flesh and the senses because sensuality is an essential element of bodily existence. Surely sensuality performs the pleasures of firm, proportionate shape. Yet, sensuality just as readily can perform what writer Yukio Mishima called the 'narcissism' of a 'bulging belly or a flat chest with protruding ribs' –irregularities of droop that display eating as overconsumption and as fat that grows through lack of movement, atrophic mid-life softness that (supposedly) distances caressability because observers fear the anaphrodisiac body's imagined stagnant innards; they warn of the imaginer's own degeneration (Mishima 1970: 15).

The anaphrodisiac older female body is more irregular than a younger female body, which itself is also more chaotic and abnormal than a male body. In the West, artists have idealized and romanticized women's bodies into the female nude – predictable patterns in which youth and shapeliness signify allure and the decency of regularity, permitting viewers the relief of not having to literally or figuratively look at what culture assumes to be human beings' natural state of defectiveness. Art historian Kenneth Clark, whose *The Nude* remains the most inclusive consideration of the subject, asserts that the nude is art's answer to 'the humiliating *im*perfection to which our species is usually condemned' (1956: 341). In effect, he accepts the body as a death trap, a loser's habitat. Some younger women escape the humiliation that Clark affirms. As one ages, this humiliation includes loss of physical strength, and, for women, the end of reproductivity. Reproductivity not only symbolizes but has also come to embody fuckability. The post-reproductive body is unfuckable – erotically taboo – because it is not a potential site of male fertility/ creativity: it is a tomb for men who seek immortality rather than the pleasures enjoyed by two mortals.

As Clark so bluntly puts it, 'on the whole there are more women whose bodies look like a potato than like the Knidian Aphrodite. The shape to which the female body tends to return is one that emphasizes its biological functions' (p. 93). According to Clark, Praxiteles's Knidia (*c.*350 BC) purified the 'bulging statuettes from paleolithic caves,' forms exemplifying tuberosity because their creators emphasized breasts, hips, and belly (p. 71). Representing beauty, sex, and fertility to the Greeks, the Knidia became the model for the female nude. Most women, unable to compete with the classical goddess and her descendants, are reversions; and atavism, for Clark, is ugly. In his terms, the older female body could only be emphatically, and naturally, tuberous with its presumably pendulous breasts and enlarged abdomen ironically stressing "biological functions" that may have ended.

The older female nude is an oxymoron if not a virtual impossibility. The tradition of both the female and the male nude almost exclusively represents a young body. The Resting Hercules, heroic and ideally robust, is a mature body without an ancient Greek female equivalent. Ripe like a fruit, in bloom like a flower: the female nude, in Clark's terms, is supremely clean of disharmonious development.[5] Disharmony is a sign of the anaphrodisiac body, which is not merely unshapely, it is misshapen as well. For the Greeks, youth was the prerequisite essence of the nude because youth meant reproductive potency.

Clark assumes the existence of natural bodies upon which natural events and forces operate. Calling this body potato-like or matronly doesn't make much difference. Within this system of values, the "natural" older female body lacks proportion and harmony. It is men's flabby sister, thanks to the erroneous notion that the "natural" male body is hard.

The "natural" older female body is also younger women's feeble grand-mother, because, "naturally," young women are powerful – sexually and alluringly visible. The mid-life body, an incarnation of the myth of the "natural" body that manifests in reality as a self-fulfilling prophecy, is, like other conventional constructions of the female body, 'easy to be intimate with.'[6] Smooth skin, slender physique, and high round breasts typify the look of desirability, of potential sexual intimacy. Wrinkles, gray hair, and untoned muscle characterize the conventional figure of the grandmother, whose body welcomes familial embraces and provides nurturance and warmth safe from – because sterilized of – sex. Femaleness as an invitation to sex (whether loving or violent) and femaleness as a provider of emotional and physical nourishments are all too familiar. But wrinkles, gray hair, and untoned muscle describe the hag as well as the grandmother. The hag is mean and hideous, is not a body that supplies intimacy, yet it is as formulaic and as familiar as the body of the sexpot, the grandmother, and the mid-life matron. The supposedly chaotic older body, with its erratic contours and unpredictable menopausal organs, keeps the order of formulaic fantasy writ as both expectation and reality.

Beauty is not natural to anyone, for people create or negate their beauty by exercising – or not – aesthetic energy. For the mid-life body-builder this creation is supremely conscious. Her exercise of pleasure creates a monster who performs a beauty that sins against the vacuous glamour that is the prettiness of "young." The mid-life bodybuilder's glamour is, in part, the provocation of her years. Glamour is her accumulation of charisma; her aging, her experience, and her aesthetic/erotic work on her body, which give it character and expressiveness and which kill conventional beauty.

The matron, like the bodybuilder, is neither an innocent nor inexpressive body, but cultural pathology has negated her possible beauties. I sound harsh about the matron, but it is so often a prototype of submission and anaphrodisia. Germaine Greer writes in *The Change* that women should enjoy becoming the invisible matron, whose interior life allows her to 'gaze outward' and see beauty, to 'at last transcend the body that was what other people principally valued her for' (1992: 378). The matron's "invisibility" releases her from the 'fretful struggle to *be* beautiful' (p. 378). According to Greer, a woman must move from incessantly laboring to be an object of desire to understanding that 'beauty is not to be found in objects of desire but in those things that exist beyond desire' (p. 377). Such is the aphrodisiac – the erotogenic body – whose bodybuilder creator, at best, has made herself *out of* her interior life, her aesthetic concentration. This kind of concentration and its product are being experienced as pleasure. Concentration and its product are comfortableness, clarity, and groundedness, and they are related to Greer's 'calm and indifference,' which she calls 'a desirable condition' (p. 378). The hyper-muscular mid-life bodybuilder deviates spectacularly from the matron model, and the less monumentally developed mid-life bodybuilder deviates as well: through monster/beauty discipline, both become visible in a way that is attractive to some observers, and it is the bodybuilder's being, as supreme aesthete/"abomination" and as felt by the observer, rather than the bodybuilder's outer beauty, that is her more complex allure.

Writing about feminist artist Mary Kelly's *Interim*, an extensive 1990 installation that investigated the subjectivity of becoming a mid-life woman, art historian Norman Bryson takes on a funereal tone: 'no social agencies step forward, like suitors, to claim the woman of middle age; time no longer urges, it hangs heavy. Identification enters on a period of vacuum and dearth. What is striking now is the stark condition of need for identification' (1990: 27). Time, hanging heavy, claims the mid-life body, enervating it, degenerating it from lassitude to sluggishness so that *it* hangs heavy.

Mid-life women could stand wooing, out of the closet of time which is the death trap of the anaphrodisiac body. Herbert Marcuse's discussion of time in *Eros and Civilization* is useful for understanding both aesthetic concentration –timelessness – and the anaphrodisiac death trap:

> Timelessness is the ideal of pleasure . . . The flux of time is society's most natural ally in maintaining law and order, conformity, and the institutions that relegate freedom to a perpetual utopia; . . . Whether death is feared as constant threat, or glorified as supreme sacrifice, or accepted as fate, the education for consent to death introduces an element of surrender into life from the beginning – surrender and submission. It stifles "utopian" efforts. The powers that be have a deep affinity to death; death is a token of unfreedom, of defeat.
>
> (1966: 231/236)

The "natural" body of the matron figure consents to the death of aphrodisia, whereas the aphrodisiac body, created in the timelessness of aesthetic concentration, may appear relatively ageless. Bodybuilders wrinkle, like everyone else. That their 'bodies know no age, or refuse to reveal the process of aging,' that they grow younger with time, is a fable (Goldberg 1997: 221). But, as bodybuilding philosopher and doyen Al Thomas told me in a letter from 1996, the 'only "organ" (apart from the liver) that is available for endless regeneration is muscle.' Thomas, a great lover of muscle, wrote too that 'there is no age at which well-developed (well-trained) muscle becomes something other than (anything other than) beautiful.' Intense training, Thomas believes, creates the 'sort of muscle which (however covered with a bit of wrinkling or flab) is erotic and eroticized and arousing, no less in an old woman than in a young woman or girl. FAR more. Far more to be cherished.'[7] This is because aesthetic concentration has created a woman whose allure is not only in her muscle but also in her agency; for she has *chosen* shape, strength, and development. Her appearance displays them, and so does her being when she is a 'body of content.'[8]

In general, the body of content and conventional beauty are not one and the same. For good reason, feminists have critiqued women's longing to be beautiful, because, as Francette Pacteau elaborates in *The Symptom of Beauty*, her resounding analysis of conventional female beauty, it is a symptom of patriarchal psychology. Naming or creating a feminist model of a real and beautiful woman who is not a 'symptom of beauty' remains. The beauty and fashion industries create the desire to be photogenic, to conform to the glamour that photographic illusions can design. I posit the erotogenic as an antidote to the photogenic and as a feminist model of beauty, rooted in aphrodisiac capacity, not simplistically reliant on appearance. The older aphrodisiac body does not strain for glamour that is only artifice, and it is not rabid with longing for youth.

The runway model and the porn icon symbolize youth itself and create longing. In addition, for the older woman, they represent loss. The mid-life bodybuilder, who asserts her will against the expectation, even the demand that she become the formulaic matron, draws on the energy of the "tabooed logic" of eros and therefore appears unreasonable (Marcuse 1966: 185). We see this in philosopher Susan Bordo's words describing bodybuilding in *Unbearable Weight*: 'adversarial relationship to the body,' 'compulsive,' 'perfection,' 'tightly managed,' 'disdain for material limits and the concomitant intoxication with freedom, change, and self-determination,' '*control . . .* total mastery of the body' (1993: 151, 152, 211–212, 246, 301). Bordo effectively analyzes the simultaneously productive and counterproductive aspects embedded in body disciplines that promise pleasure, beauty, and freedom. Yet, her chiefly negative take on bodybuilding misses the important point of *aesthetic* control, which is a process and experience of sensuous embodiment and which is particularly beneficial for older women. Granted, I speak about bodybuilding as a practitioner who perceives and interprets its best aspects, whereas Bordo presents its worst features and speaks, to my knowledge, as a non-practitioner. (Bordo did, one summer, engage in 'a little bit of casual weight-training,' at which time she came to understand its 'attractions' in terms of 'the hard and impenetrable.'[9]) Also, Bordo does not consider the mid-life bodybuilder as embodying different needs and pleasures than her younger counterpart. Bordo posits the female body-builder as a contemporary icon of fit femininity who imposes imperatives of perfection upon herself and impossible achievements of appearance on others (1993: 151, 211–212).

Perfection and aphrodisiac beauty are not equivalents. The latter is creatable – and odd. Think of Frida Kahlo and Louise Nevelson. They styled themselves through the ornaments of clothing, jewelry, and make-up. The primary self-styling mode of the bodybuilder is the artist's basic, intuitive, and sensual shaping of matter into form. Bodybuilding has been described in such conventional terms as the molding of the clay of the body and as the dexterous sculpting and chiseling of the body, metaphors that trivialize the aesthetic process of bodybuilding as it has been exercised by women bodybuilders I have interviewed. For them, these metaphors are either altogether inaccurate or imprecisely used. The bodybuilder as mid-life monster/beauty is *bizzarerie*, a form of deviant content who, like all exercisers, has worked from the inside out. Molding and chiseling shape materials from the outside, and the latter is a subtractive sculptural process. Resistance exercise as aesthetic practice is simultaneously additive and subtractive control that requires intuitive looseness as part of the discipline.

The matron model assumes that women have no control over their bodies or that women cannot or will not assert it. Damning management, as Bordo does, dashes the fitness imperative model but also segues into acceptance of matronhood, whose loose flesh becomes the contrary of taut bodies built by the tight control of fear. Let us expand both models, and say that the matron may affirm the pleasures of literally and figuratively hanging loose, while the mid-life bodybuilder may assert the necessary looseness of artistic process, which makes work fun and the aesthetic erotic.

EROTOGENESIS

I think, all too often, about the lament made to me several years ago by an artist in her fifties whose work has been instrumental in the formulation of a feminist visual erotics. She said, 'There is not an erotics for older women. You're out of the game.'[10] Personal shame, determined by cultural shame, is part of what redistributes, inhibits, and makes older women's erotic flair and flesh invisible.

I think, too, of my bodybuilder friend who, in response to society's matronizing of women, has protested, 'What are you supposed to do? Shrivel up and die?' Her body reads as aphrodisiac pleasure to me – the opulent forms, the sweaty ecstasies of gym time, her telling me, 'I feel horniest working out.' I identify: always, and especially after I've performed an exercise with heavier weight or more repetitions, I catch myself swaggering to the drinking fountain, radiating sex.

Voluptuousness is extreme comfortableness in one's body/being. Bodily ease, which is an erotic condition, is "naturally" rare in adults. Bodily ease characterizes children's more than adults' bodies, for adults must work at flexibility. The bodybuilder's contours, posture, muscle, strength – and, often, flexibility – project her body/being as an instrument and a site of pleasure. Pleasure supports and strengthens eros. If, as Marcuse argues, the 'erotic aim of sustaining the entire body as subject-object of pleasure calls for the continual refinement of the organism, . . . the growth of its sensuousness,' then the bodybuilder's developing and refining her body can be self-affirming rather than simply self-glorifying or punishing (1966: 212). Comfortableness in one's body/being may strike some as a luxury – of time, energy, and money. But erotic well-being is not a luxury; it sustains a human being, it is not dessert.[11] Erotic well-being includes elements of self-celebration, a lust for oneself that, while it cannot cancel out an observer's objectifying gaze, focuses on primary aspect of the mid-life bodybuilder's attention on her own pleasure. Here lust means enthusiasm and appetite for one's own lusciousness.[12]

Feminists have argued that female display dehumanizes a woman whether she is an object of dirty pleasures who arouses sexual desire or an object of supremely clean enjoyment who stirs aesthetic feeling. The aphrodisiac body, especially when clothed in (almost) nudity, the way we see or imagine the bodybuilder, provokes both responses. Deliberate and cognizant self-display is perhaps more problematic to feminists than is innocent exhibition, because the subject *knows* that she may be fulfilling someone else's desires.

But art is paradoxical, and often the contradictions in art objects captivate us: Kahlo's stunning self-martyrdoms, Hesse's sagging, tangled, agonizing visceral equivalents, the mid-life woman's monstrous beauty of solid form incongruous with age, of display motivation too easily perceived as repellent, undignified, ridiculous, or immature. Some may even read the mid-life monster/beauty bodybuilder as an undeserving – because not young – subject who has gratified herself.

Pacteau makes beauty a hopeless pursuit. She argues that 'the pleasure afforded by self-display arises from the subject's identification with the gaze of the other; the subject sees itself, as a picture' (1994: 149, 186). Art critic Dave Hickey insists that beauty, as art, is a rhetoric, that it has an agenda (1993: 11–24). The bodybuilder's agenda is to show the bizarre – because apparently unbelievable – spectacle of mid-life eros.

The body that lusts for itself does not lose itself and refuses to be expelled from the paradise of eros. More prosaically, this body looks good naked. Consider a David Barton gym ad with no image, only words: 'Look better naked.'[13] It may be taken as an admonishment to achieve something impossible, as a snotty, imperious comment that invites rejection, as an unsurprising acknowledgment that everyone is embarrassed by their body or hates it, as a possible means to better sex – or as a suggestion that anyone can be a nude, clothed and confident in the beauty of her own skin, like Aphrodite.

God knew better than Adam and Eve, who were beautiful in the garden, beautiful in their nakedness. But when they knew too much, they knew that they were naked, and God expelled them. Erotic shame and oblivion ensued.
We know that we are naked.

Today's bodybuilders know that they can look better naked. These words made flesh can reinstate the body in paradise.

The erotic requires connection, in which the gaze of another is essential and not necessarily alienating: *I feel pleasure because you feel pleasure in my pleasure. You mirror my pleasure in myself.* This does not separate a woman from herself, does not necessarily make her into an image, isolate her into a picture useful only as someone else's masturbatory tool. The erotic gaze derives from mother's and infant's mutually loving looks, which can be a model of the freedom to look with love and pleasure at another human being and through that erotic interactivity, to look at oneself similarly.

Older women are not supposed to show off their bodies, but the monster's purpose is to show and be shown. In her extravagant body, developed beyond the de-eroticized rationality of the body of the matron, the mid-life bodybuilder is a prophetic vision not only of the body's power against the powers that be, but also of the horror of difference and the paradox of pleasure: self-display as erotic agency and engagement and as a persuasion to self-pleasure, different from because not simply the self-estrangement of needy exhibition; age as the disruptive beauty of roundness associated with reproductive sexiness; eros in the wrong body; the shock of muscle where there should be flab, of stereotyped masculinity where there should be naturally aging femininity. Monster/beauty: a feminist nude. Monster/beauty: doom to maturity as ripe, then rotten.

Webster's New World Dictionary defines matron: a woman 'who has a mature appearance or manner.' Mature means developed, which implies sedateness, decorum, self-respect. The bodybuilder is also dignified and mature, in heretical ways. She exemplifies what historian Jan Todd, strongest woman in the world in 1977, calls 'Majestic Womanhood,' a nineteenth-century ideal of physical strength and size, independence, and intelligence produced by purposive exercise proponents, against the ideology of True Womanhood, which supported women's weakness and passivity (1998). The matron model corresponds to True Womanhood, and her *developed* body is the fullness of flab. The mid-life bodybuilder's maturity also takes up space. The bigger and stronger she becomes, the more abundantly, showily *developed* she is.

Just as nineteenth-century masculinism feared manly women and the unsexing of women achieved through means that included purposive exercise and artmaking, so today women and men, many feminists included, derogate female bodybuilders for looking like men. Bordo, for example, writes that the 'new "power look" of female body-building . . . encourages women to develop the same hulklike, triangular shape that has been the norm for male body-builders' (1993: 179). Her point that contemporary fitness and weight loss regimes produce a masculine body is well-taken: "successful" women must reject softness, equated with the (non-liberated) mother's body. However, a hulk is large, heavy, clumsy, and slow, but many female bodybuilders, including Emilia Altomare in her forties and Linda Wood-Hoyte in her fifties, are graceful and sleek, and, like Diana Dennis in her forties, extremely flexible. The triangular shape of male bodybuilders replicates an ideal female form of large chest, small waist and hips, and round buttocks. In *Foreign Bodies*, a study of bodily pleasure, pain, and competencies, philosopher Alphonso Lingis speaks of bodybuilders' 'hermaphrodite muscles,' an accurate description of bodybuilders of both sexes (1994: 42). Yet, I would add that the hermaphroditic body is other than strictly male and female; it is an unnamed sex, just as the mid-life bodybuilder may be, on sight, an undesignatable age.[14]

Discrete muscle creates equivocation. Equivocation is erotic essence, part of the paradox of (aesthetic) pleasure. Lingis asks, 'Is it not the indecisive and equivocal carnality, rather than the splendor of proportions not yet disfigured by the fatigue of years, that makes youth troubling?' (ibid.: 62). Because she is bizarrely unfatigued in flesh, the mid-life bodybuilder radiates carnality whose sex and age seem vacillating and inconclusive. Her strong and shapely hypersexuality troubles time itself as the tyrant of reasonable aging.

Like the no-effort fantasy bodies of soft porn, the mid-life bodybuilder is an epicurean spectacle, but she projects a different state of being than they do. Matron, *Playboy* ingenue at forty,[15] and bodybuilder may all love their bodies, like everyone, to varying degrees at various times. Yet, the bodybuilder's love, rooted tremendously in capacity – pleasurable work and strength, confidence in body – is narcissism as contemplation, physical education as erotic and spiritual education.

All too often, contemporary cultural critics see the gym as a site of one-dimensional Foucauldian discipline, like a barracks, school, or prison. Gym as labor camp, producing the docile body, that desperate mid-life youth-seeker. The bodybuilder does, with martial determination, protect herself against the paleolithic bulbousness that Clark and other art historians interpret as fat (not strength), and against the flabbily middle-aged and marginal Silenus, so empathetically painted by Rubens as flesh, that substance made female in Western art.[16] One mid-life bodybuilder, however, calls the gym 'heaven,' and another, Laurie Fierstein, says that if working out isn't fun, it isn't creative.[17] Training can be the same kind of experience that artmaking is. The bodybuilder's concentration, which simultaneously creates strength and shape, disproves the idea that bodybuilding is a mindless routine, such as three sets of ten reps per each designated body part during every gym stint.[18]

Looking at herself in the mirror as she trains can entail a bodybuilder's muscular and aesthetic concentration, a self-contemplation whose erotic rootedness and energy signify narcissism as connection rather than isolation or withdrawal. This aesthetic/erotic focus is related to Marcuse's idea that Narcissus's 'life is that of *beauty*, and his existence is *contemplation*' (1966: 171). Creating monster/beauty, the mid-life bodybuilder is both grounded and fluid. She may enjoy being observed, but she escapes such observation, her own included, into an interiority that is tissue and soul-deep: the barbell presses her feet to the floor as she curls the bar to develop her biceps; the barbell forces her back and shoulders to the bench as she presses the bar above her chest to strengthen her pecs; the bodybuilder's swagger balances her from mind to torso to footsteps.

At its best, bodybuilding disciplines one to live with the ground, to feel it throughout all her body at once as she struts to the drinking fountain or from the parking lot to her office; and bodybuilding simultaneously disciplines one to glide through space. Grounded and gliding, the bodybuilder can achieve clarity. Connected, grounded, gliding, and clear, the mid-life female bodybuilder, a feminist nude, is, like the nudes of Western art, an expressive body. She expresses not only a state of being but also being itself. Being is a state of gratification (p. 125).[19]

A model of aesthetic/erotic self-creation, the mid-life bodybuilder provides images and practices of living aesthetically. Time disappears and pleasure follows when one is living aesthetically. Quoting Kant, Marcuse calls the aesthetic attitude 'purposiveness without purpose' and 'lawfulness without law' (p. 177). Today's sports audience expects muscle to perform – in a game, a competition, some display of prowess. In these terms, the bodybuilder's aesthetic expertise has no value: her muscles are gratuitous, dysfunctional, purposeless. In these terms, bodybuilding, purposive though it is, is a waste of time because it is non-productive, just as art is non-productive. But non-productivity – *being* as one trains, one's *being* as a body – distinguishes eros as it does the aesthetic. We are comfortable with the muscular body that does something, for it enacts the performance principle, whose laws are utility, acquisition, competitiveness, and domination, which, crushing pleasure, generates economically useful products rather than aesthetic/erotic citizens: narcissists, contemplators of beauty; and Aphrodites, agents of their own pleasure.

The mid-life bodybuilders I interviewed began the discipline in their thirties and did so on their own. Women who take up bodybuilding in their early twenties often have done so at the instigation of their bodybuilder boyfriends, who then become Pygmalions and Svengalis. For Altomare, Fierstein, and other bodybuilders, the gym has been and continues to be a pleasure zone that provides 'challenge,' 'sensual transformation,' strength, development, and that creates bodies of content, in whose 'sacrum[s] . . . thought has become living cells.'[20] Thought, the concentration of Narcissus, made visible in the mid-life body. Thought as physical education, educating the body in eros.

I perform calf raises, seated rows, squats, and military presses more slowly than most people and linger, "wasting time," longer between sets than many experts recommend. This leisure is time to feel my muscles swelling. I love to swell like that, in a sacral joy that shapes an intellectual and psychic as well as a physical swagger. Swell and swagger: the words "erection," "phallic," and "masculine" don't apply here.

The "pump" is a pleasurable feeling brought about when a muscle is filled with blood and is short of oxygen. Muscles are engorged, like cocks about to come: that's the bodybuilding cliché. This priapic-muscular equation unrealistically masculinizes the pleasure of swellings and erections: during sexual arousal, a woman's nipples become erect and her clitoris and labia swell. We are habituated to perceiving muscle as male and monumentalizing it into phallic power; as if gender, in the extreme of hypermasculinity, needs to be bolstered or protected, and as if bodily bigness that is firm to hard can only be male.[21] Lingis writes beautifully and sensitively about bodybuilding, though I do not always agree with him. A case in point is his comparison of bodybuilders, posing in competitions, to erect penises. He puts it like this: 'whole anatomies pumped like priapic erections' (1994: 30). Dieting reduces body fat and brings out vascularity, which seems to legitimize the penis metaphor. (Yet, dieting itself, for bodybuilders, crosses gender.)[22] When we ascribe male and phallic metaphors to female bodies, we simply may be maintaining gender's rigid grip on our imaginations and behaviors.

Lingis describes bodybuilders' 'contracting poses and shifting with held violence from one pose to the next with the vaginal contractions of labor pains' (ibid.: 30). His metaphors, applied to 'whole anatomies' rather than to men or women, seem to expand gender, unlocking masculinity from the male and femininity from the female. Yet, the male metaphor figures as being whereas the female metaphor figures as pain. Masculinity is a state of achievement, whereas femininity is involuntary corporeal process. Masculinity presumably feels good, whereas femininity hurts.

I could adjust the involuntary aspect of this problematic gender asymmetry. I could say that one can control her vaginal contractions for her own and her lover's pleasure during heterosexual intercourse; that her vagina and vulva are slick during these contractions; that bodybuilders, oiled when they pose, flex like lovemaking vaginas and exhibit the slickness of aroused female sexual organs. But, as much as I enjoy my metaphor, I have just played into the gender maintenance game. "Aroused" may be a better way to understand "swell" and "swagger," which are conditions that need not be gendered. Wanting to revamp representations and discourses about masculinity, Bordo suggests that we 'allow the imagination to play with the figure of the *aroused* penis – aroused (as in a state of *feeling*), rather than "erect" (as in a state of accomplishment and readiness to perform)' (1997: 63). Arousal can be any person's, any body's pleasure.

An orgasmic body, the mid-life bodybuilder's, in which the undoing of discrete anatomies, the separated sexes, produces monster/beauty integrity. Pacteau writes that 'beauty resides in the *integrity* of the body'; she notes the derivation of integrity from Latin *integer*, intact, and from the root *tangere*, to touch (1994: 85). Orgasm can be the beauty of integrity. Orgasm not as melting, not as dismemberment, parts felt separately from other parts.

Lingis asks, 'Does not the orgasmic body figure as a body decomposed, dismembered, dissolute . . .? Is it not a breaking down into a mass of exposed organs, secretions, striated muscles, systems turning into pulp and susceptibility?' (1994: 55–56). The penis becomes "dismembered" in the vagina, "cut off" visually from the rest of a man's body depending on the physical length of thrusts and the position of bodies. The penis "dissolves," detumesces, in the female saline and mucosal genital secretions, in a sexual solution. The male "breaks down" as he comes, his penis and perhaps his entire body going limp. He becomes "pulp," looking soft and juicy all over – from sweat – and because the skin of his penis is moist with his own and his lover's cum. He exhibits utmost susceptibility to swelling, for his exposed organ, his penis, has changed form, "decomposing" from erection to a soft, still very sensitive tissue. This is one kind of orgasmic body and being. There are many.

An orgasmic body and being different from the one in Lingis' description might 'figure as a body' continually remembering itself. Acute local pleasures – a kissed toe, a back of the knee caressed by three fingers, a cervix under the pressure of a penis, chest prickling to the graze of a two-day-old beard – accentuate awareness of anatomical details, which are galvanized as a global sensation when luxuriously hard thrusts of a penis in a vagina centralize these specific pleasures in the vulval–vaginal area. Aphrodisiac beauty is coming together, all parts organized for and resonant with erotic leisure. This leisure is a condition and process through which one discovers orgasmic being.

> *Counting reps is measuring productivity. Counting makes one tense, expectant, and takes her away from pleasure. Thought becomes the living cells of disengagement. A reason for being in the gym is to come and to come and come, to swell again and again. Orgasm, from Greek orgasmos, to swell with lust.*

Visual pattern, force field, holy middle, flux of muscular transformations, viable vehicle of lust, *ecorché* and Aphrodite, hair 'dyed and fried' or going gray, the mid-life bodybuilder is a creation not a picture, an abundance not a lack, a fulfillment ready to be more fulfilled.[23]

She is Emilia Altomare, Christa Bauch, Diana Dennis, Laurie Fierstein, Linda Wood-Hoyte.[24] "Paradise now".

This chapter is a little more than half of Chapter One in my book *Monster/Beauty: Building the Body of Love* (2001: 59–88), which was an expansion of my performance "Monster/Beauty: Mid-life Bodybuilding as Aesthetic Discipline," which I presented at the Women and Aging: Bodies, Cultures, Generations conference organized by the Center for Twentieth Century Studies, University of Wisconsin, Milwaukee, Wisconsin, April 1996. I have left references to time, such as "several years ago," as they are in *Monster/Beauty*.

Notes

1 Both the bodybuilder who heard what this gym owner said and repeated it to me, and the gym owner must remain anonymous. A Portuguese translation of Marshall Blonsky, 'I Could Love Them All,' was published in 'Hipermulheres,' *Mais!* (January 1996). I was one of the women in her forties who participated – speaking, not flexing – in *Evolution F: A Surreal Spectacle of Female Muscle*, which was organized by bodybuilder Laurie Fierstein.

2 Robert A. Wilson (1966) advocates estrogen replacement therapy for menopausal women so that they can stay feminine forever.

3 In my essay (2000), 'The Real Nude,' I argue that, despite art historians' conceptualization of the nude as an abstraction, the female bodybuilder is a real nude.

4 Joan Semmel (1995) *Joan Semmel: A Passion for Painting*. New York: Inner-Tube Video.

5 See Clark (1956): 106, 111, 115, 124, 128, for fruit and flower metaphors for the female nude.

6 A student, Grady Schieve, made this comment about women's bodies in my course Monster/Beauty, spring 1995.

7 This statement and the previous ones in this paragraph by Al Thomas are all from a letter of his to me dated 1996.

8 'Body of content' was a phrase used by Al Thomas in a conversation with me in May 1995.

9 Bordo describes her experience in 'Reading the Male Body' (1997: 60–61).

10 The artist, who wishes to remain anonymous, said this to me in a telephone conversation, June 1993.

11 Erotic well-being provides a kind of 'social security.' See my 'The Erotic as Social Security' (1994: 66–72).

12 Alphonso Lingis (1985: 34) asks, 'Might not pleasure's incessant movement of self-affirmation have an affective and not objectifying form – self-affirmation as adhesion to self, itself pleasurable – a lust lusting with regard to itself?'

13 I saw the ad in the program for *Celebration of the Most Awesome Female Muscle in the World*, a bodybuilding performance organized by Laurie Fierstein in 1993.

14 I stick with the "undesignatable age" description even though a student in one of my classes said that mid-life bodybuilder Christa Bauch looked like she was in her forties. He was correct. I was showing a slide of her and asked what age the class thought she was. For Scott, Bauch's face indicated her age.

15 See 'Life Begins at Forty,' *Playboy* (February 1995), which was that month's cover story as well as being a Valentine's Day feature.

16 Svetlana Alpers (1995) makes an exquisite case for the complexity of Rubens' gender embodiment in his painting.

17 I interviewed Laurie Fierstein and the other bodybuilder, who wishes to remain anonymous, in May 1995. Fierstein has said to me that the fun, the pleasure of the process, derives from doing, whereas often the fun or pleasure of the result derives from others' reactions.

18 Alan M. Klein (1993: 41) suggests that the 'oft-overlooked seduction of weight training lies in the very mindlessness of the routine, which is as compelling as the physical alteration.'

19 Marcuse writes: 'Being is essentially the striving for pleasure,' and 'Being is experienced as gratification' (1966: 166).

20 'Challenge' was used by a bodybuilder who wishes to remain anonymous and 'sensual transformation' by Fierstein in separate conversations with me in May 1995. Al Thomas (1995: 16) meditates on the bodybuilder, in whose 'sacrum . . . thought has become living cells.'

21 Stephen D. Moore deals with bigness in sections titled 'Gigantic God' and 'Colossal Christ' (1996: 86–91, 108–17). Jonathan Goldberg (1997) considers more mundane aspects of bigness and male bodybuilding.

22 Anne Bolin (1997: 201) argues that female and male bodybuilders 'pursue the same diet. Differences between the sexes on the diet were regarded as differences of degree, not kind.'

23 'Dyed and fried' is Fierstein's phrase.

24 Photos of these midlife bodybuilders appeared in the original publication of this chapter. See Frueh (2001: 75, 76, 98, 103, 113).

Contributors

Rebecca Andrews is a photographer, film and graphic designer, and competitive female bodybuilder. Previous work has included life-size prints of bodybuilders exhibited at The Old Truman Brewery (Brick Lane, London) and other 'taboo' areas of body modification. Rebecca has also completed a project focusing on young Olympic Athletes for the 2012 games commissioned by the Maidstone Arts development. She has recently completed her MA in Artist's Film, Video and Photography at the University for the Creative Arts (UCA), Maidstone, UK.

Anne Bolin received her Ph.D. in Anthropology from the University of Colorado. She is a Professor of Anthropology in the Department of Sociology and Anthropology at Elon University, Elon, North Carolina and is the recipient of the Elon University Distinguished Scholar Award. Anne has presented and published extensively in the research areas of sport ethnography and bodybuilding, gender and the body, human sexuality, and gender variance. Her books include *In Search of Eve: Transsexual Rites of Passage* (Bergin and Garvey); *Perspectives on Human Sexuality* (State University of New York Press, 1999, with Patricia Whelehan) and *Athletic Intruders: Women, Culture and Exercise* (State University of New York Press, 2003, with Jane Granskog). Her most recent book with co-author Patricia Whelehan is titled *Human Sexuality: Biological, Psychological and Cultural Perspectives* (Routledge, 2009). Her current research is focused on gender and embodiment including ethnographic research with physique competitors. Anne is an avid bodybuilder and has competed for over 22 years. She is a professional in the Natural Physique Association.

Brian Bailey is a Ph.D. candidate in the department of Sociology at McMaster University. His dissertation research examines the intersection of male bodybuilding, health and masculinity, and he credits his competitive bodybuilding experiences for broadening his perspectives on health.

Joanne Batey is a Senior Lecturer in Sport and Exercise Psychology and a BASES accredited Sport Psychologist at the University of Winchester, England. She is Programme Leader for Sports Science and Director of the Sport Science Consultancy Unit (SSCU) which provides Sports Science support to athletes of all levels and sports. Jo is BASES accredited Sport Psychologist and has experience of working with team sports in professional rugby, national league hockey, academy football and development squads, as well as working with individual performers in a variety of sports.

Tanya Bunsell studied for her Ph.D. at the University of Kent in the School of Social Policy, Sociology and Social Research. Her publications include, 'The female bodybuilder as a gender outlaw,' *Qualitative Research in Sport and Exercise*, 1(2): 141–159 (2009, with C. Shilling), 'Confessions of a female bodybuilder apprentice: Exploring moral dilemmas' (forthcoming, Bristol University, Connections 8 conference) and 'Running [the 400 m] with Jon Silman: a phenomenological insight' (2009, British library online). Tanya is currently teaching sociology at The Sixth Form College Farnborough. Her main academic interest is in the Sociology of the Body, in addition, she is also interested in qualitative research methods, gender studies, sociology of health and illness, and aspects of deviance. Tanya is a qualified personal trainer and an enthusiastic weight trainer.

Nicholas Chare is a Visiting Research Fellow at the School of Fine Art, History of Art and Cultural Studies at the University of Leeds. His upcoming book *Auschwitz and Afterimages* (IB Tauris, 2011) provides a critical reappraisal of Julia Kristeva's concept of abjection. He has recently published articles in *Art History, Convergence, Cultural Critique, Journal of Cultural Research* and *Visual Culture in Britain*.

Kenneth R. Dutton is an Emeritus Professor of the University of Newcastle, Australia, where he held the Chair of French from 1969 to 1998, also serving as Pro-Vice-Chancellor and Deputy Vice-Chancellor. Following his retirement, he worked in an honorary capacity as President of Alumni, member of the University Council and Deputy Chancellor. He is the author of 20 books and over 50 articles and monographs, chiefly in the fields of literary and cultural history and biography.

Joanna Frueh is a writer, performance artist, and scholar whose work expands into photo, video, and audio pieces. Her most recent book is *Clairvoyance (For Those In The Desert): Performance Pieces, 1979–2004* (2008). She is Professor of Art History Emerita at the University of Nevada, Reno.

James Gillett Ph.D. is an Associate Professor at McMaster University, in Hamilton, Ontario, Canada. He is jointly appointed in the Department of Sociology and the Department of Health Aging and Society.

Leslie Heywood is Professor of English and Creative Writing at State University of New York, Binghamton. She is the author of, among others, *Bodymakers: The Cultural Anatomy of Women's Bodybuilding* (Rutgers University Press), *Built to Win: The Female Athlete as Cultural Icon* (University of Minnesota Press), and *Pretty Good for a Girl: A Memoir* (Free Press/Simon & Schuster*)*.

Adam Locks is Senior Lecturer in Media Studies at the University of Chichester. He has been a guest speaker on aspects of bodybuilding four times at the Annual International Society of Sports Nutrition (ISSN) conference held in America. He is currently writing a book with Adrian Smith on cult British horror director Norman J. Warren, and has recently published a chapter on Warren in *British Culture And Society In The 1970s* (eds. Laurel Forster and Sue Harper, 2010, Cambridge Scholars) and for the online film journal *Senses of Cinema* (2010). Other current projects include an in-depth study of Hammer Horror actor John Carson, and operating as co-ordinator for a celebration of the iconic television show *The Avengers* held at the university in June 2011.

Lee F. Monaghan is Senior Lecturer in Sociology, Department of Sociology, University of Limerick. He teaches the sociology of health, illness and the body, social theory, and qualitative research. He has published extensively on body-related issues, including bodybuilding, the obesity debate and violence in Britain's night-time economy. He is the author of *Bodybuilding, Drugs & Risk* (Routledge, 2001) and *Men & the War on Obesity* (Routledge, 2008). He is currently working on the second edition of *Key Concepts in Medical Sociology* (Sage, edited with Jonathan Gabe), and *Debating Obesity: Critical Pespectives* (Palgrave, edited with Emma Rich and Lucy Aphramor).

Gareth Owen Ph.D. is a Research Fellow at the Peninsula School of Medicine, University of Exeter, England. His doctoral research was an ethnographic study of a gay rowing club participating in mainstream competitive events. His analysis focused on the dynamic tension between pride and shame in the construction of competitive masculinities. Gareth is currently researching public involvement in suicide prevention.

Niall Richardson teaches Film Studies at the University of Sussex where he is convenor of MA Gender and Media. He is the author of *The Queer Cinema of Derek Jarman: Critical and Cultural Readings* (IB Tauris, 2009), *Transgressive Bodies: Representations in Film and*

Popular Culture (Ashgate, 2010), *Studying Sexualities: Theories, Representations, Practices* (Palgrave, 2011, with Angela Werndly and Clarissa Smith) and *Aged Femininity and Gentility: Representations in Popular British Cinema* (forthcoming). Once a competitive body-builder, he now remains a committed "gym rat."

Chris Shilling is Professor of Sociology and Director of Graduate Studies (Research) at the School of Social Policy, Sociology and Social Research, University of Kent, UK. He was one of the main figures involved in establishing the sociology of the body, and has for over 20 years been prominent in developing the interdisciplinary field of body studies. Chris's main publications include *The Body and Social Theory* (Sage, 1993, 2nd edition 2003), *Re-forming the Body* (Sage, 1997, with P.A. Mellor), *The Sociological Ambition* (Sage 2001, with P.A. Mellor), *The Body in Culture, Technology and Society* (Sage, 2005), *Embodying Sociology* (ed., Blackwell, 2007), and *Changing Bodies. Habit, Crisis and Creativity* (Sage, 2008). Among his present projects, he is currently working on a 3rd edition of *The Body and Social Theory*.

Andrew C. Sparkes Ph.D. is Professor of Sport and Body Pedagogy in the Faculty of Education, Community and Leisure at Liverpool John Moores University, England. His recent work has focused on performing bodies and identity formation; interrupted body projects and the narrative reconstruction of self; ageing bodies; and the lives and careers of marginalized individuals and groups. These interests are framed by a desire to develop interpretative forms of understanding via the use of life history, ethnography, and narrative approaches.

Works Cited

Introduction

Adams, Mark (2009) *Mr. America: How Muscular Millionaire Bernarr Macfadden Transformed the Nation Through Sex, Salad, and the Ultimate Starvation Diet* (New York: Harper).

Budd, Michael Anton (1997) *The Sculpture Machine: Physical Culture and Body Politics in the Age of Empire* (Basingstoke: MacMillan).

Butler, George and Gaines, Charles (1991 [1974]) *Pumping Iron: The Art and Sport of Bodybuilding* (London: Sphere).

Cashmore, Ellis (2000) *Making Sense of Sports* (London and New York: Routledge).

Chapman, David (1994) 'Bodybuilding Pioneers', *Muscle and Fitness* (November): 174–177.

Chapman, David (1997) *Adonis: The Male Physique Pin-Up 1870–1940* (London: Heretic).

Cooper, Emmanuel (1990) *Fully Exposed: The Male Nude in Photography* (London, Sydney and Wellington: Unwin Hyman).

Dobbins, Bill (1997a) 'Arnold and Franco', *Muscle and Fitness* (July): 94–99.

Dobbins, Bill (1997b) 'Arnold and Jo', *Muscle and Fitness* (July): 62–67.

Dutton, Kenneth R (1995) *The Perfectible Body: The Western Ideal of Male Physical Development* (London: Cassell).

Dyer, Richard (1997) *White: Essays on Race and Culture* (London and New York: Routledge).

Ewing, William A. (1996) *The Body: Photoworks of the Human Form* (London: Thames and Hudson).

Fitness, Johnny (1998) ''97 Ms Olympia', *MuscleMag* (March): 50–54.

Fitness, Johnny (2001) 'Editorial', *MuscleMag* (July): 9, 188.

Fortney, Ed (1995) 'Guest Editorial', *MuscleMag* (October): 7, 189.

Fussell, Sam (1991) *Muscle: Confessions of an Unlikely Bodybuilder* (London: Abacus).

Grannis, Lori (1998) 'Larry Scott: Master of Biceps', *MuscleMag* (March): 58–62.

Harris, Ron (1995) 'Guest Editorial', *MuscleMag* (September): 7.

Hunter, Jack (1995) *Inside Terrordome: An Illustrated History of the Freak Film* (London: Creation Books).

Koetzle, Michael (1994) *1000 Nudes: Uwe Schied Collection* (Hohenzollernring: Benedikt Taschen).

Leamer, Laurence (2005) *Fantastic: The Life of Arnold Schwarzenegger* (New York: St. Martin's Press).

McGough, Peter (1997) 'Anatomy of an American Icon', *Muscle and Fitness* (July): 48, 50, 52, 54, 56–58, 60.

Ray, Shaun (1997) 'Venice Beach', *Muscle and Fitness* (September): 131–133.

Roark, Joe (1997) 'Arnold Schwarzenegger Timeline', *Muscle and Fitness* (July): 71–74, 76, 78, 80, 82, 84, 86, 88, 90, 92.

Roark, Joe (1999) 'Factoids', *Flex* (August): 134–136.

Romano, John (1996) 'Drugs Versus Natural', *Muscular Development* (February): 134–137.

Sandow, Eugene (1904) *Bodybuilding* (London: Gale and Polden).

Schwarzenegger, Arnold (1993) *Arnold: The Education of a Bodybuilder* (New York: Simon and Schuster).

Tang, Isabel (1999) *Pornography: The Secret History of Civilization* (London: Channel Four Books).

Thomas, Alan Berkeley (1978) *The Expanding Eye: Photography and the Nineteenth-Century Mind* (London: Croom Helm).

Thorne, Gerard and Embleton, Phil (1997) *Encyclopedia of Bodybuilding: The Ultimate A-Z Book On Muscle Building!* Mississauga: MuscleMag International.

Webster, David (1982) *Bodybuilding: An Illustrated History* (New York: Arco Publishing).

Weider, Joe, Weider, Ben with Steere, Mike (2006) *Brothers of Iron: How the Weider Brothers Created the Fitness Movement and Built a Business Empire* (Champaign: Sports Publishing L.L.C.).

Woodland, Les (1980) *Dope: The Use of Drugs in Sport* (Newton Abbot: David and Charles).

Zulak, Greg (1999) 'Uncensored', *MuscleMag* (December): 96.

Introduction to Part 1: What is the "Practice" of Bodybuilding?

Brady, Jacqueline (2001) 'Is a Hard Woman Good to Find? Reconsidering the Amazon Project', *Studies in Gender and Sexuality*, 2(3): 215–241.

Bridges, Tristan S. (2009) 'Gender Capital and Male Bodybuilders', *Body & Society* 15(1): 83–107.

Brook, B. (2001) 'Feminist Readings of Bodybuilding' in Brook *Feminist Perspectives on the Body* (London: Longman) (118–135).

Chare, Nicholas (2008) 'Admirable Muscles: Male Beauty, Sex, Schmoes, and *Pumping Iron II*' in Steven L. Davis and Maglina Lubovich (eds.) *Hunks, Hotties and Pretty Boys: Twentieth Century Representations of Male Beauty* (Cambridge: Cambridge Scholars Press) (143–175).

Coles, Fen (1999) 'Feminine Charms and Outrageous Arms', in Janet Price and Margrit Shildrick (eds.) *Feminist Theory and the Body: A Reader* (Edinburgh: Edinburgh University Press) (445–453).

Gillett, James and White, Philip G. (1992) 'Male Bodybuilding and the Reassertion of Hegemonic Masculinity: A Critical Feminist Perspective', *Play & Culture*, 5: 358–369.

Grogan, S., Evans, R., Wright, S. and Hunter, G. (2004) 'Femininity and Muscularity: Accounts of Seven Women Body Builders', *Journal of Gender Studies*, 13(1): 49–61.

Guthrie, Sharon R. and Castelnuovo, Shirley (1992) 'Elite Women Bodybuilders: Models of Resistance or Compliance?', *Play & Culture*, 5: 401–408.

Holmlund, Christine (1989) 'Visible Difference and Flex Appeal: The body, sex, sexuality and race in the *Pumping Iron* films', *Cinema Journal*, 28(4): 38–51.

Ian, Marcia (2001) 'The Primitive Subject of Female Bodybuilding: Transgression and Other Postmodern Myths', *Differences: a Journal of Feminist Cultural Studies*, 12(3): 69–99.

Locks, Adam (2003) *Bodybuilding and the Emergence of a Post Classicism* (unpublished Ph.D. thesis).

Patton, Cindy (1994) 'Rock Hard: Judging the Female Physique', *Journal of Sport & Social Issues*, 25(2): 118–140.

Richardson, Niall (2004) 'The Queer Activity of Extreme Male Bodybuilding: Gender Dissidence, Auto-Eroticism and Hysteria', *Social Semiotics*, 14(1): 49–65.

Richardson, Niall (2008) 'Flex-rated! Female bodybuilding: feminist resistance or erotic spectacle?', *Journal of Gender Studies*, 17(4): 289–301.

Schulze, Laurie (1990) 'On the Muscle' in Jane Gaines and Charlotte Herzog (eds.) *Fabrications* (London and New York: Routledge) (59–78).

Shippert, Claudia (2007) 'Can Muscles be Queer? Reconsidering the Transgressive Hyper-built Body', *Journal of Gender Studies*, 16(2): 155–171.

Simpson, Mark (1994) 'Big Tits! Masochism and Transformation in Bodybuilding' in Mark Simpson *Male Impersonators* (London: Cassell).

St. Martin, Leena and Gavey, Nicola (1996) 'Women's Bodybuilding: Feminist Resistance and/or Femininity's Recuperation?', *Body & Society*, 2(4): 45–57.

Turner, Victor (1992) *Blazing the Trail. Way Marks in the Exploration of Symbols* (Tuscan: The University of Arizona Press).

Wiegers, Yvonne (1998) 'Male Bodybuilding: The Social Construction of a Masculine Identity', *Journal of Popular Culture*, 32: 2 (141–161).

1 Buff Bodies and the Beast: Emphasized Femininity, Labor, and Power Relations among Fitness, Figure, and Women Bodybuilding Competitors 1985–2010

Advisory Notice 101409 (Oct. 14, 2009). IFBB Professional League. Online: http://www.ifbbpro.com/category/news (accessed April 15, 2010).

Aliotti, Gina (2007) 'The Fine Details of Figure: Effective Presentation and Etiquette Figure Athlete'. Online: http://figureathlete.tmuscle.com/free_online_article/figure_competition/the_fine_details_of_figure (accessed February 8, 2010).

Arnault, Manuel (2009) 'Curva e Contracurva', *Vogue Portugal* 78 (April): 168–171.

Bavington, Lisa (2004) 'A Show Solidarity Against GNC: GNC Replaces Female Bodybuilding with Women's Figure', 1–3. Online: http://Compebodybuilding.about.com/cs/women/a/gncsos.htm (accessed July 30, 2004).

Bolin, Anne (1992) 'Vandalized Vanity: Feminine Physiques Betrayed and Portrayed' in Francis Mascia-Lees and Patricia Sharpe (eds.) *Tattoo, Torture, Adornment and Disfigurement: The Denaturalization of the Body in Culture and Text* (Albany, NY: State University of New York Press) (79–99).

Bolin, Anne (1994) 'Transcending and Transgendering: Male to Female Transsexuals, Dichotomy and Diversity' in Gilbert Herdt (ed.) *Third Sex, Third Gender: Beyond Sexual Dimorphism in Culture and History* (New York: Zone Books) (447–486).

Bolin, Anne (1996) 'Bodybuilding' in David Levinson and Karen Christensen (eds.) *The Encyclopedia of World Sport: From Ancient Times to the Present Volume I* (Santa Barbara, CA: ABC-CLIO) (107–130).

Bolin, Anne (1997) 'Flex Appeal, Food and Fat: Competitive Bodybuilding, Gender and Diet' in Pamela L. Moore (ed.) *Building Bodies* (New Brunswick, NJ: Rutgers University Press) (184–208). Reprinted from *Play and Culture*, 5(4): 378–400, 1992.

Bolin, Anne (1998) 'Muscularity and Femininity: Women Bodybuilders and Women's Bodies in Culturo-Historical Context' in Karin A. Volkwein (ed.) *Fitness as Cultural Phenomenon* (New York, NY: Waxmann Munster) (187–212).

Bolin, Anne (2003) 'Beauty or the Beast: The Subversive Soma' in Anne Bolin and Jane Granskog (eds.) *Athletic Intruders: Ethnographic Research on Women, Culture and Exercise* (Albany, NY: State University of New York Press) (107–130).

Bolin, Anne (2004) 'Testy and Docile Bodies: Her-Stories of Compliance and Defiance in Women's Bodybuilding' in *Body/Gender: The Proceedings of the Sixth International Super-Slim Conference on Politics of Gender and Sexuality* (1–7 English).

Burstyn, Varda (1999) *The Rites of Men: Manhood, Politics, and the Culture of Sport* (Ontario: University of Toronto Press).

Butler, George and Gaines, Charles (1985) *Pumping Iron II: The Women* (Cinecom International films, Inc. Barbelle Productions).

'Choosing the Right Figure Shoes' (n.d.) HardBodyFigure.com. Online: http://www.hardbodyfigure.com/Figure12.html (accessed February 3, 2010).

Clive, Teagan (1997) 'Joe Weider's Olympia Weekend: Sole Survivor', *Joe Weider's Muscle and Fitness*, 58(1): 84–97, 237.

Connell, Robert W. (1987) *Gender and Power* (Stanford: Stanford University Press).

Connell, Robert W. (2000) *The Men and the Boys* (Berkeley: University of California Press).

Connell, Robert W. (2002) *Gender* (Cambridge: Polity Press).

Contest Activity Report (2005) *NPC News*, 19(5): 234–243.

Dayton, Laura (1994) 'Raye Hollitt: New and Improved', *Powerhouse* 8(8): 70–73.

Dobbins, Bill (n.d.a) 'Kim Chizevsky: The Best Female Bodybuilder of all Time'. Online: http//:www.billdobbins.com/PUBLIC/pages/coolfree/Kimbest.html (accessed April 15, 2010).

Dobbins, Bill (n.d.b) 'What Kind of Body Should Win Fitness Contests?' Online: http//:www.billdobbins.com (accessed October 10, 2004).

Dobbins, Bill (n.d.c) 'Fitness and Figure competitors: The Struggles, The Pain, and the Beauty'. Online: http//:www.bodybuilding.com/fun/billdobbins2.htm (accessed July 22, 2004).

Dobbins, Bill (n.d.d) 'The evolution of bodybuilding judging'. Online: http://www.billdobbins.com/public/pages/coolfree/judgevo.html.

Dobbins, Bill (1997) 'Muscle...or Fitness?', *Joe Weider's Muscle and Fitness* 58(5): 158–161, 239.

Dobbins, Bill (1999) 'Professional Bodybuilding for Women: A Victim of its Own Success'. Online: http//:www.billdobbins.com (accessed July 22, 2004).

Downs, Steve (1994) 'Taj Mahl Fitness Pageant', *Women's Exercise*, 2(4): 52–58.

Dworkin, Shari L. and Wachs, Faye Linda (2009) *Body Panic: Gender, Health and the Selling of Fitness* (New York: New York University Press).

Faludi, Susan (1991) *Backlash: The Undeclared War Against American Women* (New York: Anchor Books).

Gallagher, Marty (1997) 'Designing Delts', *Joe Weider's Muscle and Fitness* 58(8): 115–121.

Hard Body News (2008) 'It's official – NPC rule changes announced for 2009'. Online: http://www.bodybuildingweekly.com/hardbodies_news/bodybuild-ing_fitness_figure_industry_news/its-official-npc-rule-changes-announced-for-2009.html (accessed September 21, 2009).

Herdt, Gilbert (2009) *Moral Panics, Sex Panics: Fear and the Fight over Sexual Rights: Intersections, Transdisciplinary Perspectives on Genders and Sexualities* (New York: New York University Press).

IFBB (2001) 'Amateur Rules for Bodybuilding', 2001 edition. Online: http://www.ifbb.com/amarules/indes.html (accessed October 6, 2004).

IFBB (2001) 'Amateur Rules for Women's Fitness', 2001 edition. Online: http://www.ifbb.com/amarules/indes.html (accessed October 6, 2004).

IFBB (2006) 'Amateur Rules for Bodybuilding, Women's Fitness, Body Fitness, Men's Fitness, Code of Ethics, Directives, The Deviation Method, Judging Forms'. Online: http//:www.ifbb.com/amarules/index.html (accessed April 15, 2010).

IFBB (2009) '2010 IFBB Pro League Contest Schedule', *NPC News*, 23(5): 217–218.

IFBB (2010) 'IFBB Rules Men and Women Bodybuilding, Men Classic Bodybuilding, Women Fitness, Men Fitness, Women Body Fitness,' 2009 edition. Online: http://www.ifbb.com/pdf/IFBBrulebook.pdf (accessed December 15, 2009).

IFBB Professional League (2009) 'IFBB Professional League Rules for Bodybuilding, Fitness, and Figure 2009'. Online: http://www.ifbbprofessional-league.com/IFBBProRules.pdf (accessed January 22, 2010).

Kanner, B (1994) 'Body Flattering Lingerie: How Much Science, How Much Fiction?' *Glamour*, (October): 197–198.

Kelly, Brenda (n.d.) 'Do I have to Wear High Heels?'. Online: http://www.bodybuilding.com/fun/brenda17.htm (accessed April 15, 2010).

Kindela, Jerry (1996) 'Odyssey', *Flex*, 13(12): 159–166, 188, 190, 222, 230.

Lafferty, Yvonne and McKay, Jim (2004) 'Suffragettes in Satin Shorts? Gender and Competitive Boxing', *Qualitative Sociology*, 27(3): 249–276.

Lindsay, Jon (2009) 'NPC Women's Figure Competition Guidelines'. Online: http//: www.lindsayproductions.com/figureguidelines.htm (accessed September 11, 2009).

Manion, Jim (2000) *Letter January 5, to NPC Female Bodybuilding Competitors*. *Subject*: Bodybuilding Criteria. President National Physique Committee.

McCaughey, Martha (1997) *Real Knockouts: The Physical Feminism of Women's Self-Defense* (New York University Press).

McGough, Peter (ed.) (1998) 'The First 15 and All That', *Flex*, 16(2): 18–20.

McGough, Peter (2000) 'Work in Progress', *Flex* 18(9): 99–100, 102, 104, 106, 108–110.

McGough, Peter (2001) '180 Degrees of Separation: Kim Chizevsky's Moment of Truth', *Joe Weider's Flex*, 19(5): 186–188, 190.

Messner, Michael A. (2004) 'Barbie Girls versus Sea Monsters: Children Constructing Gender' in Michael S. Kimmel and Michael A. Messner (eds.) *Men's Lives* (Boston: Pearson AB) 87–102.

NPC (2004) 'New NPC Rule Changes for 2004; New NPC Rule Changes for 2003; New Rule Changes for NPC Bodybuilding and Fitness and the Creation of a New Division-Figure; Bodybuilding; Fitness, NPC Internet Event Press Policy'. Online: http//:www.npcnewsonline.com/new/npcrules.html (accessed October 6, 2004).

NPC (2009a) 'NPC 2010 Division Rules', *NPC News*, 23(4): 132–152.

NPC (2009b) 'NPC Amateur Bikini Division Competition at the 2009 Arnold Sports Festival'. Online: http://arnoldsportsfestival.com/2009/01/07/npc-amateur-division-competition-at-2009-arnold/ (accessed July 6, 2009).

NPC (2009c) 'NPC 2009 Rule Changes and Bikini Division Guidelines'. Online: hyperlink has been removed, see http//:www.posingswimsuits.com (accessed May 12, 2011).

NPC (2009d) 'National Physique Committee Rules and Guidelines for Judging Competitions, 2009'. Online: http://getbig.com/info/npc/npcrules.htm (accessed March 3, 2010).

NPC (2009) 'NPC Bikini Division', *NPC News On-Line*. Online: http://www. npcnewsonline.com/new/npcrules_bikini.html (accessed July 6, 2009).

NPC Women's Figure Competition Guidelines (n.d.) MuscleContest.com. Online: http://lindsayproduction.com/figureguidlines.htm, (accessed February 3, 2010).

New Inflatable Bikini Will Pump!-You Up (1992) *The Greensboro News and Record*, (July) 30: 1.

Potter, Peter (2003) 'NPC Junior USA', *Southern Muscle* 5(6): 50–59.

Richardson, Niall (2004) 'The Queer Activity of Extreme Male Bodybuilding: Gender Dissidence, Auto-eroticism and Hysteria', *Social Semiotics*, 14(1): 49–65.

Rosenthal, J.R (2000) 'Something about Mary', *Flex*, 18(1): 236–39, 41–42.

Salzman, Philip C. (1999) *The Anthropology of Real Life: Events in Human Experience* (Prospect Heights, IL: Waveland).

Schippert, Claudia (2007) 'Can Muscles be Queer? Reconsidering the Transgressive Hyper-built Body', *Journal of Gender Studies*, 16(2): 155–171.

Thomas, Al (1999) 'Toward a New Aesthetics of Body for the Modern Woman' in Joanna Frueh, Lauri Fierstein and Judith Stein, (eds.) *The Modern Amazon* (Rizzoli, NY: New Museum Books) (86–99).

Schmaltz, Jim (2003) 'Suzie Curry: Buh-bye: Hard Times', *Flex* 21(10): 41–50.

Teper, Lonnie and Silverman, Ruth (1996) 'Who's Sexier? Women Bodybuilders or Fitness Women?', *Australian Ironman* 3(1): 52–63.

Vogue (1994) 'Waist Case', (September) 184(9): 244.

Weber, Carol Ann (1992) 'Fitness Wars', *Muscular Development*, 29(5): 8–9.

Wennerstrom, Steve (2004) 'The Light-Heavyweight Class: A History', *Joe Weider's Flex*, 22(4): 219.

Wilkins, Rob (n.d.) 'All About the New IFBB Figure Division. Bodybuilding. COM Articles, Fitness and Figure Competitions'. Online: http//:www. bodybuilding.com/fun/rob7.htm (accessed October 3, 2004).

2 Outside and Inside the Gym: Exploring the Identity of the Female Bodybuilder

Bartky, Sandra (1988) 'Foucault, Feminism and Patriarchal Power', in Irene Diamond and Lee Quinby (eds.), *Feminism and Foucault* (Boston, MA: Northeastern University Press).

Beauvoir, de Simone (1993 [1949]) *The Second Sex* (London: Everyman).

Becker, Howard (1997 [1963]) *Outsider* (London: Simon and Schuster).

Bourdieu, Pierre (1978) 'Sport and Social Class', *Social Science Information*, 17: 819–840.

Connell, Robert (1987) *Gender and Power* (Cambridge: Polity).

Cooley, Charles (1922 [1902]) *Human Nature and Social Order* (New Brunswick: Transaction Publishers).

Crossley, Nick (2006) 'In the Gym: motives, meanings and moral careers', *Body & Society*, 12(3): 23–50.

Douglas, Mary (1966) *Purity and Danger* (London: RKP).

Durkheim, Emile (1995 [1912]) *The Elementary Forms of Religious Life* (New York: Free Press).

Felshin, Jan (1974) 'The social view', in E.R. Gerber et al. (eds.), *The American Woman in Sport* (Reading, MA: Addison-Wesley).

Fisher, Leslee (1997) 'Building One's Self Up', in Pamela Moore (ed.) *Building Bodies* (New Brunswick, NJ: Rutgers University Press).

Frueh, Joanna (2001) *Monster/Beauty Building a Body of Love* (Berkeley: University of California Press).

Goffman, Erving (1963) *Stigma* (London: Penguin).

Goffman, Erving (1969) *The Presentation of Self in Everyday Life* (London: Penguin).

Goffman, Erving (1974) *Frame Analysis* (New York: Harper and Row).

Goffman, Erving (1979) *Gender Advertisements* (London: Macmillan).

Goffman, Erving (1983) 'The Interaction Order', *American Sociological Review*, 48: 1–17.

Goffman, Erving (1987) 'The Arrangement Between the Sexes', in Mary Jo Deegan and Michael Hill (eds.), *Interaction* (Winchester, MA: Allen and Unwin).

Heywood, Leslie (1998) *Bodymakers: A Cultural Anatomy of Women's Bodybuilding* (New Brunswick, NJ: Rutgers University Press).

Ian, Marcia (1995) 'How Do You Wear Your Body?: Bodybuilding and the sublimity of drag', in Monica Dorenkamp and Richard Henke (eds.), *Negotiating Lesbian and Gay Subjects* (London and New York: Routledge).

Kessler, Suzanne and McKenna, Wendy (1978) *Gender: An Ethnomethodological Approach* (Chicago: University of Chicago Press).

Koskela, Hille (1997) '"Bold Walk and Breakings": Women's spatial confidence versus fear of violence', *Gender, Place & Culture*, 4(3): 301–320.

Leder, Drew (1990) *The Absent Body* (Chicago: Chicago University Press).

Lowe, Maria R. (1998) *Women of Steel* (New York: New York University Press).

Mansfield, Alan and McGinn, Barbara (1993) 'Pumping Irony: The muscular and the feminine', in Sue Scott and David Morgan (eds.), *Body Matters* (London: Falmer).

Mead, George Herbert (1962 [1934]) *Mind, Self and Society* (Chicago: Chicago University Press).

Merleau-Ponty, Maurice (1962) *Phenomenology of Perception* (London and New York: Routledge).

Mills, Charles Wright (1940) 'Situated Actions and Vocabularies of Motive', *American Sociological Review*, V: 904–913.

Monaghan, Lee (2001) 'Looking Good and Feeling Good', *Sociology of Health and Illness*, 23(3): 330–356.

Nelson, Mariah Burton (1994) *The Stronger Women Get, The More Men Love Football* (New York: Harcourt).

Paris, Bob (1997) *Gorilla Suit – My Adventures in Bodybuilding* (St. Martins Press: New York).

Sassatelli, Roberta (1999) 'Interaction Order and Beyond: A field analysis of body culture within fitness gyms', *Body & Society*, 5(2–3): 227–248.

Shilling, Chris (2003) *The Body and Social Theory, 2nd edition* (London: Sage).

Shilling, Chris and Bunsell, Tanya (2009) 'The Female Body Builder as a Gender ouTlaw', *Qualitative Research in Sport and Exercise*, 1(2): 141–159.

St. Martin, Leena and Gavey, Nicola (1996) 'Women's Bodybuilding: Feminist resistance and/or femininity's recuperation?' *Body & Society*, 2(4): 45–57.

Tate, S. (1999) 'Making your Body your Signature: Weight-Training and Transgressive femininities' in Roseneil, Sasha and Seymour, Julie (eds.) *Practising Identities: Power and Resistance* (Basingstoke: Macmillans).

Thomas, J. (2005) 'Bulked-up Barbie Girl Waging War on Her Body', *The Independent*, October 15.

Turner, Victor (1957) *Schism and Continuity in an African Society: A Study of Ndembu Village Life* (Manchester: Manchester University Press).

Turner, Victor (1977) 'Variations of the Theme of Liminality', in S. Moore and B. Myerhoff (eds.) *Secular Ritual* (Assen: Van Gorcum) (36–52).

Turner, Victor (1969) *The Ritual Process: Structure and Anti-Structure* (Chicago: Aldine Publishing Co.).

Turner, Victor (1974) *Dramas, Fields and Metaphors* (Ithaca, NY: Cornell University Press).

Turner, Victor (1992) *Blazing the Trail. Way Marks in the Exploration of Symbols* (Tuscan: The University of Arizona Press).

Waskul, Dennis and Vannini, Philip (eds.) (2006) *Body/Embodiment: Symbolic Interactionism and the Sociology of the Body* (Hampshire: Ashgate Publishing Ltd.).

Young, Iris M. (1990) *Throwing Life a Girl* (Bloomington, IN: Indiana University Press).

3 Accounting for Illicit Steroid Use: Bodybuilders' Justifications

Adler, Patricia A. and Adler, Peter (1987) *Membership Roles in Field Research*. London: Sage.

Baker, Millard (2009) 'United Kingdom Expands Anabolic Steroid Laws for 2012 London Olympics'. Online: http://www.ironmagazine.com/blog/2009/united-kingdom-expands-anabolic-steroid-laws-for-2012-london-olympics/ (accessed August 27, 2010).

Bloor, Michael, Monaghan, Lee, Dobash, Russell P. and Dobash, Rebecca E. (1998) 'The Body as a Chemistry Experiment: Steroid Use Among South Wales Bodybuilders' in Sarah Nettleton and Jonathan Watson (eds.) *The Body in Everyday Life* (London and New York: Routledge).

Davis, Fred and Munoz, Laura (1968) 'Heads and Freaks: Patterns and Meanings of Drug Use Among Hippies', *Journal of Health and Social Behavior* 9(2): 156–64.

Davis, Kathy (1995) *Reshaping the Female Body: The Dilemma of Cosmetic Surgery* (London and New York: Routledge).

Dunning, Eric and Waddington, Ivan (2003) 'Sport as a Drug and Drugs in Sport: Some Exploratory Comments', *International Review for the Sociology of Sport* 38(3): 351–368.

Elliot, Diane L. and Goldberg, Linn (2000) 'Women and Anabolic Steroids' in Charles E. Yesalis (ed.) *Anabolic Steroids in Sports and Exercise*, 2nd edition (Champaign, IL: Human Kinetics).

Featherstone, Mike (1991) 'The Body in Consumer Culture' in Mike Featherstone, Mike Hepworth and Bryan S. Turner (eds.) *The Body: Social Process and Cultural Theory* (London: Sage).

Gabe, Jonathan; Kelleher, David and Williams, Gareth (eds.) (1994) *Challenging Medicine* (London and New York: Routledge).

Glassner, Barry (1990) 'Fit For Postmodern Selfhood' in Howard S. Becker and Michal M. McCall (eds.) *Symbolic Interaction and Cultural Studies* (Chicago: University of Chicago Press).

Goffman, Ervin (1968) *Stigma: Notes on the Management of Spoiled Identity* (Middlesex: Penguin Books).

Grogan, Sarah, Shepherd, Sarah, Evans, Ruth, Wright, Sam and Hunter, Geoff (2006) 'Experiences of Anabolic Steroid Use: In-depth Interviews with Men and Women', *Journal of Health Psychology*, 11(6): 845–856.

Hart, Graham and Carter, Simon (2000) 'Drugs and Risk: Developing a Sociology of HIV Risk Behaviour' in Simon J. Williams, Jonathan Gabe and Michael Calnan (eds.) *Health, Medicine and Society* (London and New York: Routledge).

Herlitz, Leal C., Markowitz, Glen S., Farris, Alton B., Schwimmer, Joshua A., Stokes, Michael B., Kunis, Cheryl, Colvin, Robert B. and D'Agati, Vivette D. (2010) 'Development of Focal Segmental Glomerulosclerosis After Anabolic Steroid Abuse', *Journal of the American Society of Nephrology* 21(1): 163–172.

Kashkin, Kenneth B. (1992) 'Anabolic Steroids' in Joyce H. Lowinson, Pedro Ruiz, Robert B. Millman and John G. Langrid (eds.) *Substance Abuse: A Comprehensive Textbook*, 2nd edition (Baltimore: Williams and Wilkins).

Klein, Alan M. (1993) *Little Big Men: Bodybuilding Subculture and Gender Construction* (Albany, NY: State University of New York Press).

Klein, Alan (1995) 'Life's too Short to Die Small: Steroid Use Among Male Bodybuilders' in Donald F. Sabo and David F. Gordon (eds.) *Men's Health and Illness: Gender, Power, and the Body* (London: Sage).

Korkia, Pirkko K. and Stimson, Gerry V (1993) *Anabolic Steroid Use in Great Britain: An Exploratory Investigation* (London: The Centre for Research on Drugs and Health Behaviour).

Lupton, Deborah (1997) *The Imperative of Health: Public Health and The Regulated Body* (London: Sage).

Mansfield, Alan and McGinn, Barbara (1993) 'Pumping Irony: The Muscular and the Feminine' in Sue Scott and David Morgan (eds.) *Body Matters* (London: Falmer Press).

McKeganey, Neil and Barnard, Marina (1992) *AIDS, Drugs and Sexual Risk: Lives in the Balance* (Buckingham: Open University Press).

Monaghan, Lee (1999) 'Challenging Medicine? Bodybuilding, Drugs and Risk' *Sociology of Health & Illness*, 21(6): 707–734.

Monaghan, Lee F. (2001a) *Bodybuilding, Drugs and Risk* (London: Routledge).

Monaghan, Lee F. (2001b) 'Looking Good, Feeling Good: The Embodied Pleasures of Vibrant Physicality', *Sociology of Health & Illness*, 23(3): 330–356.

Monaghan, Lee F. (2002) 'Vocabularies of Motive for Illicit Steroid Use among Bodybuilders', *Social Science & Medicinei*, 55(5): 695–708.

Monaghan, Lee F. (2009) 'The Normalization of Steroid Use', *Addiction*, 104(12): 1979–1980.

Monaghan, Lee, Bloor, Michael, Dobash, Russell P. and Dobash, Rebecca E. (2000) 'Drug-taking, "Risk Boundaries" and Social Identity: Bodybuilders' Talk about Ephedrine and Nubain', *Sociological Research Online*, 5(2). Online: http://www.socresonline.org.uk/5/2/monaghan.html.

Pates, Richard and Barry, Cindy (1996) 'Steroid Use in Cardiff: A Problem for Whom?' *The Seventh International Conference on the Reduction of Drug Related Harm* (Hobart, Tasmania).

Rhodes, Tim (1997) 'Risk Theory in Epidemic Times: Sex, Drugs and the Social Organisation of Risk Behaviour', *Sociology of Health & Illness*, 19(2): 208–227.

Schaps, Eric and Sanders, Clinton R. (1970) 'Purposes, Patterns, and Protection in a Campus Drug-using Community', *Journal of Health and Social Behavior*, 11: 135–145.

Schutz, Alfred (1964) *Collected Papers II: Studies in Social Theory* (The Hague: Martinus Nijhoff).

Scott, Marvin B. and Lyman, Stanford M (1968) 'Accounts', *American Sociological Review*, 33(1): 46–62.

Sparkes, Andrew C. (2009) 'Ethnography and the Senses: Challenges and Possibilities', *Qualitative Research in Sport and Exercise*, 1(1): 21–35.

Sykes, Gresham and Matza, David (1957) 'Techniques of Neutralization: A Theory of Delinquency', *American Sociological Review*, 22(6): 664–670.

Uzych, Leo (1992) 'Anabolic Androgenic Steroids and Psychiatric Related Effects: A Review', *Canadian Journal of Psychiatry Review*, 37(1): 23–28.

Waddington, Ivan (2000) *Sport, Health and Drugs: A Critical Sociological Perspective* (London: E & FN Spon).

Weber, Max (1930 [1905]) *The Protestant Ethic and the Spirit of Capitalism* (London: Unwin & Hyman).

Weinstein, Raymond M. (1980) 'Vocabularies of Motive for Illicit Drug Use: An Application of the Accounts Framework', *The Sociological Quarterly*, 21(4): 577–593.

Wright Mills, Charles (1940) 'Situated Actions and Vocabularies of Motive', *American Sociological Review*, 5(6): 904–913.

4 Bodybuilding and Health Work: A Life Course Perspective

Atkinson, Michael (2007) 'Playing With Fire: Masculinity, Health, and Sports Supplements', *Sociology of Sport Journal*, 24: 165–186.

Becker, Howard S. (1963) *Outsiders: studies in the sociology of deviance* (London: Free Press of Glencoe).

Blaxter, Mildred (2000) 'Class, Time and Biography' in Simon J Williams, Jonathan Gabe and Michael Calnan (eds.) *Health, Medicine and Society: Key Theories, Future Agendas* (London and New York: Routledge) (27–50).

Bridges, Tristan S. (2009) 'Gender Capital and Male Bodybuilders', *Body & Society*, 15: 83–107.

Connell, Raewyn (2008) 'Masculinity Construction and Sports in Boys' Education: a framework for thinking about the issue', *Sport, Education and Society*, 13: 131–145.

Connell, Robert W. (1987) *Gender and Power* (Cambridge: Polity Press).

Connell, Robert W. and Messerschmidt, James W. (2005) 'Hegemonic Masculinity: Rethinking the concept', *Gender and Society*, 17: 829–859.

Conway, Stephen and Hockey, Jenny (1998) 'Resisting the "Mask" of Old Age?: The social meaning of lay health beliefs in later life', *Ageing and Society*, 18: 469–494.

Cooley, Charles Horton (1964) *Human Nature and the Social Order* (New York: Schocker Books).

Crawford, Robert (1980) 'Healthism and Medicalization of Everyday Life', *International Journal of Health Services*, 10: 365–388.

Crawford, Robert (1984) 'A Cultural Account of Health: Control, Release and the Social Body' in John B. McKinlay (ed.) *Issues in the Political Economy of Health Care* (New York: Tavistock) (61–103).

Elling, Agnes and Knoppers, Annelies (2005) 'Sport, Gender and Ethnicity: Practises of Symbolic Inclusion/Exclusion', *Journal of Youth and Adolescence*, 34: 257–268.

Gill, Rosalind, Henwood, Karen and McLean, Carl (2005) 'Body Projects and the Regulation of Normative Masculinity', *Body & Society*, 11: 37–62.

Gillett, James (1995) 'The Reclaiming of Social Space: A study of amateur male Bodybuilders', in Otmar Weiss and Wolfgang Schultz (ed.) *Sport in Space and Time* (Vienna: University of Vienna Press) (163–169).

Gillett, James, and White, Philip G. (1992) 'Male Bodybuilding and the Reassertion of Hegemonic Masculinity: A Critical Feminist Perspective', *Play & Culture*, 5: 358–369.

Goldstein, Michael S. (2000) 'The Growing Acceptance of Complementary and Alternative Medicine' in Chloe E. Bird, Peter Conrad, and Allen M. Fremont (eds.) *Handbook of Medical Sociology*, 5th edition (New York: Prentice Hall) (284–297).

Gray, Ross E., Fitch, Margaret I., Fergus, Karen D., Mykhalovskiy, Eric and Church, Kathryn (2002) 'Hegemonic Masculinity and the Experience of Prostate Cancer: A Narrative Approach', *Journal of Aging and Identity*, 7: 43–62.

Gray, Ross E., Klotz, Laurence, Iscoe, Neil, Fitch, Margaret, Fransen, Edmee, Johnson, Beverly and Labrecque, Manon (1997) 'Results of a Survey of Canadian Men with Prostate Cancer', *Canadian Journal of Urology*, 4: 359–365.

Grogan, Sarah (1999) *Body Image: Understanding Body Dissatisfaction in Men, Women and Children* (London and New York: Routledge).

Gruneau, Richard (1997) 'The Politics of Ideology of Active Living in Historical Perspective', in James E. Curtis and Storm J. Russell (ed.) *Physical Activity in Human Experience* (Champaign, IL: Human Kinetics) (191–228).

James, Alison and Hockey, Jenny (2007) *Embodying Health Identities* (New York: Palgrave Macmillan).

Keane, Helen (2005) 'Diagnosing the Male Steroid User: drug use, body image and disordered masculinity', *Health: An Interdisciplinary Journal for the Social Study of Health, Illness and Medicine*, 9: 189–208.

Klein, Alan M. (1981) 'The Master Blaster: Bodybuilding and Empire Building', *Arena Review*, 5: 21–28.

Klein, Alan M. (1985) 'Pumping Iron', *Society, Transactions, Social Sciences and Modern*, 22: 68–75.

Klein, Alan M. (1986) 'Pumping Irony: Crisis and Contradiction in Bodybuilding', *Sociology of Sport Journal*, 3: 112–133.

Klein, Alan M. (1992) 'Man Makes Himself: Alienation and Self-Objectification in Bodybuilding', *Play & Culture*, 5: 326–337.

Klein, Alan M. (1993) *Little Big Men: Bodybuilding Subculture and Gender Construction* (Albany, NY: State University of New York Press).

Lawton, Julia (2003) 'Lay Experiences of Health and Illness: past research and future agendas', *Sociology of Health and Illness*, 25: 23–40.

Leder, Drew (1990) *The Absent Body* (Chicago: University of Chicago Press).

Miller, Kathleen E., Sabo, Donald F., Farrell, Michael P., Barnes, Grace M. and Melnick, Merrill J. (1999) 'Sports, Sexual Behavior, Contraceptive Use, and Pregnancy Among Female and Male High School Students: Testing Cultural Resource Theory', *Sociology of Sport Journal*, 16: 366–387.

Monaghan, Lee F. (1999a) 'Creating the Perfect Body', *Body & Society*, 5: 267–290.

Monaghan, Lee F. (1999b) 'Challenging Medicine? Bodybuilding, drugs and risk', *Sociology of Health & Illness*, 21: 707–734.

Monaghan, Lee F. (2001a) *Bodybuilding, Drugs and Risk* (London: Routledge).

Monaghan, Lee F. (2001b) 'Looking Good, Feeling gOod: the embodied pleasures of vibrant physicality', *Sociology of Health and Illness*, 23: 330–356.

Monaghan, Lee F. (2002) 'Vocabularies of Motive for Illicit Steroid Use Among Bodybuilders', *Social Science & Medicine*, 55: 695–708.

Oliffe, John (2009) 'Health Behaviors, Prostate Cancer, and Masculinities: A Life Course Perspective', *Men & Masculinities*, 11: 346–366.

Pawluch, Dorothy, Cain, Roy and Gillett, James (2000) 'Lay Constructions of HIV and Complementary Therapy Use', *Social Sciences & Medicine*, 51: 251–264.

Robertson, Steve (2006) '"Not Living Life in Too Much of an Excess": lay men understanding health and well-being', *Health: An Interdisciplinary Journal for the Social Study of Health, Illness and Medicine*, 10: 175–189.

Smith, James A., Braunack-Mayer, Annette, Wittert, Gary and Warin, Megan (2007) '"I've been Independent for so Damn Long!": Independence, masculinity and aging in a help seeking context', *Journal of Aging Studies*, 21: 325–335.

Sparkes, Andrew C. and Smith, Brett (2002) 'Sport, Spinal Cord Injury, Embodied Masculinities, and the Dilemmas of Narrative Identity', *Men and Masculinities*, 4: 258–285.

White, Philip G. and Gillett, James (1994) 'Reading the Muscular Body: A Critical Decoding of Advertisements in *Flex* Magazine', *Sociology of Sport Journal*, 11: 18–39.

White, Phil, Young, Kevin and Gillett, James (1995) 'Bodywork as Moral Imperative: Some Critical Notes on Health and Fitness', *Loisir et Societe/Society and Leisurei*, 18: 159–181.

5 The Shame–Pride–Shame of the Muscled Self in Bodybuilding: A Life History Study

Barbalet, Jack (2002) *Emotions and Sociology* (Oxford: Blackwell).

Bramham, Peter (2003) 'Boys, Masculinities and PE', *Sport, Education and Society*, 8(1): 57–71.

Carrington, Ben (2000) 'Double Consciousness and the Black British Athlete' in Kwesi Owusu (ed.) *Black British Culture and Society* (London and New York: Routledge).

Cooley, Charles (1983 [1922]) *Human Nature and Social Order* (London: Transaction).

Davidson, Judy (2006) 'The Necessity of Queer Shame for Gay Pride' in Jayne Caudwell (ed.) *Sport, Sexualities and Queer/Theory* (London and New York: Routledge).

Drummond, Murray (2003) 'The Meaning of Boys' Bodies in Physical Education', *The Journal of Men's Studies*, 11(2): 131–143.

Frank, Arthur (1991) 'For a Sociology of the Body: An analytical review' in Mike Featherstone, Mike Hepworth, and Bryan S. Turner (eds.) *The Body* (London: Sage).

Freund, Peter (1990) 'The Expressive Body: a common ground for the sociology of emotions and health and illness', *Sociology of Health and Illness*, 12(4): 454–477.

Giddens, Anthony (1991) *Modernity and Self-Identity* (Cambridge, MA: Polity Press).

Hoschschild, Arlie (1983) *The Managed Heart: Commercialization of Human Feeling*. Berkeley, CA: University of California Press.

Hylton, Kevin (2009). *'Race' and Sport: Critical Race Theory* (London and New York: Routledge).

Klein, Alan (1995). 'Life's too Short to Die Small: steroid use among male body-builders' in Donald Sabo and David Gordon (eds.) *Men's Health and Illness* (London: Sage).

Majors, R. (1990) 'Cool pose: Black masculinities in sport' in M. Messner and D. Sabo (eds.) *Sport, Men and the Gender Order: Critical Feminist Perspectives* (Champaign, IL: Human Kinetics).

Mercer, Kobena (1994) *Welcome to the Jungle: New Positions in Black Cultural studies* (London and New York: Routledge).

Messner, Michael (1992). *Power at Play: Sports and the Problem of Masculinity* (Boston: Beacon Press).

Monaghan, Lee (2001) *Bodybuilding, Drugs and Risk* (London and New York: Routledge).

Munt, Sally (2007) *Queer Attachments: The Cultural Politics of Shame* (Hampshire: Ashgate Publishing Ltd.).

Nathanson, Donald L. (1992) *Shame and Pride: Affect, Sex and the Birth of Self* (New York: W.W. Norton).

Owen, Gareth (2006) 'Catching Crabs: Bodies, emotions and gay identities in mainstream competitive rowing', in Jayne Caudwell (ed.) *Sport, Sexualities and Queer/Theory* (London and New York: Routledge).

Probyn, Elspeth (2000) 'Sporting Bodies: dynamics of shame and pride', *Body & Society*, 6(1): 13–28.

Sabo, Donald (1994) 'Doing Time Doing Masculinity: sports and prison' in Michael Messner and Donald Sabo (eds.) *Sex, Violence and Power in Sports* (Freedom: The Crossing Press).

Scheff, Thomas (2003) 'Shame in Self and Society', *Symbolic Interaction*, 26(2): 239–262.

Sewell, Tony (1997) *Black Masculinities and Schooling* (Stoke on Trent: Trentham Books).

Shilling, S. (1993) *The Body and Social Theory* (London: Sage).

Sparkes, Andrew, Batey, Joanne and Brown, David (2005) 'The Muscled Self and Its Aftermath: A life history study of an elite, black, male bodybuilder', *Auto/Biography*, 13(2): 131–160.

Wellard, Ian (2006) 'Able Bodies and Sport Participation: social constructions of physical ability for gendered and sexually identified bodies', *Sport, Education and Society*, 11(2): 105–119.

Wesley, Jennifer (2001) 'Negotiating Gender: bodybuilding and the natural/unnatural Continuum', *Sociology of Sport Journal*, 18: 162–180.

White, Philip and Gillett, James (1994) 'Reading the Muscular Body: A critical decoding of advertisements in *Flex* magazine', *Sociology of Sport Journal*, 11: 18–39.

Wolke, Dieter and Sapouna, Maria (2008) 'Big Men Feeling Small: childhood bullying experience, muscle dysmorphia and other mental health problems in bodybuilders', *Psychology of Sport and Exercise*, 9: 595–604.

6 Building Otherwise: Bodybuilding as Immersive Practice

Arnoldi, Katie (2001) *Chemical Pink* (New York: Forge Books).

Brown, Chris (2005) 'Westfailure?' in David Held and Antony McGrew (eds.) *The Global Transformations Reader* (New York: Polity Press).

Conrad, Joseph (1988). *Heart of Darkness*, ed. Robert Kimbrough, 3rd edition (New York: Norton Critical Editions).

CrossFit, Inc (n.d.) 'The CrossFit Training Guide'. Online: http://journal.crossfit.com/2010/05/crossfit-level-1-training-guide.tpl.

Csikszentmihalyi, Mihaly (1990) *Flow* (New York: Harper).

Derrida, Jacques (1991) 'Signature Event Context', in Peggy Kamuf (ed.) *Between the Blinds: A Derrida Reader* (New York: Columbia University Press) (82–111).

Fussell, Samuel Wilson (1991) *Muscle: Confessions of an Unlikely Bodybuilder* (New York: Avon Books).

Hardt, Michael and Negri, Antonio (2000) *Empire* (Cambridge, MA: Harvard University Press).

Hay, Peter R (2002) *Main Currents in Western Environmental Thought*, (Bloomington, IN: Indiana University Press).

Heywood, Leslie (1998) *Bodymakers: A Cultural Anatomy of Women's Bodybuilding.* (New Brunswick: Rutgers University Press).

Heywood, Leslie (2000) 'Ghettos of Obscurity: Individual Sovereignty and the Struggle for Recognition in Female Bodybuilding', in Joanna Frueh, Laurie Fierstein, and Judith Stein (eds.) *Picturing the Modern Amazon* (NY: Rizzoli) (72–85).

Kaye, Kristin (2005) *Iron Maidens: The Celebration of the Most Awesome Female Muscle in the World* (New York: Thunder's Mouth Press).

Klein, Alan M. (1993) *Little Big Men: Bodybuilding Subculture and Gender Construction* (Albany, NY: State University of New York Press).

Kuntsler, James Howard (1994) *The Geography of Nowhere* (New York: The Free Press).

Kuntsler, James Howard (2005) *The Long Emergency* (New York: Atlantic Monthly Press).

Macnaghten, Phil (2003) 'Embodying the Environment in Everyday Life Practices', *The Sociological Review*, 51(1): 63–84.

Mellor, Mary (2005) 'Ecofeminism and Environmental Ethics: A Materialist Perspective', in Michael E. Zimmerman, J. Baird Callicot, Karen J. Warren, Irene J. Klaver, and John Clark (eds.) *Environmental Philosophy: From Animal Rights to Radical Ecology* (Upper Saddle River, NJ: Pearson/Prentice Hall).

Monaghan, Lee (2000) *Bodybuilding, Drugs, and Risk* (London and New York: Routledge).

Parry, Jim, Robinson, Simon, Watson, Nick J. and Nesti, Mark (2007) *Sport and Spirituality: An Introduction* (London and New York: Routledge).

Pease, Donald E (2009) *The New American Exceptionalism* (Minneapolis: University of Minnesota Press).

Richardson, Niall (2008) 'Flex Rated! Female Bodybuilding: Feminist Resistance or Erotic Spectacle', *Journal of Gender Studies*, 17(4): 289–301.

Solotaroff, Paul (2010) *The Body Shop* (New York: Little, Brown).

Introduction to Part 2: Bodybuilding *as* Representation

Baudrillard, Jean (1983) *Simulacra and Simulation* (Ann Arbor: University of Michigan Press).

Daum, Patrick (ed.) 2006 *Impressionist Camera: Pictorial Photography in Europe, 1888–1918* (London: Merrell Publishers).

Frueh, Joanna (2003) 'The Aesthetics of Orgasm', *Sexualities*, 6(3–4): 459–478.

Goggin, G. (2006) *Cell Phone Culture: Mobile Technology in Everyday Life* (Oxford: Routledge).

Klein, Alan M. (1993) *Little Big Men* (Albany, NY: State University of New York Press).

Richardson, Niall (2008) 'Flex-rated! Female bodybuilding: feminist resistance or erotic spectacle?', *Journal of Gender Studies*, 17(4): 289–301.

7 The Self-Contained Body: The Heroic and Aesthetic/ Erotic Modes of Representing the Muscular Body

Bayley, Stephen (1991) *Taste: The Secret Meaning of Things* (London: Faber and Faber).

Brain, Robert (1979) *The Decorated Body* (London: Hutchinson).

Butler, George (1990) *Arnold Schwarzenegger: A Portrait* (New York: Simon and Schuster).

Chatwin, Bruce and Mapplethorpe, Robert (1983) *Lady: Lisa Lyon* (London: Blond and Briggs).

Clark, Kenneth (1960) *The Nude: A Study of Ideal Art* (Harmondsworth: Pelican).

Delph, Edward William (1978) *The Silent Community: Public Homosexual Encounters* (Beverly Hills, CA: Sage).

Gunn, Freja (1973) *The Artificial Face: A History of Cosmetics* (Newton Abbot: David and Charles).

Guthrie, R. Dale (1976) *Body Hot Spots: The Anatomy of Human Social Organs and Behavior* (New York: Van Nostran Reinhold).

Hollinghurst, Alan (1983) *Robert Mapplethorpe 1970–1983* (London: Institute of Comtpemporay Arts).

Kennedy, Robert (1985) *Reps!* (New York: Sterling Books).

Lucie-Smith, Edward (1972) *Eroticism in Western Art* (New York: Praeger).

Montagu, Jennifer (1963) *Bronzes* (London: Weidenfeld and Nicholson).

Morris, Desmond (1971) *The Human Zoo* (London: Corgi Books).

Mostyn, Suzanne (1991) 'In Trim for the Hair-free Alternative', *Sydney Morning Herald*, October 10.

Passmore, John (1970) *The Perfectibility of Man* (London: Duckworth*)*.

Polhemus, Ted (ed.) (1973) *Social Aspects of the Human Body* (Harmondsworth: Penguin).

Rudofsky (1971) *The Unfashionable Human Body* (New York: Doubleday).

Walters, Margaret (1978) *The Nude Male: A New Perspective* (London and New York: Paddington Press).

8 Flayed Animals in an Abattoir: The Bodybuilder as Body-Garde

Best, Stephen and Kellner, Douglas (1997) *The Postmodern Turn* (New York and London: Guilford Press).

Blake, Andrew (1996) *The Body Language: The Meaning of Modern Sport* (London: Lawrence and Wishart).

Bordo, Susan (1999) *The Male Body* (New York: Farrar, Straus and Giroux).

Budd, Michael Anton (1997) *The Sculpture Machine: Physical Culture and Body Politics in the Age of Empire* (Basingstoke: MacMillan).

Bukatman, Scott (1994) 'X-Bodies (the torment of the mutant superhero)', in Rodney Sappington and Tyler Stallings (eds.) *Uncontrollable Bodies: Testimonies of Identity and Culture* (Seattle: Bay Press).

Clare, Anthony (2000) *On Men: Masculinity in Crisis* (London: Arrow).

Dobbins, Bill (1994) The Women: Photographs Of The Top Female Bodybuilders (New York: Artisan).

Dutton, Kenneth R. (1995) *The Perfectible Body: The Western Ideal of Physical Perfection* (London: Cassell).

Ewen, Stuart (1985) *All Consuming Images: The Politics of Style in Contemporary Culture* (New York: Basic).

Farson, Daniel (2000) *Gilbert and George: A Portrait* (London: Harper Collins).

Featherstone, Mike (1991) *The Body: Social Process and Cultural Theory* (London: Sage).

Featherstone, Mike (2000) (ed.) *Body Modification* (London: Sage).

Fitness, Johnny (2002) 'Editorial', *MuscleMag* (February): 14, 204.

Fussell, Sam (1991) *Muscle: Confessions of an Unlikely Bodybuilder* (London: Abacus).

Giddens, Anthony (1991) *Modernity and Self-Identity: Self and Society in the Late Modern Age* (Cambridge: Polity).

Graham-Dixon, Andrew (1996) *A History of British Art* (London: BBC Books).

Hall, James (1999) *The World As Sculpture: The Changing Status of Sculpture from the Renaissance to the Present Day* (London: Chatto and Windus).

Harris, Ron (2002) 'Thunder Thighs', *MuscleMag* (September): 110–112, 114–115.

Hesse, Eric (2001) 'Titanic Mass Training with Greg Kovacs', *MuscleMag* (July): 178–180, 182, 184–185.

Hotten, Jon (2004) *Muscle: A Writer's Trip Through a Sport With No Boundaries* (London: Yellow Jersey Press).

Klein, Alan M. (1993) *Little Big Men: Bodybuilding Subculture and Gender Construction* (Albany, NY: State University of New York Press).

Kostelanetz, Richard (2001) *Dictionary Of The Avant-Gardes* (London and New York: Routledge).

Locks, Adam (2003) *Bodybuilding and the Emergence of a Post Classicism* (unpublished Ph.D. thesis).

Merrit, Greg (2000) 'Things To Come?', *Flex* (February): 86–88, 90–91.

Morrisroe, Patricia (1995) *Mappelthorpe: A Biography* (London: Papermac).

O'Brien, Daniel (2000) *SF: UK – How British Science Fiction Changed The World*. London: Reynolds and Hearn and Channel Four Later.

O'Connell, Jeff (2000) 'Future Shock', *Muscle and Fitness* (February): 42–50.

Pegrum, Mark (2000) *Challenging Modernity: Dada between Modern and Postmodern* (New York and Oxford: Berghahn Books).

Persaud, Raj (2001) *Staying Sane: How To Make Your Mind Work For You* (London, New York, Toronto, Sydney and Auckland: Bantam).

Philips, Bill (1995) 'No Holds Barred', *Muscle Media 2000* (September): 10–14.

Pope, Harrison G., Phillips, Katherine A. and Olivardia, Roberto (2002) *The Adonis Complex: The Secret Crisis of Male Body Obsession* (New York: Simon and Schuster).

Rineheart, Robert and Sydnor, Synthia (2003) *To The Extreme: Alternative Sports, Inside And Out* (Albany, NY: New York Press).

Robert, Karl Frederick (1988) *Modern and Modernism: The Sovereignty of the Artist 1885–1925* (New York: Atheneum).

Robinson, Dave (1999) *Nietzsche and Postmodernism* (Cambridge: Icon Books).

Romano, John (2003) 'The New IFBB Rules: Put Up And Shut Up', *Muscular Development* (October): 240–244.

Rosenthal, Jim (2002) 'Wonder Woman', *Flex* (February): 110–114, 116.

Rutherford, John (1992) *Men's Silences: Predicaments in Masculinity* (London: Routledge).

Schmidt, Julian (1997) 'Kovacs Going Where No Man Has Gone Before', *Flex* (August): 146–148, 150, 152–154, 156–158.

Solotaroff, Paul (1998) 'Addicted to Death', *The Observer* (September 27): 8–9.

Stein, Judith (1999) 'Object Lessons', in Joanna Frueh et al. (eds.) *Picturing the Modern Amazon* (New York: newmuseumbooks).

Tasker, Yvonne (1994) *Spectacular Bodies: Gender, Genre and the Action Cinema* (London: Routledge).

Walters, Margaret (1978) *The Male Nude* (London and New York: Paddington Press).

Webster, David (1982) *Bodybuilding: An Illustrated History* (New York: Arco Publishing).

Whitehead, Stephen M. and Barrett, Frank J. (eds.) (2001) *The Masculinities Reader* (Oxford: Polity).

Zulak, Greg (1997) 'Too Ripped?', *MuscleMag* (May): 59.

9 Strategies of Enfreakment: Representations of Contemporary Bodybuilding

Adams, Rachel (2001) *Sideshow USA: Freaks and the American Cultural Imagination* (Chicago: University of Chicago Press).

Benzie, Tim (2000) 'Judy Garland at the Gym – gay magazines and gay bodybuilding', *Continuum: Journal of Media & Cultural Studies*, 14(2): 159–169.

Berger, John (1972) *Ways of Seeing* (London: Penguin).

Bogdan, Robert (1988) *Freak Show: Presenting Human Oddities for Amusement and Profit* (Chicago: University of Chicago Press).

Bordo, Susan (1993) *Unbearable Weight: Feminism, Western Culture, and the Body* (Berkeley: University of California Press).

Bordo, Susan (1999) *The Male Body* (New York: Farrar, Straus and Giroux).

Durbach, Nadja (2009) *Spectacle of Deformity: Freak Shows and Modern British Culture* (Berkeley: University of California Press).

Dutton, Kenneth (1995) *The Perfectible Body: The Western Ideal of Physical Development* (London: Cassell).

Fiedler, Leslie (1978) *Freaks: Myths and Images of the Secret Self* (New York: Simon and Schuster).

Gamson, Joshua (1998) *Freaks Talk Back: Tabloid Talk Shows and Sexual Nonconformity* (Chicago: University of Chicago Press).

Hevey, David (1992) *The Creatures That Time Forgot: Photography and Disability Imagery* (London: Routledge).

Hotten, Jon (2004) *Muscle: A Writer's Trip Through a Sport With No Boundaries* (London: Yellow Jersey Press).

Jones, Meredith (2008) 'Makeover Culture's Dark Side: Breasts, Death and Lolo Ferrari', *Body & Society*, 14(1): 89–104.

Kaplan, E. Ann (1997) *Looking for the Other: Feminism, Film, and the Imperial Gaze* (London: Routledge).

Lindsay, Cecile (1996) 'Bodybuilding: A Postmodern Freak Show' in Rosemarie Garland-Thomson (ed.) *Freakery: Cultural Spectacles of the Extraordinary Body* (New York: New York University Press) (356–367).

Locks, Adam (2003) *Bodybuilding and the Emergence of a Post Classicism* (unpublished Ph.D. thesis).

Matarazzo, Mike (1992) 'Freaky', *Flex* (August): 42–47.

Mayne, Judith (2000) *Framed: Lesbians, Feminists, and Media Culture* (Minneapolis: University of Minnesota Press).

Mercer, John (2003) 'Homosexual Prototypes: Repetition and the Construction of the Generic in the Iconography of Gay Pornography', *Paragraph: Journal of Modern Critical Theory*, 25(1–2): 280–290.

Merck, Mandy (2007) 'Mulvey's Manifesto', *Camera Obscura*, 22(366): 1–23.

Mulvey, Laura (1975) 'Visual Pleasure and Narrative Cinema', *Screen*, 16(3): 6–18.

Newton, Lee (1988) 'The Things People Say', *Sport & Fitness: Incorporating Health & Strength*, (December): 42–43.

Pope, Harrison G., Phillips, Katherine A. and Olivardia, Roberto (2002) *The Adonis Complex: The Secret Crisis of Male Body Obsession* (New York: Simon & Schuster).

Paris, Bob (1991) *Beyond Built* (New York: Warner Books).

Paris, Bob (1997) *Gorilla Suit: My Adventures in Bodybuilding* (New York: St. Martin's Press).

Paris, Bob and Jackson, Rod (1994) *Straight from the Heart: A Love Story* (New York: Warner Books).

Richardson, Niall (2010) *Transgressive Bodies: Representations in Film and Popular Culture* (Hampshire: Ashgate Publishing Ltd.).

Rodowick, David N. (1982) 'The Difficulty of Difference', *Wide Angle*, 5(1): 5–15.

Schmidt, Julian (1989) 'Yo, Franco!', *Flex*, 59–62.

Shildrick, Margrit (2002) *Embodying the Monster: Encounters with the Vulnerable Self* (London: Sage).

Silverman, Kaja (1992) *Male Subjectivity at the Margins* (London: Routledge).

Spelman, Elizabeth (1982) 'Woman as Body: Ancient and Contemporary Views', *Feminist Studies*, 8(1): 108–131.

Stephens, Elizabeth (2006) 'Cultural Fictions of the Freak Body: Coney Island and the Postmodern Sideshow', *Continuum: Journal of Media & Cultural Studies*, 20(4): 485–498.

Thomson, Rosemarie Garland (1996) 'Introduction: From Wonder to Error – A Genealogy of Freak Discourse in Modernity' in Rosemarie Garland Thomson (ed.) *Freakery: Cultural Spectacles of the Extraordinary Body* (New York: New York University Press) (1–19).

Thomson, Rosemarie Garland (1997) *Extraordinary Bodies: Figuring Physical Disability in American Culture and Literature* (New York: Columbia University Press).

Thomson, Rosemarie Garland (2009) *Staring: How We Look* (Oxford: Oxford University Press).

Yuan, David D. (1996) 'The Celebrity Freak: Michael Jackson's "Grotesque Glory"' in Rosemarie Garland Thomson (ed.) *Freakery: Cultural Spectacles of the Extraordinary Body* (New York: New York University Press) (368–384).

10   Getting Hard: Female Bodybuilders and Muscle Worship

Alvarez, Erick (2008) *Muscle Boys* (London and New York: Routledge).

Baxandall, Michael (1988) *Painting and Experience in Fifteenth-Century Italy* (Oxford: Oxford University Press).

Benjamin, Walter (1997) *Charles Baudelaire* (London: Verso).

Campbell, John Edward (2004) *Getting it on Online* (New York: Harrington Park Press).

Chare, Nicholas (2008) 'Admirable Muscles: Male Beauty, Sex, Schmoes, and *Pumping Iron II*', in Stephen L. Davis and Maglina Lubovich (eds.) (2008) *Hunks, Hotties and Pretty Boys* (Newcastle: Cambridge Scholars Publishing).

Chare, Nicholas (2010) *'Sexing the Canvas', in Dana Arnold (ed.) Art History: Contemporary Perspectives on Method* (Chichester: John Wiley & Sons).

Connolly, Pamela H (2006) 'Psychological Functioning of Bondage/Domination/ Sado-Masochism (BDSM) Practitioners', *Journal of Psychology and Human Sexuality*, 18(1): 79–120.

Connor, Steven (2005) 'Michel Serres's *Les Cinq Sens*,' in Niran Abbas (ed.) *Mapping Michel Serres* (Ann Arbor: University of Michigan Press).

Denham, Bryan E. (2008) 'Masculinities in Hardcore Bodybuilding', *Men and Masculinities*, 11: 2: 232–42.

Dutton, Kenneth R. (1995) *The Perfectible Body* (London: Cassell).

Dworkin, Shari L. and Wachs, Faye Linda (2009) *Body Panic* (New York: New York University Press).

Frueh, Joanna (2001) *Monster Beauty* (Berkeley: University of California Press).

Haraway, Donna (1991) 'A Cyborg Manifesto' in *Simians, Cyborgs and Women: The Reinvention of Nature* (New York: Routledge), pp. 149–182.

Hardt, Micheal and Negri, Antonio (2005) *Multitude* (London: Hamish Hamilton).

Heywood, Leslie (1998) *Bodymakers* (New Brunswick: Rutgers).

Ihde, Don (2007) *Listening and Voice. Phenomenologies of Sound*, 2nd edition (New York: State University of New York).

Johnston, Lynda (1996) 'Flexing Femininity: female bodybuilders refiguring "the body"', *Gender, Place and Culture*, 3(3): 27–40.

Kaye, Kristin (2005) *Iron Maidens* (New York: Thunder's Mouth Press).

Klein, Alan M. (1993) *Little Big Men* (Albany, NY: State University of New York Press).

Lingis, Alphonso (1994) *Foreign Bodies* (London and New York: Routledge).

Lowe, Maria R. (1998) *Women of Steel* (New York: New York University Press).

Parker, Suzi (2003) *Sex in the South* (Boston: Justin, Charles & Co.).

Plummer, John (2001) 'Up the Amazon', *Bizarre*. 45: 8–83.

Richardson, Niall (2004) 'The Queer Activity of Extreme Male Bodybuilding: Gender Dissidence, Auto-eroticism and Hysteria', *Social Semiotics*. 14(1): 49–65.

Richardson, Niall (2008) 'Flex-rated! Female bodybuilding: feminist resistance or erotic spectacle?', *Journal of Gender Studies*, 17(4): 289–301.

Robinson, Laura (2002) *Black Tights* (Toronto: Harper Collins).

Rose, Nikolas (2000) 'Identity, Genealogy, History', in P. Du Gay, J. Evans and P. Redman (eds.) *Identity: A Reader* (London: Sage).

Rubin, Patricia (2007) *Images and Identity in Fifteenth-Century Florence* (New Haven: Yale University Press).

Screech, Timon (1999) *Sex and the Floating World* (Honolulu: University of Hawaii Press).

Serres, Michel (2008) *The Five Senses* (trans. M. Sankey and P. Cowley) (London: Continuum).

Thrift, Nigel (1997) 'The rise of soft capitalism', *Journal for Cultural Research*, 1(1): 29–57.

11 Aphrodisia and Erotogenesis

Alpers, Svetlana (1995) *The Making of Rubens* (New Haven and London: Yale University Press).

Bolin, Anne (1997) 'Flex Appeal', in Pamela Moore (ed.) *Building Bodies* (New Brunswick, NJ: Rutgers University Press).

Bordo, Susan (1993) *Unbearable Weight: Feminism, Western Culture, and the Body* (Berkeley: University of California Press).

Bordo, Susan (1997) 'Reading the Male Body', in Pamela Moore (ed.) *Building Bodies* (New Brunswick, NJ: Rutgers University Press).

Bryson, Norman (1990) 'Interim and Identification', in Mary Kelly (ed.) *Interim* (New York: The New Museum of Contemporary Art).

Clark, Kenneth (1956) *The Nude: A Study in Ideal Form* (Princeton: Princeton University Press).

Frueh, Joanna (1994) 'The Erotic as Social Security', *Art Journal*, 53(1): 66–72.

Frueh, Joanna (2000), 'The Real Nude', in Joanna Frueh et al. (eds.) *Picturing the Modern Amazon* (New York: Rizzoli).

Frueh, Joanna (2001) *Monster/Beauty: Building the Body of Love* (Berkeley, Los Angeles: University of California Press).

Goldberg, Jonathan (1997) 'Recalling Totalities: The Mirrored Stages of Arnold Schwarzenegger', in Pamela Moore (ed.) *Building Bodies* (New Brunswick, NJ: Rutgers University Press).

Greer, Germaine (1992) *The Change: Women, Aging and the Menopause* (New York: Alfred A. Knopf).

Hickey, Dave (1993) *The Invisible Dragon: Four Essays on Beauty* (Los Angeles: Art Issues Press).

Klein, Alan M. (1993) *Little Big Men: Bodybuilding Subculture and Gender Construction* (Albany, NY: State University of New York Press).

Lingis, Alphonso (1985) *Libido: The French Existential Theories* (Bloomington, IN: Indiana University).

Lingis, Alphonso (1994) *Foreign Bodies* (London and New York: Routledge).

Marcuse, Herbert (1966) *Eros and Civilization: A Philosophical Inquiry into Freud* (Boston: Beacon).

Mishima, Yukio (1970) *Sun and Steel* (Tokyo: Kodansha International Ltd.).

Moore, Stephen D. (1996) *God's Gym* (London and New York: Routledge).

Pacteau, Francette (1994) *The Symptom of Beauty* (Cambridge: Harvard University Press).

Thomas, Al (1995) 'Some Thoughts on Spirit: Its Source and "Uses" in the Best of Games', *Iron Game History*, 4(2): 14–19.

Todd, Jan (1998) 'Majestic Womanhood vs. "Baby Faced Dolls": The Debate over Women's Exercise', in Jan Todd (ed.) *Physical Culture and the Body Beautiful: Purposive Exercise in the Lives of American Women 1800–1870* (Macon, GA: Mercer University Press).

Wilson, Robert A. (1966) *Feminine Forever* (New York: M. Evans).

Index